Linguistic Fieldwork

A handy beginner's guide, this textbook introduces the various stages of
linguistic fieldwork, from the preparation of the work to the presentation of
the results. Drawing on over forty years of fieldwork experience between
them, in over two dozen languages, the authors pack the book with examples and anecdotes from their experiences, and include practical exercises for students to test what they have learnt. Independent of any particular perspective, the methods can be applied to a wide range of fieldwork
settings, for projects with very different theoretical backgrounds, and without the need to travel too far. The book covers 'traditional fieldwork' such
as language description and documentation, as well as less typical methods, including language contact and quantitative studies with experiments
or questionnaires.

JEANETTE SAKEL is Senior Lecturer in Linguistics at the University of
the West of England, Bristol.

DANIEL L. EVERETT is Dean of Arts and Sciences at Bentley University
in Waltham, Massachusetts.

CAMBRIDGE TEXTBOOKS IN LINGUISTICS

General editors: P. AUSTIN, J. BRESNAN, B. COMRIE, S. CRAIN,
W. DRESSLER, C. EWEN, R. LASS, D. LIGHTFOOT, K. RICE,
I. ROBERTS, S. ROMAINE, N. V. SMITH.

Linguistic Fieldwork

Linguistic Fieldwork
A Student Guide

JEANETTE SAKEL

University of the West of England, Bristol

DANIEL L. EVERETT

Bentley University, Massachusetts

CAMBRIDGE
UNIVERSITY PRESS

CAMBRIDGE UNIVERSITY PRESS
Cambridge, New York, Melbourne, Madrid, Cape Town,
Singapore, São Paulo, Delhi, Tokyo, Mexico City

Cambridge University Press
The Edinburgh Building, Cambridge CB2 8RU, UK

Published in the United States of America by Cambridge University Press, New York

www.cambridge.org
Information on this title: www.cambridge.org/9780521545983

First published 2012

Printed in the United Kingdom at the University Press, Cambridge

A catalogue record for this publication is available from the British Library

Library of Congress Cataloging in Publication data
Sakel, Jeanette, 1973–
Linguistic fieldwork : a student guide / Jeanette Sakel, Daniel L. Everett.
    p.   cm. – (Cambridge textbooks in linguistics)
Includes bibliographical references and index.
ISBN 978-0-521-83727-9 (hardback)
1. Linguistics – Fieldwork.   2. Languages, Modern – Study and teaching – Handbooks,
manuals, etc.   I. Everett, Daniel Leonard.   II. Title.
P128.F53S24   2012
410.72 – dc23   2011041742

ISBN 978-0-521-83727-9 Hardback
ISBN 978-0-521-54598-3 Paperback

Additional resources for this publication at www.cambridge.org/sakel-everett

Contents

Preface

This guide emerges from a combined forty years of field research in over two dozen languages of the Brazilian and Bolivian Amazon, Greenland and Europe, including immigrant languages in Europe. The authors have been teaching field methods courses and seminars in Brazil, the USA, the UK, Germany and Denmark. They have had the enjoyable experience of taking graduate students and seasoned linguists from Brazil, the USA, Israel, Germany and the Netherlands to the field in order to train them in fieldwork methods. The authors thoroughly enjoy the intense challenge of field research and the presentation of the lessons learned thereby to the international linguistics community. Many of the suggestions included within this guide are ones we wish someone had made to us before we began our field research careers.

This book is intended for upper-division undergraduates, graduate students and above. It can be used in class or for self study. The book presumes basic knowledge of most areas of linguistics. To lighten up the reading and make it more personal, we have added anecdotes from our own and others' experience. Depending on what you are setting out to do (or learn), some sections will be more relevant than others, though generally all chapters should be of interest to the field researcher.

The major theme to be developed in this book is how to do fieldwork, independent of any particular theoretical perspective. Not just 'prototypical fieldwork' is considered, but other ways of working with first-hand language data are explored. The book's major thesis is that *linguistic fieldwork can be successful with proper preparation and execution, bringing deep personal and professional satisfaction for the researchers and their native-speaker teachers*. The book's purpose is to help linguists do, enjoy, and succeed at field research.

This book began with an invitation from Andrew Winnard to Dan Everett to write an introductory book on fieldwork. In 2006, while a visitor at the Max Planck Institute for Evolutionary Anthropology in Leipzig, Everett completed the first draft. Subsequently, Everett began work on another book, *Don't sleep, there are snakes*. In the meantime, it was recognized that the original draft of the book needed to take on a different focus, since Everett had conceived of the book as a manual rather than as a textbook. Sakel joined the project and made numerous and profound changes to the manuscript to bring it more in line with the objectives of a textbook. Her work has been sufficiently extensive to warrant our joint decision to list her as first author.

Acknowledgements

We are grateful to Andrew Winnard at Cambridge University Press for making this book possible and for his valuable comments along the way. We are furthermore indebted to a number of anonymous reviewers, who have given constructive comments with great promptness, and helped to shape the book in its current form.

We are thankful to a range of people who have commented on drafts of this book: Patrick Thornhill, Miguel Oliveira Jr, Ingrid Turner, Julia Reinbold, Robert Van Valin, Caleb Everett, Jeanine Treffers-Daller, Viveka Velupillai, Clare Ferguson, Gary Dicks, Virginia Marchioro, Munira Hashmi, Ben Wainwright, Megan Peters, Samantha Goodall, Caroline Lucas and Matthew Hale.

Too many to name, numerous other students and PhD students at the University of the West of England and the University of Manchester have given us valuable feedback during field methods courses.

Dan Everett would especially like to thank Bernard Comrie for making it possible to write the first draft of this book as a visitor at the Max Planck Institute for Evolutionary Anthropology in Leipzig, Germany.

Finally, Jeanette Sakel is forever indebted to Maya Thornhill, who shared her mum with this book during the first months of her life.

1   Introduction
What is linguistic fieldwork?

Are you ready to 'go to the field'? This book is written to prepare you for a great adventure: to discover a language, to use the skills you have learnt studying linguistics to document, describe and analyse how people use language. Your adventure may take you far away to a place you never heard of before, or you may simply talk to your next door neighbour. Linguistic fieldwork can be many things!

Have you ever wondered why your neighbour, who speaks both Urdu and English, sometimes switches between the two within the same sentence? Or have you always wanted to work on an 'exotic' language in a far-flung place? Or are you interested in a particular linguistic theory and want to figure out whether a theoretical notion can be found in language? In all three cases, doing linguistic fieldwork would be a way of finding out. You could record people's speech, carry out linguistic experiments or ask the speakers questions about their language use. These methods can be used on their own or in combination with one another.

Apart from being one of the most satisfying ways to engage with linguistics, fieldwork is essential in expanding our knowledge of how language works. We would not be able to get new ideas by theorizing alone. Real data is needed to make valuable discoveries. In this way fieldwork is indispensable for theoretical development.

Fieldwork can confirm what you suspected or lead to surprising results. You may end up with ideas completely different from those you started out with. Answering one question during fieldwork may lead to a hundred further questions. Yet, it is enormously satisfying to eventually find out how the language works.

Finally, fieldwork can be time out from the other things you may do. While the idea of being an 'armchair linguist' (Crowley 2007: 11) may be appealing (it sounds comfortable!), having a change of scene can be a very good experience.

Linguists choose to do fieldwork for various reasons. The first reason may be a university assignment. Sometimes the main reasons are not linguistic. For example, one of the authors, Dan Everett, was originally a missionary. Fieldwork was his way of learning the language to be able eventually to translate The Bible. As it turns out, fieldwork has not only changed his views on Christianity, but has also altered his preconceived ideas about the grammatical theories he was following at the time (Everett 2008).

Jeanette Sakel

For me it all started when I was a student writing my BA dissertation. Living in Denmark at the time, I decided to carry out sociolinguistic fieldwork on the maintenance of the Greenlandic language among Greenlanders living in Denmark. It was primarily a questionnaire-based study, which some may argue is not 'fieldwork' at all. However, for me it was the beginning of my career doing field research. I discovered that I loved working with speakers on their language. Subsequently, I decided to collect data on aspects of the grammar of Greenlandic for my MA thesis. I successfully applied for a small university travel grant to go to Greenland, which paid for my airfare. My Greenlandic teacher in Denmark put me in contact with a *højskole*, a type of residential school for adults in Sisimiut, just north of the Arctic Circle on the west coast of Greenland. Paying a small fee, I was allowed to stay at the school. The setting was ideal for my study, as I had easy access to speakers of various ages and dialectal backgrounds. On the professional level, the fieldwork went very well: I collected interesting data and learnt more about the structures I was studying. But there was a surprise in store that I could never have anticipated, the details of which I will go into in section 5.2.9.

1.1   A definition of fieldwork

You will probably have an understanding of what fieldwork is and an idea as to the kinds of activities that take place. Before we go into detail defining our subject matter, have a short think about your understanding of the term.

Exercise 1.1

(a)   What do you understand by the notion of *fieldwork*?
(b)   How does your understanding relate to the following points:
 – interviewing somebody?
 – interviewing yourself?
 – working in a setting far away?
 – working with your next door neighbour?
 – working on an undescribed or little-described language?
 – working on a well-known language?
 – documenting a language or writing a grammar?
 – looking at a particular aspect of a language?

If we were to ask ten people how they define fieldwork, we would probably get ten different answers. Indeed, many linguists have diverging views, centring on a common core of 'prototypical' fieldwork, which involves collecting data on an endangered language in a remote and usually 'exotic' setting. Hyman (2001), discussing the ways in which the term *fieldwork* is used in the literature, distinguishes prototypical and non-prototypical fieldwork at various levels. Prototypical field-work entails the linguist working with speakers in a small setting far away for a long period of time. The language is spoken in its natural language context, the data are naturalistic and the motivation for conducting fieldwork is entirely language-driven. The opposite of each of these points would be non-prototypical fieldwork, namely the linguists interviewing themselves or being observed by others in a large setting close to home. The fieldwork would only last a short time, the language under scrutiny being well known. The subject matter would be the formal system of a language, the language data controlled and the entire study driven by theory.

Indeed, many instances identified as linguistic fieldwork are not prototypical, but lie somewhere in between the two extremes.

Exercise 1.2

(a)   To what degree were the two types of fieldwork carried out by J. Sakel prototypical or non-prototypical?

(b)   Imagine the different fields of linguistics that use language data – what type of fieldwork would they require to collect their data?

    Discuss, for example, the type of data-collection needed in fields such as generative grammar, sociolinguistics, typology, documentation of endangered languages, second language acquisition and bilingualism.

Depending on your background in linguistics, you may agree with the prototypical definition of fieldwork. However, many linguists refer to their work as fieldwork even though it is far from prototypical. Where should we draw the line between what is fieldwork and what is not? Imagine a generative lin-guist, who often uses introspection to theorize about grammatical structures in English. Would this person be conducting fieldwork by doing so? How many people would say that the native-speaker grammaticality judgements of the early generative grammarians (e.g. Chomsky 1965) are indeed fieldwork? As a matter of fact, this type of work almost totally fits Hyman's (2001) categorization of non-prototypical fieldwork.

Take, for example a variationist sociolinguist like William Labov, who works on varieties of English in the USA (e.g. Labov 1966). He is not only close to home, but also working on a large, well-described language which is also his native tongue. Still, often linguists refer to his work, as well as others' work in sociolinguistics, as fieldwork (see also Milroy 1987 for the use of naturalistic data in sociolinguistics, which again is usually referred to as fieldwork).

Consider then the typologist Marianne Mithun, who conducts fieldwork on a variety of endangered North American indigenous languages, many of which are spoken close to her home in California. Even though most people would agree that this should be considered fieldwork, it does not fulfil all of Hyman's (2001) prototypicality criteria, for example she may indeed work with her neighbours on a particular structure of a language.

Finally, let us consider the fields of second language acquisition and bilingualism, which rely heavily on the analysis of actual language data, but where research sometimes involves experiments in controlled settings. Furthermore, at least one of the languages is usually well known. Language data in these fields can range from natural to artificial, spontaneous or semi-spontaneous speech, and researchers may be using elicitation or conducting experiments (Nortier 2008: 46). Still, many researchers in this area refer to their data-collection as fieldwork, in particular if it involves primarily naturalistic data (see Moyer 2008: 27 and Dörnyei 2007: 130).[1]

As you can see, very different disciplines within linguistics conduct fieldwork, some more 'prototypical' than others. For this reason, definitions of what fieldwork *is* vary considerably. In order to reach our definition of fieldwork, let us briefly acknowledge the history of linguistic fieldwork and how others have defined fieldwork before us.

Linguistic fieldwork as a discipline began with Franz Boas (1858–1942), who trained a core of linguistically aware anthropologists and thereby was (indirectly) responsible for the birth and growth of North American linguistics. During the years of Boas's influence, roughly during his life and following his death until the 1950s, North American linguistics was concerned with describing specific languages in detail, producing integrated studies of texts keyed to cultural studies, grammars and dictionaries. Other influential forerunners were Boas's student Edward Sapir, as well as Leonard Bloomfield. For a more detailed discussion of the history of fieldwork in the Americas, see appendix 1.

Over the following decades, a number of publications appeared to help the linguist or anthropologist learn and figure out the grammar of a language. These were guides on how to extract information about grammar from spoken language data (e.g. Nida 1947), sometimes focusing on particular language groups (e.g. Bouquiaux & Thomas 1976; see also later works on particular language groups, e.g. Abbi 2001). A notable exception was Samarin's (1967) book on field methods, which also gave information on more practical issues, such as what makes a good language teacher. Samarin's view of fieldwork is rather broad, e.g. regarding the place of study: 'Field linguistics can be carried on anywhere, not just *in the field*, as its name implies. [emphasis Samarin's] A "field archaeologist" must go out to where he expects to collect his data, but a linguist can bring his data to himself. Thus, some fieldwork is done by bringing jungle dwellers to a city and is conducted in an office instead of a lean-to.' (Samarin 1967: 1–2).

As interest in linguistic fieldwork has increased, a range of publications on modern fieldwork methods have appeared (e.g. Vaux & Cooper 1999; Newman & Ratliff 2001; Crowley 2007; Gippert, Himmelmann & Mosel 2006; Aikhenvald 2007; Bowern 2008; Chelliah & de Reuse 2011). There is also a plethora of online resources on fieldwork. These published materials present fieldwork methods, including modern concerns such as fieldwork ethics. Still, the type of fieldwork focused on is in many cases close to the prototypical 'ideal'.

Newman & Ratliff (2001: 1) refer to fieldwork as 'the complex and involved business of describing language as it is used by actual speakers in natural settings'. The focus on 'natural settings' means that working in an office, as mentioned by Samarin (1967), would not count unless that is where the speakers generally use their language.

Crowley (2007) sets fieldwork ethics high on his agenda. He focuses on the documentation and description of endangered languages and views fieldwork as a means to record the languages that are in danger of disappearing. Crowley acknowledges less prototypical work, e.g. with only one speaker as part of a university field methods course, as a '*kind* of fieldwork' (Crowley 2007: 14, his emphasis), agreeing that 'Any work that you do with a speaker of a language other than English with a view to publishing the resulting linguistic analysis can legitimately be referred to as fieldwork.' (2007: 14). However, he is reluctant to endorse this type of work. Similarly, while mentioning sociolinguistic data-collection, he does not include this in his definition of linguistic fieldwork (2007: 18).

In a similar way, Bowern (2008: 7) stresses the humane and ethical perspective of fieldwork, which also shines through in her definition of fieldwork: 'It involves the collection of accurate data in an ethical manner. It involves producing a result which both the community and the linguist approve of. [. . .] The third component involves the linguist interacting with a community of speakers at some level.' According to Bowern, linguistic experiments would not be considered fieldwork *per se*, neither would working with a speaker removed from his language community.

Chelliah and de Reuse (2011) focus on descriptive fieldwork and language documentation, but are more inclusive than other publications in asserting that fieldwork can be carried out in one's home town, among one's own relatives. This is to cover cases where native-speaker linguists work on their own language. Nonetheless, the general focus of the book is on prototypical fieldwork.

Our own definition aims to encompass both prototypical and less prototypical types of fieldwork:

> **Fieldwork** *describes the activity of a researcher systematically analysing parts of a language, usually other than one's native language and usually within a community of speakers of that language.*

It is useful to consider this definition in more detail. Again, by dwelling on our own definition, we are not claiming that it is 'right' in some absolute sense. But it does raise issues worth considering, however one ultimately comes to understand the essence of field research.

'Systematically analysing' should be clear. We go into field research with a system of ideas that guide our research. How does this system guide, then, what we are going to study? What are the subparts of the system? How do the different subparts of the system, projected onto the language of study, interact? For example, perhaps we are conducting research to test a specific claim in the literature, e.g. 'language **x** lacks embedding'. What system could there be to our investigation? First, if a claim has been made to this effect, we want to check with native speakers the data that were adduced on its behalf. Do native speakers agree with all the grammaticality judgements offered to support the claims being tested? Are there discrepancies across speakers? And so on. To check data requires a plan. How many speakers should one check the data with? How should one subcategorize and test discrepancies in speaker judgements? How can one design and test alternative hypotheses? Second, if a language lacks embedding, it should be reflected at several places in the grammar, not merely, say, in the absence of complement clauses. Does the language have disjunction? Coordination? Verb phrases? Complex noun phrases? Adjectival phrases? And so forth. In other words, field research is like any other large, complex task. It requires planning, administration, progress checks, self-evaluation and reports (at least to oneself).

Continuing with a discussion of our definition, why does it refer to 'parts of a language', rather than a 'whole language'? First of all, it is impossible to study a whole language. Just consider the thousands of studies of the English language and the fact that there is no sign that research on English is coming to an end. A language is vast and beyond any single researcher's ability to study in a human lifetime. Language is everything: semantics, sociolinguistics, phonetics, phonology, syntax, morphology, ethnography of communication, and so on. Second, language as an object of study is unclear, unfocused – there are no boundaries to identify either a coherent beginning or end of the study if its object is 'documentation of English' or some such. Additionally, languages change, and in that way no language can be studied conclusively. The goal of 'parts of language' requires a lowering of the sights from *language* to *selected components*. Their selection requires a coherent vision of how the parts fit together, assuming that the study is to fit together at the end, that it is not strategically opportunistic.[2] Having said this, linguists are usually aware of this fact, and when they say that they are 'writing a grammar of a language' they often do so because it is easier to say than 'writing a grammar of parts of the language, the way we understand the language at this particular time, with the structures found in the corpus that we managed to investigate, considering that we may not have been able to record every last speaker's idiolect of the language, etc.'. The linguist could resort to saying that they are 'writing part of a grammar of a language', but that may be understood as focusing on certain aspects (e.g. the verbal paradigm), rather than doing a general overview. Talking about a 'sketch' of a grammar may also be an option, but such sketches can be of a few pages, while the linguist may aim to make the grammar as comprehensive as possible. For the sake of simplicity, in what follows we refer to 'writing a grammar' or 'documenting a language' with the understanding that one can only ever record 'part of a language'.

Coming back to our definition of fieldwork, the last two parts of the definition state that something would 'usually' be the case. By this we try to delimit field-work from other types of data-collection, while not excluding non-prototypical forms of fieldwork. For example, the language under scrutiny would in many cases be other than one's native language. Yet, many modern fieldworkers train speakers to conduct fieldwork on their own language, or speakers study linguistics to eventually be able to work on their own language. The work carried out by these speakers would still be considered fieldwork. They would probably use the same methods as other fieldworkers, for example not relying too heavily on introspection but analysing the language of a variety of other speakers. Indeed, this type of fieldwork is very rewarding, as the speakers' insight into their language may lead to further insights into the language that a non-native linguist may not spot when studying the language 'from the outside'.

The last part of the definition states that field research would usually be conducted 'within a community of speakers of that language'. This means in the place and among the people where the language is usually spoken. Thus, you could be living among an indigenous group far afield, or if you study the language behaviour of your neighbour mixing Urdu and English, that community may merely involve the neighbour and his family.

Let us briefly go back to Samarin's (1967) statement that fieldwork can also be conducted away from the speech community. Indeed, the locus of language, the speaker, can easily move to a different place and therefore a linguist is not as restricted as an archaeologist when it comes to the place of work. Indeed, in many cases, circumstances make linguists work elsewhere than in the original speech community. Imagine for example a language spoken by refugees, whose original home is torn by war. As linguists, we can still study the language by bringing one or more speakers to us. But will we miss out on something? By working with only one speaker, we may not capture the entire language, but rather document an idiolect. Think, for example, about the way in which young speakers differ from old speakers in their language use. Furthermore, we may not be able to check the data with other speakers. If our speaker has contact phenomena or idiosyncratic behaviour in his language (such as a lisp), we may not pick up on it and may instead assume this is how the language is spoken by others as well. On the other hand, imagine we had access to a range of different speakers in our setting away from the original place where the language is spoken. This would open up the opportunity to be able to check the data, but there might still be issues that could have been different had the fieldwork been done *in the field*. If we assume that language and culture are inextricably intertwined (Everett 2005), one would not be able to understand one without the other. Taking speakers out of their communities or studying parts of languages outside their cultural contexts may lead to very different results from studying a language in its natural environment. The language may not be the same as it is when being used on a regular basis. Grammar and culture can affect, and to some degree effect, each other. Coming back to our definition: where fieldwork is possible within a community of speakers, it is a good idea to conduct as much fieldwork as possible in that community. Nonetheless, there are cases where it is necessary or advantageous for fieldwork to take place in other settings.

Summarizing, our definition is kept rather broad in order to include various linguistic pursuits dealing with empirical data. It encompasses prototypical fieldwork on the grammar of a language, as well as fieldwork in areas such as sociolinguistics and bilingualism.

1.2   Overview: the following chapters

The chapters of this book deal with the different considerations surrounding any type of fieldwork – hence every chapter will be relevant on its own account. While we include quite diverse types of fieldwork, some sections within individual chapters may be more relevant to you than others. As most subsections are generally readable on their own, you can easily pick those you are interested in, skipping less relevant aspects.

In chapter 2 we present you with two examples of fieldwork, with hands-on exercises to try out some of the techniques. You will first learn about the basic skills of text-collection, transcription, analysis and elicitation to study the language Mosetén from the Bolivian Amazon. Then, you will be introduced to how to set up a fieldwork project on language contact between Somali and English among members of the UK Somali immigrant community in Bristol.

Chapter 3 focuses on the languages involved in fieldwork. We discuss ways of finding a language to work on, lingua francas, as well as the ins and outs of monolingual and bilingual fieldwork.

Chapter 4 deals with the people involved in the fieldwork, including the researcher, the speakers of the language or variety under scrutiny, as well as other stakeholders. We discuss how to find appropriate speakers and we go into detail concerning fieldwork ethics.

Chapter 5 is about the preparation of the fieldwork. Our discussion ranges from preparing your research questions and literature review to applying for funding and preparing for fieldwork in remote places.

In chapter 6 we go into detail on a wide range of fieldwork methods, including the collection of texts, elicitation, linguistic experiments and participant observation.

Finally, chapter 7 examines the outcomes of fieldwork, including corpora, grammars and dictionaries. We also discuss how to archive fieldwork data.

1.3   Summary and further reading

In this chapter we introduced the concept of linguistic fieldwork and discussed our definition of the subject. For further reading on the distinction between prototypical and non-prototypical fieldwork, see Hyman (2001). For a detailed overview of the history of linguistic fieldwork with a wealth of references to earlier works on linguistic fieldwork, see Chelliah & de Reuse (2011). The latter book is also a modern, general introduction to fieldwork, alongside Bowern (2008) and Crowley (2007). A book aimed at a general readership, which discusses numerous aspects of linguistic fieldwork among the Pirahã, is Everett's (2008) *Don't sleep, there are snakes.*

2 Fieldwork projects
Two examples

This chapter guides you through aspects of two very different fieldwork projects:

1. Fieldwork on the morphosyntax of an Amazonian language from Bolivia: how to begin extracting information about the grammar from spoken language

2. Fieldwork on the language contact situation between Somali and English among immigrants in the UK: how to set up a research project, and what to take into account before starting the data-collection

This is a first opportunity to learn about – and try out – some of the fieldwork techniques discussed in this book. It will be an introduction to many of the techniques and terms discussed in later chapters. These include text recording, elicitation and transcription in **1.** and how to find speakers, use picture stories, use sociolinguistic questionnaires, apply for funding and ethics applications in **2.**

2.1 Fieldwork project 1. Mosetén in Bolivia: text-collection, transcription, analysis and elicitation

In this chapter we will introduce the basic principles of text-collection, transcription, analysis and elicitation. These are the cornerstones of 'prototypical fieldwork', generally employed in describing the morphosyntax of a language in order to write a grammar, but aspects of these methods are present in all types of fieldwork.

The data are taken from Sakel's fieldwork on Mosetén in Bolivia, a language spoken by approximately 800 people in the Alto Beni region of the foothills of the Andes and the Amazon Basin. Sakel's aim was to write a grammar of this language. This is how she spent her first weeks in the field.

Jeanette Sakel

When I first started working on Mosetén I sussed out people who would be willing to work with me and who would be good teachers. Within my first week of living among the Mosetenes I was contacted by Juan Huasna, a Mosetén man in his late forties who had been working with anthropologists and biologists doing fieldwork in the past. He had also participated in a workshop run by the linguist Colette Grinevald some years prior to my own fieldwork, with the aim of developing orthographies for various languages of the Bolivian lowlands, where he had learnt to read and write his language. Juan had since attempted to write his own Mosetén-Spanish dictionary, as well as volunteering to teach Mosetén at the local school. He soon became the most important contact for me in the Mosetén area, as he was inquisitive and eager to learn about the structures of his own language. An added bonus was that he could write the language, so I could set aside the work on the sound system to a later date when I was more familiar with the language.

Juan, like most other Mosetenes, was a fluent speaker of Spanish, the official language of Bolivia and the language I used as a lingua franca (i.e. the intermediate language that both of us spoke) in order to conduct fieldwork. In the examples given below, I translate our Spanish conversations into English to make them accessible to the reader.

The text we are going to look at now is from my very first fieldwork session with Juan. I asked Juan to tell me about himself. This is generally a good way to start, as you learn more about the people you are going to work with and at the same time most teachers will be able to talk for a good few minutes on this topic, so you are likely to get some usable data. It certainly worked for me in this case, as Juan spoke for quite a while, and I recorded all of it. When he stopped we had a chat about what I had understood (which at that stage was very little).

Exercise 2.1

You can access the recordings for this section on the following website: www.cambridge.org/Sakel-Everett. Listen to track 1 and try to note down what (if anything) you understand. Why do you understand this?

(The key to the exercise is also available at www.cambridge.org/Sakel-Everett.)

Transcription

From now on, let us go through the fieldwork techniques used with this initial text. At first, we need to go back to the recording to *transcribe* what Juan said. Normally, the first transcription of a text is done phonetically, in IPA. For now, however, let us make use of Juan's writing skills and return to the phonology of the language at a later stage.

As anybody who has attempted this will certify, transcribing, even in your mother tongue, takes a long time: you have to play and replay short chunks of the spoken text, trying to copy it down on paper as accurately as possible.

Spoken language – even a monologue – is very different from written language. There are false starts, hesitations and repetitions. This was also the case in Juan's text, particularly as this was his very first recording and he may have been a little nervous. This is completely normal, and will happen to most people (unless they are experienced BBC reporters!). It is important to tell a speaker-cum-transcriber that it does not matter to you, and that you are merely interested in the way language is spoken. Having said this, it is a good idea to transcribe everything the way it is said on the tape. If transcribing together with a teacher – as in this case – they may come up with 'more appropriate' alternatives. It is a good idea to write those down as well, as they will give the speaker's judgements about the correctness of his language. You may end up with two different transcriptions, one word-by-word as it was said and the other as corrected by the teacher.

The following transcriptions are the first three chunks of the Mosetén text from Sakel's recording. We could call these chunks 'sentences', even though sentences are not as straightforward in spoken language as in written language.[1]

Jeanette Sakel

For the transcription I did not use IPA, which would be common practice in most fieldwork situations on previously little-described languages. I was 'lucky' in that Mosetén had been part of the project to develop orthographies for various Bolivian languages. The resulting orthography was based on a careful study of the phonology of Mosetén, and since Juan was able to write down recorded texts straight away, I decided to start off using this writing system – revisiting the phonology of Mosetén once I had a better understanding of the language.

(a)   Transcription the way it was said:

Yäe yäerä' yoshropaiyeyak jin mi'ïn jäe'mä sobakityi' ichhe' öchhe' öichhe' jakh Bolivia. Yäesï' ti'i nash ti'i, yäesï' ti'i chhata' ti'iyäe Fan Juan Huasna Bozo. Nä'iyäe Santa Anaya' de Mosetensi' khäkï jike tse'yäe mö'yä'sï'.

(b)   Transcription 'corrected' by the teacher:

Yäerä' yoshropaiyeyak in mi'ïn sobakityi' öichhe' jakh Bolivia. Yäesï' ti'i nash, yäesï' ti'i, chhata' ti'iyäe Juan Huasna Bozo. Nä'iyäe Santa Anaya' de Mosetensi' khäkï jike tse'yäe mö'yä'sï'.

Exercise 2.2

Try to listen to the recording again, while reading what Juan has written down. Can you guess what the apostrophes ['] and the two dots on some of the vowels [ï, ä, ö] mean?

(The key to the exercise is available at www.cambridge.org/Sakel-Everett.)

Since the two versions are very similar, we can conflate the two transcriptions, presenting mistakes, hesitations and false starts in brackets.

(c)   Transcription, finalized:

(Yäe) yäerä' yoshropaiyeyak (j)in mi'ïn (jäe'mä) sobakityi' (ichhe' öchhe') öichhe' jakh Bolivia. Yäesï' ti'i nash (ti'i), yäesï' ti'i, chhata' ti'iyäe (Fan) Juan Huasna Bozo. Nä'iyäe Santa Anaya' de Mosetensi' khäkï jike tse'yäe mö'yä'sï'.

If you worked through the key to exercise 2.2 you will have learnt that the glottal stop is marked by an apostrophe /'/ and nasal vowels are marked by two dots on the vowel (or first vowel of a vowel combination) /ï, ä, ö/ in the Mosetén orthography.

Other particularities of the Mosetén spelling you may have noticed after hearing the recording are:

- consonants followed by /h/ are aspirated e.g. /chh/ in *öichhe'*
- *j* is pronounced [h] – written *j* because that is the way it is done in Spanish, the language many Mosetenes can write.
- /ty/ (in *sobakityi'*) is a palatalized *t*
- /ch/ is an affricate [tʃ]

While figuring out the phonology of a language is very important at the beginning of fieldwork of this type, for our current purpose we will leave it aside and concentrate on the analysis of the morphosyntax of this language.

Exercise 2.3

Now that the text is written down, can you understand what Juan is talking about? What could the translations of the three first sentences be?

(The key to the exercise is available at www.cambridge.org/Sakel-Everett.)

Again, the proper nouns help us in finding out what Juan is talking about (see exercise 1). You will notice that some of them, e.g. *Santa Ana-ya' de Moseten(e)s*, appear with extra morphology. It would be good to find out what these morphemes mean. We will come to the grammatical analysis in a while, but first we will have to translate the text.

Translation: overall and word-by-word

The next step is to do a rough translation. Above, we divided the text up into chunks. This can be difficult, since spoken language does not always have clear sentence boundaries. When these boundaries are unclear, it may help to divide up the text into shorter chunks of related meanings. It is common practice to present the original text in italics and put the translation into single inverted commas:

(1) *(Yäe) yäerä' yoshropaiyeyak (j)in mi'in (jäe'mä) sobakityi' (ichhe' öchhe') öichhe' jakh Bolivia.*
'I want to thank you, visiting this land Bolivia.'

(2) *Yäesi' ti'i nash (ti'i), yäesi' ti'i, chhata' ti'iyäe (Fan) Juan Huasna Bozo.*
'My name is Juan Huasna Bozo.'

(3) *Nä'iyäe Santa Anaya' de Mosetensi' khäkï jike tse'yäe mö'yä'si'.*
'I was born in Santa Ana de Mosetenes because my mother was from there.'

The rough translation is an important step, because now we understand what the text is about, but this is still not enough to understand the grammar of the language. In order to do so, we need to go one step further and do a word-by-word translation. It is a good idea, and common practice in linguistics, to align the Mosetén word with the translation underneath from now on, so that it is clear what belongs to what.

(1) *Yäe* *yäerä'* *yoshropaiyeyak*
   I   I will thank you
   (j)in *mi'in* *(jäe'mä)* *sobakityi'*
   ?   you uh   visitor
   (ichhe' *öchhe')* *öichhe'* *jakh* *Bolivia.*
   in this in this in this earth Bolivia
   'I want to thank you visiting this land Bolivia.'

(2) *Yäesï'* *ti'i* *nash (ti'i)* ... *chhata'* *ti'iyäe*
   my name is name well   my name
   Fan *Juan Huasna Bozo.*
   Juan Juan Huasna Bozo
   'My name is Juan, Juan Huasna Bozo.'

(3) *Nä'iyäe* *Santa Anaya' de Mosetensi'*
   I was born in Santa Ana de Mosetenes
   khäkï *jike tse'yäe* *mö'yä'sï'.*
   because then my mother from there
   'I was born in Santa Ana de Mosetenes because my mother was from there.'

The way the data are presented here is called 'glossed'. The general way to present glosses is as follows:

(example number) *The original text in the first line (in italics).*
         A word-by-word translation in the second line
         'The translation in inverted commas in the last line.'

The second line is what we will focus on next. We will have to work on our data for a while before we need to get back to Juan to ask more questions.

Analysis
We are now at the *analysis* stage: we want to figure out which grammatical structures are found in the text we are dealing with. You may be surprised: already from this very short text we can find out about a number of grammatical structures of Mosetén.

Exercise 2.4

Look at the word-by-word translations above and try to find out how Mosetén expresses:

(a)	'I' (i.e. first person singular)
(b)	possession

In order to carry out the first bit of the analysis, you can go through your word-by-word translation to see if anything looks 'suspicious'. For example sentence (1):

(1) *Yäe yäerä' yoshropaiyeyak...*
     I   I will thank you
     'I want to thank you . . . '

Here we find the word for 'I', namely *yäe*. It is repeated twice, in the second case with the suffix *-rä'* appearing together with it. In the translation *yäe-rä'* is translated as 'I will', so let us – for now – assume that *-rä'* means something like 'will, personal intention' or the like.

Findings
yäe   'I'
-rä' 'will, personal intention' (or similar)

Check
-rä' 'will, personal intention' (or similar): what exactly does it mean in other contexts, is my initial analysis okay?

Now that we have established that *yäe* is 'I', let us find more instances of this in the text. We can do this by searching for the actual form *yäe*, as well as by looking at the translation to see if the first person singular is mentioned elsewhere. Indeed, the next two sentences contain various occurrences of 'I' or related words:

(2) *Yäesï' ti'i   nash (ti'i) ...chhata' ti'iyäe*
     my   name is name well   **my** name
     Fan   Juan Huasna Bozo.
     Juan   Juan Huasna Bozo
     'My name is Juan, Juan Huasna Bozo.'

(3) *Nä'iyäe   Santa Anaya' de Mosetensi'*
     I was born in Santa Ana de Mosetenes
     khäkï   jike tse'yäe   mö'yä'sï'.
     because   then **my** mother from there
     'I was born in Santa Ana de Mosetenes because my mother was from there.'

We can copy out these instances, and add 'hyphens' [-] that indicate morpheme boundaries with other elements:

yäe-sï'   'my'
ti'i-yäe 'my name'
nä'i-yäe 'I was born'
tse'-yäe 'my mother'

It seems that there is a possessive pronoun *yäe-sï'* 'my', which consists of 'I' and another element, potentially some kind of marker indicating possession. Possession seems to be expressed in other ways as well, though, as we can see in *ti'i-yäe* 'my name' and *tse'-yäe* 'my mother'. In these cases the personal pronoun *yäe* is simply added to the nouns *ti'i* 'name' and *tse'* 'mother'. We would have to check if these really are the basic forms of these nouns (one could imagine, for example, that there is a possession marker hidden in there somewhere). Finally, *yäe* also appears with a verb, *nä'i-yäe* 'I was born', indicating that the subject of the verb is first person.

We can now extend our list of findings and things to check later to include the new insights.

Findings

nä'i	'was born'
nä'i-yäe	'I was born'
tse'	'mother'
tse'-yäe	'my mother'
ti'i	'name'
ti'i-yäe	'my name'
-yäe	Expresses possession 'my' when added to a noun and subject when added to a verb.
'my'	Can be expressed in at least two ways: by *yäe-sï'* or by adding *-yäe* to the end of the possessed noun.

Check

nä'i	Does it really mean 'be born'? Can it be used with other persons, e.g. 'he was born'?
tse'	Does it really mean 'mother'? Can it be used with other persons, e.g. 'his mother'?
ti'i	Does it really mean 'name'? Can it be used with other persons, e.g. 'his name'?
-yäe	Find more examples where *-yäe* is used with nouns and verbs.
	Check what the function of *-sï* is and whether it can be used with other elements to express possession.
possession	Do the two different strategies to express possession have different functions?

By going through how 'I' is expressed in Mosetén, we have already answered the second question of exercise 2.4, namely how possession can be expressed. There seem to be two strategies: a possessive pronoun *yäe-sï'* or adding *yäe* to the end of the possessed noun.

In order to answer the question as to how – if at all – the two strategies differ, we have to try to find more examples of possession in the text. Skimming through these first three sentences of our story, there do not seem to be any other cases of possession. However, a close look will reveal that what could be our marker *-si'* appears again in (3):

(3)   *Nä'iyäe   Santa Anaya' de Mosetensi'*
        I was born in Santa Ana de Mosetenes
        khäki   jike   tse'yäe   mö'yä'si'.
        because   then my mother from there

The form *-si'* in *Moseten-si'* does not appear with a nasal vowel, as in the other two cases, but there may be a reason for vowels being nasalized in some cases and not in others. In order to keep an open mind (the most important thing in fieldwork), let's look at both of these in closer detail.

*   *mö'yä'-**si'*** means 'from there', very similar to 'of there' – in the same way as *yäe'-si'* could be translated 'of me'. Hence, if our analysis is correct, *mö'yä'* would mean 'there'.
*   *Santa Ana-ya' de Moseten-**si'*** means 'in Santa Ana de Mosetenes'. The *de* is Spanish, meaning 'of, from'. We could imagine that the suffix *-si'* also means 'of, from', as in the other cases above.

When we look at the place name in more detail, we find the morpheme *-ya'* added to *Santa Ana*. This form seems to express 'in', as given in the translation. Let us not be fooled by the difference in 'in' being a preposition while *-ya'* is a suffix: what is a preposition in English can easily be a suffix in another language!

When we look at the other form, e.g. *mö'-**yä'**-si'*, there is actually a *-yä'* in there as well. Again, the only difference is that this form appears with a nasal vowel. Could this also mean 'in'? It is possible, since we established above that *mö'yä'* means 'there', i.e. it expresses a spatial relationship, in the same way as 'in'.

Findings
-si' / -si'   Seem to express a wider 'possession' relationship that could be expressed by 'of', e.g. 'of me', 'of the Mosetenes', etc.
-ya' / -yä'   Seems to express 'in' or some other spatial meaning.

Check
-si' / -si'   Is this the same morpheme, appearing in different forms or are we dealing with two different morphemes? In the case of the former, what triggers vowels to be nasal / oral?
-ya' / -yä'   Does *-yä'* really mean 'in'? In which other contexts can it be used? Again, what triggers the vowels to be nasal / oral?

We have already found out quite a lot. We also stumbled upon other aspects that we did not consider before, such as the function of *-ya' / -yä'* when we analysed the possessive suffix. Still, almost every time we had a finding, we had to add something to the box to check, ending up with more questions than we set out with!

Corpus search

There are many ways of carrying out such 'checks'. One is to look through the texts that are transcribed and translated. This is a *corpus search*, as all of our transcribed and translated text forms our corpus. Initially, it is a good idea to find more examples and do a detailed corpus search. Still, not all questions will be answered in this way.

Elicitation

Another way of finding the answers to our questions is to go back to Juan – or other speakers – and ask them. This process is a type of *elicitation* (see chapter 6.4). Elicitation is a skill, and benefits from careful preparation. For example, if we asked Juan 'do you think *–si''* is a possessive suffix?' we would probably not get a satisfactory answer. Unless he is a trained linguist, he will probably not know what a possessive suffix is. Even linguists can struggle to analyse their language *ad hoc*. Elicitation is most reliable when it has been thought through carefully. For example, our question above may lead to the teacher answering 'yes', not necessarily because they understand the question, or believe the answer to be 'yes', but because they are eager to please us. Similar problems can arise when asking things like 'can you say . . . in your language?', for example being creative with the morphemes we identified above and saying 'can you say *Santa-ya' Ana-si'' de Moseten*?' Even though the teacher may not consider this correct, we have indeed just said it, so it *is* possible to say it in the language (just that he wouldn't use it). It is sometimes difficult to avoid such problems in elicitation, but we could, for example, follow up the question with 'can you give me an example of *Santa-ya' Ana-si'' de Moseten* being used in a sentence?' If your teacher struggles or gives you an alternative form, you know that it is probably not considered correct in the language. Still, asking 'can you say . . . in your language' can be a way of doing elicitation (as long as you make it clear to the teacher what you are interested in).

Exercise 2.5

Try to formulate questions that we could use in our elicitation with Juan, regarding the things we have noted down to check so far. How would you formulate these questions?
  (The key to the exercise is available at www.cambridge.org/Sakel-Everett.)

Elicitation with Juan

Before beginning the elicitation session, it is a good idea to check the corpus and find as many instances as possible of the morphemes and constructions we are interested in. This can save some valuable time during the elicitation session (e.g. knowing that certain constructions are indeed possible as they exist in the corpus).

This is the way in which we can carry out our first elicitation with Juan:

1.   *-rä'*: We can ask Juan about the difference between *yäe* and *yäe-rä'*, and ask him to give examples in clauses. His answer: *yäe-rä'* means 'I will'. He adds that there is no big difference between the two forms. Thus, for now, we can mark *-rä'* as possibly a future tense marker, but will have to check this carefully in the corpus.

2.   *nä'i, tse', ti'i*: We can ask Juan what each of these words means and he answers 'he was born', 'mother' and 'name'. Hence, these words mean what we had expected. Still, his comment that *nä'i* means 'he' rather than 'I' is interesting, since in the transcribed text it is translated 'I was born'. When asking Juan how to say 'I was born', he gives us the form *nä'i*. He then says that it could also be *nä'i* 'she was born', depending on whether the person speaking is a man or a woman. There seems to be an additional glottal stop in the feminine form. Let us note this down for now and get back to it in a later elicitation session. For now, let us check the rest of the forms from our transcribed text.

3.   We can ask Juan what *yäe-si' ti'i* and *ti'i-yäe* mean. In both cases he says 'my name'. We could now ask for examples of both in different sentences. Juan gives us a number of examples, but says that the two forms *yäe-si' ti'i* and *ti'i-yäe* are mutually exchangeable, and that there would be no difference in meaning using one or the other. In this situation, it may be worth asking if he could imagine people of different ages, occupations, or people from different villages, using one rather than the other. He thinks about it and declines this as well.

That tells us that it is likely that the two are used interchangeably, but we would have to check this in the corpus, in particular the frequency of each of the forms and whether speakers from different backgrounds prefer one or the other form.

4.   The next question targets the form *mö'-yä'-si'* 'from there'. If our analysis is correct, it would be possible to say *mö'-yä'*. Indeed, when asking Juan what *mö'yä* means, he answers 'there'. Hence, the marker *-si'* in *mö'-yä'-si'* 'from there' again expresses a meaning related to 'of, from'. Taking this one step further, we can ask Juan if we can say *mö'* and *mö'-si'*? Again, his answer is affirmative. According to Juan, *mö'* means 'she' and *mö'-si'* 'her'. Thus, our results are that this place adverb is expressed by combining the feminine third person pronoun *mö'* with a suffix *-yä'*, which seems to express location. The suffix *-si'* can also be added to the different forms, expressing a 'from, of' relationship of belonging.

5.   Finally, let us ask Juan to give us examples with the nasal and oral forms in *-si'* / *-si'* and *-ya'* / *-yä'*. We can also search our corpus to find further forms to analyse. So far, we have the impression that the

nasal only ever appears in phonological environments where other nasals are present, but that needs to be investigated further.

Where to go from here: further elicitation and text analysis

These are the first results of our elicitation. As you may have noticed all the way through this chapter, one question leads to another, i.e. when we have found out something, we usually end up with more questions than we started out with! This is what characterizes many types of fieldwork. It can be difficult at times, but in the long run this kind of work is very satisfying:

- It is great when you have found out how a specific structure works (allow yourself a treat for every major breakthrough!).
- You get to know the language better after a while, know how some structures work and understand more and more.
- Using the language as much as possible, you will try out constructions and gain a more detailed knowledge of how the language works.

The next step is to continue what we have been doing in this chapter: go out and record more texts, ideally by different speakers, transcribe and translate them, analyse them, do a corpus analysis and finally go back to elicitation. It is also a good idea to work with several different speakers in elicitation, in order to get a better overview of how the language works.

Exercise 2.6

We have only looked at a number of constructions so far. Can you make a list of what we have not looked at yet in our text? There are still a number of morphemes and constructions in our three sentences that could be examined in elicitation. Can you find them and formulate questions for future elicitation?

(The key to the exercise is available at www.cambridge.org/Sakel-Everett.)

This example of starting fieldwork on the grammar of Mosetén is just one way to beginning 'prototypical' fieldwork. Another popular way to commence is to go through wordlists with speakers, such as the Swadesh list (Swadesh 1971). Such a list of words gives you the basic vocabulary of a language.[2]

2.2   Fieldwork project 2. Somali in contact with English: setting up a fieldwork project

In this section we will focus on another example of fieldwork, namely on how to set up a fieldwork project on language contact. The example is based on a study by Sakel of language contact between the immigrant language Somali and English in the city of Bristol (UK). This is what she said about her initial reason to carry out the study.

Jeanette Sakel

I had worked extensively on language contact in far-flung places when one day, on a bus ride through Bristol (my current home), I realized how many different language contact situations were going on right around me: there were Polish people speaking with the Polish driver upon getting on the bus, switching between Polish greetings (*dzień dobry* 'good morning') and English expressions (*return ticket to Broadmead*). There were two Somali teenagers, who were having a heated discussion mainly in Somali, though I understood the words *boyfriend*, *cinema* and *problem*. Finally, there was myself, writing a text message to a friend in my native language German, automatically typing *the* instead of the German equivalent *der*, only noticing this when reviewing my message before sending it.

I started thinking about the ways in which immigrants communicate, and how contact phenomena arise when the native language (henceforth L1) meets the language of the new home country (henceforth L2), as well as how the children of immigrants are dealing with their bilingualism.[3]

After some deliberation, I decided that it would be interesting to study these phenomena in various immigrant languages spoken in Bristol. For practical reasons, I decided to study one language at a time, with a long timeframe in mind. I thought I would eventually build up a corpus of data from various languages that I could compare. The language I decided to start working on first was Somali. I chose it for a number of reasons. First, there had been very little research on language contact between Somali and English in the diaspora (i.e. outside Somalia), so it was a good topic to explore in greater detail. Second, the main community was still very new: after the civil war broke out in Somalia in the 1990s, many Somalis fled to Europe and more than 20,000 came to Bristol. The Somali community in Bristol was small prior to the civil war, which means that today the vast majority of adults are first-generation immigrants. Many of their children are second-generation immigrants. This difference in the generations opened up a number of opportunities, as I expected first-generation immigrants to differ in their language use from second-generation immigrants.

Finally, I found a number of colleagues in other departments at my university who also studied the Somali community in Bristol. This promised great networking and collaboration possibilities.

Now that I had an idea for a project, I needed to look at the practical issues relating to my study.

Exercise 2.7

How would you start such a task? Assume that you have some background knowledge on language contact, but you do not know any Somalis. List as many different aspects you can think about that should be taken into account when starting this project.

Your list of aspects to take into consideration before embarking on this new fieldwork project could include 'how to find speakers', 'which fieldwork methods to use', 'funding and paying speakers', 'background reading on the subject', and many more. The current chapter will give you – step by step – the example of how the Somali project was started.

Funding

Together with a colleague, Sakel applied for a small start-up grant that was available at her research centre. They received a small amount of funding to pay some of their Somali speakers. Now they only had to find them!

Ethics approval

Before embarking on any study, you should consider the ethics relating to your research. Most universities and funding organizations require you to apply for ethics approval. This means you have to outline your study and how it would impact on the people involved. A committee considers your application to make sure it follows ethical guidelines. These include making sure that you anonymize the speakers by changing their names, if they wish it (see chapter 4.4). Sakel and her colleague applied for, and were subsequently granted, ethics approval from their university.

Finding speakers

One of the most crucial aspects of fieldwork is to find speakers to work with. When, as in this case, you do not yet know any speakers, there are various ways to proceed (see also chapter 4 for a comprehensive discussion of how to find speakers). First of all, Sakel contacted her colleagues already working with Somalis. Two Somali speakers were recommended (henceforth these will be referred to as the research assistants). Sakel contacted them and both were interested in the project. The meetings took place in places convenient to them. In one case an office at the university, in the other a local library. The research assistants were told about the project, and what it was intended to achieve. Furthermore, the topic of what they could get out of the project was discussed.

Exercise 2.8

Think about this discussion with the research assistants. What could you say about the possible achievements of the project? Furthermore, what could the speakers get out of the project themselves? How could the wider Somali community benefit from the research?

Goals and beneficiaries

Sakel had thought carefully about where she wanted the project to lead, prior to talking to the research assistants. She prepared by reading about language contact and immigrant languages and by looking at the methodologies used by similar studies. She also started to learn Somali. In order to get an overview of the linguistic situation, she decided to carry out a pilot study first.

Pilot studies are also good ways to test one's methodology, and to see whether one's general approach works. For this pilot study, Sakel decided to record a wide variety of speakers of different ages and backgrounds.

Once she had talked to the assistants about this, they discussed what they and the community to which they belonged would be able to get out of the project. The assistants would be paid for their work. Yet, Sakel also wanted to make sure that they would find some other interest in the project. Both assistants were keen on the subject, in particular with respect to finding out more about the language behaviour of their children, who had been born in Britain. Furthermore, both had recently received their degrees and wanted to continue their academic careers. Finally, they discussed how the research could be relevant to the wider community. One potential outcome would be to engage with policymakers relating to bilingual education, as well as providing information to the community on how the younger generations could maintain their Somali, if they indeed wished to do so.

Fieldwork methods

Now there is a direction for the project, we can look at the methods to use in the pilot study.

Exercise 2.9

Sakel decided to record a variety of speakers in order to get an overview of the language situation. Now it is up to you: how would you find speakers from different backgrounds? What type of recordings would you do in order to get an overview of the language situation?

Sakel asked the two assistants to find a wide variety of speakers from their extended social networks. The speakers they found were from different geographical backgrounds, of a variety of ages, had different proficiencies in Somali and English as well as varying immigration histories.[4] The project recorded a total of nineteen speakers, which was within the target of collecting data from fifteen to twenty speakers. The two assistants arranged meetings at their own houses, as well as at some of the speakers' houses, for the recordings.

When it came to the linguistic data, Sakel had to find a way of getting an overview of the situation without recording hours and hours of language data. She decided to use picture stories, cartoons without words, that the speakers would study and then tell the story. The idea was that by using pictures, rather than words, the speakers' language use would not be influenced, while all the speakers would tell comparable stories. She used one picture story to be retold in Somali, and another to be retold in English. This was followed by a structured interview in which she asked the speakers about their languages and other information on their backgrounds, such as age, gender, immigration history, and so on. The interviews were based on a short questionnaire to make sure the same basic information was collected from everybody, but apart from that there was room to explore interesting topics in more detail, or to simply have a chat. This way free speech could be recorded, alongside the more formal picture stories. Most of the interviews were in English rather than Somali, as it gave Sakel a chance to take part in the discussion. However, it turned out that for some speakers at least, carrying out the interview in Somali would be a better option. For example, younger speakers who have grown up in Britain and whose English is excellent often speak Somali heavily influenced by English. These speakers tended to retell the picture stories with only a few words in Somali, not leaving much linguistic material to work with. For this reason, Sakel changed her plan during the field sessions and asked the assistants to carry out the interviews with young speakers in Somali. She also noted down that she would have to review whether the picture stories used were appropriate, or if she could find stories that required even less proficient speakers to talk for longer.

Exercise 2.10

How would you thank the speakers for taking part in the study? Would payment be appropriate, and in which case how much? What about the work done by the two research assistants?

Altogether, the retelling of the picture stories and the interviews took no longer than thirty minutes. Sakel wanted to thank the speakers for taking part in the study, and decided to buy small presents (popular chocolates worth £5). An alternative could have been to pay them (see 4.4.2 on payment), but after looking into it in more detail she quickly rejected this idea: the speakers would have had to pay tax on their earnings, which would have involved considerable paperwork for them at the end of the year. Likewise, nineteen one-off payments would have been a huge amount of work for the university finance department administering the grant. In addition to this, some speakers might have been offended if they had been offered a payment of £5.[5] Paying the two assistants was done through the finance department, as they had worked for several hours. They had helped to set up the fieldwork and had carried out some interviews in Somali. The main part of their work was the subsequent transcription and translation of the Somali data. They also helped to analyse the different contact phenomena encountered in the data.

Jeanette Sakel

Somebody once said that every fieldwork situation is different, and this is certainly true for the types of fieldwork I have conducted. Comparing my fieldwork on Somali in Bristol with that on Mosetén in Bolivia, differences not only involve the linguistic aspects studied, but one of the most striking differences for me was in the planning and preparation. When conducting fieldwork on Mosetén, I had to make sure that I took all relevant equipment to Bolivia, including spares. While there was the possibility of having some electronic items repaired in big cities like La Paz, if something broke (e.g. got wet in a heavy downpour or fell into the river while crossing in a dugout canoe) or if I had left something at home, I would have had to do without it when working in the Mosetén area. It took me a lot of planning prior to each fieldtrip to make sure I had all the equipment I needed, and that all was sealed in waterproof bags.

When conducting fieldwork on Somali in the town where I live, I took a much more relaxed approach. Still, I prepared the contents of my fieldwork as meticulously as in the case of fieldwork in Bolivia, but I could relax a bit more with the equipment. There was one point when I was interviewing a number of Somali-speakers and I realized that the hard-drive of my solid state recorder was rapidly filling up. If this had been in Bolivia, I wouldn't have had a way to save the data onto another device and I would have been in trouble. In Bristol, all I did was call my husband, asking him to bring my laptop round. Within fifteen minutes the problem was solved. I would probably not have appreciated how 'easy' this was, had I not been doing fieldwork in the Amazon beforehand!

2.3 Summary and further reading

This chapter gave examples of the beginnings of two different fieldwork projects. In the first case, we discussed one way of starting a project with the aim of describing the grammar of a language. We looked at the methods of text-collection, transcription, translation, glossing, analysis and elicitation. In the second example, we discussed how to start a new fieldwork project on language contact in an immigrant situation. Prior to starting recording, considerable thought had to go into preparing to apply for funding, gaining ethics approval, formulating the research questions, putting together materials to be used in fieldwork and eventually finding speakers.

A number of publications deal with the setting up of fieldwork projects, including the following: Hale (2001) discusses how he started a project to analyse a language from Nicaragua, giving examples from his first page of field notes. Dixon (2011) describes his efforts to conduct fieldwork among speakers of Aboriginal languages in Australia. Craig (1979) describes her fieldwork among speakers of a Mayan language in Guatemala. Bowern (2008) also has a chapter on starting to work on a prototypical fieldwork project.

3   The languages

This chapter is about the languages studied, as well as the other languages used during fieldwork. Apart from the target language, which is the term we will be using for the language or languages under scrutiny, the other languages may include a lingua franca you and the speakers have in common. Of course, you may not need a lingua franca if you are conducting fieldwork in or on your native tongue, or you may choose to do monolingual fieldwork, in which case only the target language will be spoken in the fieldwork setting.

In the second part of the chapter we will discuss the advantages of learning the target language. Whether you analyse an aspect of a language, write a grammar or investigate a multilingual situation, some knowledge about the target language is very helpful prior to embarking on your study. That does not, by any means, imply that you have to be a native-like speaker of the language or languages in your study! In some cases, having access to grammars or other materials may suffice; in others you may learn the languages at the same time as carrying out your fieldwork. In the following sections we will explore differences in spoken and written data. Then we proceed to the challenges involved in working with small and large language groups, endangered languages versus viable languages and purely oral languages versus those with a rich literary tradition. The final part of this chapter deals with ways in which you can find a language or languages to work on.

3.1   Bilingual and monolingual fieldwork

If you are studying a language you already speak, such as your mother tongue, then you may be able to carry out your fieldwork monolingually, i.e. by exclusively using that language in the fieldwork setting. In this case, the question as to whether to carry out monolingual or bilingual fieldwork may not be directly relevant to you. However, for those who study a language they do not know or do not know well, a choice has to be made between carrying out monolingual or bilingual fieldwork. Bilingual fieldwork means that you have another language in common with the speaker of the target language. The common language, or lingua franca, could be your own mother tongue, or a language you have only just learnt with the aim of being able to carry out your fieldwork, and that both you and the speaker know well enough to be able to communicate in. In any case, you need to speak the lingua franca sufficiently well to be able to communicate, while you may have none or very restricted knowledge of the target language.

Monolingual fieldwork, on the other hand, requires the linguist to speak and understand enough of the language studied to make sense of the data. It cuts out the layer of the lingua franca, but can at times be like working on the hieroglyphics of lost languages – except without a Rosetta Stone.

There are advantages and disadvantages to both types of fieldwork. The authors of this book have done both types of fieldwork, and which one to choose is often dependent on the situation.

3.1.1   Bilingual fieldwork

Bilingual fieldwork means that you use a language other than the target language in order to communicate with the speakers.

If you want to study the language contact phenomena found in the English and Somali used by Somali immigrants (see 2.2), your study is inherently bilingual. You may carry out your fieldwork in English, Somali or any other language (indeed, many Somalis currently living in Britain came via another country, such as the Netherlands or Sweden. If you and the speakers feel more at home in Dutch or Swedish, you could choose to use one of those languages.)

If you want to study a South American language, you may end up using Spanish or Portuguese as a lingua franca, as most speakers of South American indigenous languages speak one or both of those languages. Likewise, you could use German to communicate with the speakers of the Slavic language Sorbian, which is spoken in East Germany.

Exercise 3.1

Think about the advantages and disadvantages of using a lingua franca in different types of fieldwork situations.

What is the advantage of using a lingua franca? Well, you may already speak the lingua franca, but not the target language. In this way the lingua franca gives you access to the other speech community. You will find that the speakers will be able to explain complex concepts and in contrast to a situation where you do not have a language in common, you will find that you can cut out a lot of the hard work of trying to figure out what something means. Even if you do not speak the lingua franca well, there may be advantages in using one. For example, you may be able to find materials to enable you to learn the lingua franca prior to conducting your fieldwork, while you may not be able to prepare for learning the target language if there are no (or only few) available materials on that language.

The study discussed in chapter 2.1. (Mosetén) is a typical case of bilingual fieldwork: the common language between researcher and speaker is Spanish, the lingua franca, while Mosetén is the language under investigation. Analysis of the language data is facilitated by the Spanish translations. Furthermore, during elicitation the linguist is able to ask the speaker questions about the target language in Spanish.

The drawback of using a lingua franca is that it may make you study the target language through tinted glasses. You may not understand all the subtleties of the target language, merely because they do not exist in the lingua franca. Furthermore, the speakers may show interference from the lingua franca in their language if it is used as a working language. For example, if you were to ask how to translate 'I'd like to go for a walk today', the speaker may translate this using the same word order as in the lingua franca. This resultant word order may be acceptable in the target language, but may not be the unmarked word order. Or imagine you are studying language contact phenomena; your speakers may be influenced by your using one of the contact languages and they may end up using more features of that contact language because of your input.

This is just one of the reasons why it is important to use a variety of methods when collecting data, and not rely solely on elicitation, in particular when working bilingually. Yet, contact influence may still be present even in most other types of data. For example in Mosetén (see 2.1), Spanish influence is present in the language of most speakers and is not necessarily triggered by the use of Spanish as a lingua franca but rather by the bilingualism of the speakers. Consider also Grosjean's (2008) claim that a speaker may assume a bilingual mode through simply knowing that the interviewer speaks both languages, even if the other language is never explicitly used in the situation. If this were true, even monolingual fieldwork could bring up interference from another language. There are some strategies the linguist can use to avoid interference from another language. Thus, if a truly monolingual mode is desired, the linguist could make sure that the speakers never hear another language spoken by the interviewer (be it the linguist or someone else hired to interview the speakers).

Of course, how this is solved depends largely on the goals of your fieldwork; if you want to describe the language as it is used by its speakers, be it in a bilingual or monolingual mode, some interference from another language will probably arise. If, on the other hand, you want to get a notion of what the language is without too much interference from another language, for example when documenting a language, you may have to prepare carefully for how you will collect your data in order to avoid interference. In this case you could ask a native speaker to collect the data from proficient, possibly older, speakers who have less contact phenomena in their language (though this will only give you a partial picture of the use of the language).

Jeanette Sakel

When collecting data on Mosetén, I bought a tape-recorder for my main teacher and trained him in fieldwork ethics. He enthusiastically recorded many older speakers from remote areas. This had many advantages: he recorded speakers gradually, whenever it was convenient. Furthermore, he was able to ask questions in Mosetén, and put the speakers at ease. It led to a much more monolingual mode than if I had interviewed them. Indeed, quite a few interviews I did often ended up with speakers giving explanations in Spanish while telling a story, in an effort to accommodate me.

Coming back to the concept of bilingual fieldwork, even though there may be interference from the lingua franca, bilingual fieldwork can be advantageous, for example in short studies where it may not be feasible to learn the target language sufficiently well to carry out monolingual fieldwork. Also, working bilingually at the beginning of a study may help the linguist to negotiate more easily about payment or working conditions.

3.1.2   Monolingual fieldwork

Dan Everett

I first learned of monolingual fieldwork in 1976, when I took my first course in linguistics from Kenneth Pike, one of the pre-eminent linguists of the first half of the twentieth century. In one of my first linguistics classes, a speaker of a language that Pike had never studied was brought in to the classroom. Pike switched to Mixtec, which this person did not know. Pike then proceeded to speak to her in Mixtec, showing her a number of natural objects, e.g. fruit, sticks, stones, leaves, etc. and doing things with them, such as dropping them, throwing them, breaking them, using them to hit people, etc. Within thirty minutes he had filled all the available blackboard and overhead projector space with data. He then stopped and thanked the teacher. He proceeded to tell us about the phonemic structure of her language, the grammar (basic word structure and sentence structure), and even was able to classify the language. For a new linguistics student, or even for an old hand, it was most impressive.

To much applause, the speaker left, quite impressed with herself.

Since then I myself have done such 'monolingual demonstrations' many times, at the University of Pittsburgh, Presidency College in Madras, India, the University of Campinas, Brazil, the University of Manchester and other places. The two that most stand out in my mind, however, are demonstrations that I did at the annual meeting of the Linguistic Society of America, in Manhattan, and a special forum to honour the memory of Kenneth Pike at the University of Michigan. Both of the latter lasted two hours and involved two speakers of the same language in each, man and woman, on Kisi and Nepali, respectively. Those were languages I knew absolutely nothing about beforehand. At the LSA meeting, over 110 professional linguists were present, many of whom had more field experience than I did (though not necessarily more monolingual field experience). In fact, there were specialists on the Kisi language in the crowd. In Michigan, there were specialists on Nepali in the audience and Pike's family was present. There is a considerable amount of pressure on you each time you do such a demonstration and many people hope that you will really get something wrong, or at least, the possibility that you might adds to the entertainment value and the suspense. But these 'shows', though I consider them legitimate and very important teaching tools, using them now in most of my introductory linguistics classes, do not begin to bring you as a linguist under the same amount of pressure to perform as real fieldwork in a community of speakers where you have research objectives crucial to a particular state of your career and crucial to the language community (perhaps) or to the relevant funding agency.

Before my demonstration at the LSA meeting, I flew to Dallas to meet with Ken Pike, not long before he died as it turned out, and to ask him why he thought monolingual fieldwork was so important. The main reason that stood out to me from our conversations on the subject was that monolingual fieldwork and monolingual demonstrations teach us about language as a holistic experience. They involve making sense out of interdependent facts about communication, e.g. gesture, intonation, body orientation, facial expression, accent, etc. in ways that simple elicitation, discourse studies, or investigating natural corpora, all of these mediated through a lingua franca, simply could never do. Pike's view of the importance of monolingual fieldwork thus follows from his own theory of language as part of human behaviour (Pike 1967).

Monolingual fieldwork may not be suitable in many fieldwork situations, but it is an important method if your aim is to write a grammar. By being forced to figure out how language, grammar, the body and the social environment are all integrated in communication, the grammar in a sense (regardless of theoretical perspective) becomes more 'concrete' or more intuitive and more easily learnable. There are other advantages to monolingual fieldwork, but this is a very important reason – the 'phenomenology of language'.

There are various reasons why one might work monolingually. Here are some of the more important ones.

First, it could be that you *must* work monolingually. This was the case with the Pirahã. It is very rare today to find an entire people group that speaks no outside language, except for a few phrases and lexemes. But the Pirahã, for important cultural reasons (Everett 2005), have chosen not to learn Portuguese or any other language and have insisted on remaining monolingual. Therefore, there was no choice. Either one conducted monolingual research or one would have been forced to move on to another group.

Another reason for working monolingually is that you may want to learn the language better than you might under normal fieldwork conditions, even though you might plan to move eventually to a lingua franca. In this sense, the monolingual method of fieldwork is just a starting point for you.

A reason that some people work monolingually is because they believe that it is superior all round to using a lingua franca, as difficult as it may be for some field researchers to believe. That is, working through texts, semantics, pragmatics and so on, in only the language of study, is seen by some to give ultimately a better grasp of the language, culture, grammar and people than the 'cheat' of working through another language. Even though not everybody agrees with this, it can be a very well-reasoned position and it is not one to set aside lightly. Usually, it is the view of people (such as missionaries) who have much longer-term goals than the average linguist. But if you want to work intensively to understand one language and people, and are willing to commit many years to the effort, a case can be made that working monolingually is the better option.

If Pike was right in his own writings and lectures on the subject, a researcher might adopt the monolingual method in order to develop a deeper intuitive grasp of the language. How does monolingual research deepen intuitions about a language? Well, it does this by (summarizing Pike) forcing the researcher to approach the language, the grammar and the people holistically, learning all simultaneously. It does this because when there is no lingua franca, the researcher must pay attention to every gesture, every expression, every outsider remark, every response, all nuances of the utterance as a communicative and cultural event (see again Everett 2005), in order to begin to make sense of what is said and begin to make inroads into the understanding of this new language and culture. To put this in terms that Pike invented, and that have been quite influential, especially in the anthropological literature, the fieldworker is trying to move from an *etic* perspective to an *emic* perspective, i.e. from seeing only the surface, physical character of events and states, to understanding the meaning of what is heard and seen, as someone on the inside of the system (though, realistically, of course, one never *is* going to become an insider).

Yet another reason for working monolingually is to demonstrate greater respect for the people whose language you aim to study. This respect emerges as the people see that you are avoiding what may be to them 'languages of domination'. That is, the national language of the country in which they are found, usually the language of the 'conquerors' (or the dominant group), perhaps still having very negative connotations. Moreover, by forcing yourself to learn the people's language and use it as the (reflexive) medium for studying itself, you demonstrate very clearly and publicly a willingness to subordinate yourself to these people. One way, of course, that this is shown, is that you willingly subject yourself to becoming a laughing stock, at least temporarily during language-learning, as a by-product of a genuine effort to learn, and thus, attribute value to the people.

There is an additional reason for working monolingually argued for elsewhere by Everett (2005), which is admittedly very controversial: that it is not always possible to translate between languages, i.e. that not all languages have the same expressive power. In other words, a lingua franca may simply fail you in two ways: (i) by not having the wherewithal to talk about concepts in the target language; and (ii) by misleading the linguist into putting concepts that are in fact not understood in terms of the concepts expressed in another language and culture, which are roughly – but too roughly – equivalent, or in fact very different.

Thus, looking at (i), if you try to speak Portuguese to study Pirahã, the concept of *xibipiio* will be difficult to grasp, because it is difficult to learn what it means without actually using it by speaking Pirahã. The concept means something like 'the experiential liminality of an object', such as when a bird flies out of sight or a man walks into sight from the jungle, or you first hear the sound of an approaching boat or plane. It means to leave or enter sensory perception. But it has cultural connotations that are difficult to express – especially the excitement that a Pirahã feels when they utter it. It would be nearly impossible to figure out a word like this – that corresponds to no concept of English – without using the word and developing an intuition for it that could later guide analysis.

With respect to (ii), in translating a concept like 'to save' someone, this is a general concept in English that even carries religious meaning for some. Someone can save you from sin, save you from drowning, save you from a bad investment. But many languages would use separate words for each. The word *save* has to be learned by using it, not by translating it.

We cannot learn the meanings of words, especially those for concepts very different from those we work with, without using them in speaking the language and understanding culture in which they are embedded.

Of course, there are reasons why a field researcher might legitimately choose not to work monolingually. These include at least the following. First, time is always limited and it may be that in a particular research project there is simply not time to work monolingually, that the researcher simply must use a lingua franca to get at the data they need in the amount of time available. This is fine. But then, of course, all the other advantages of monolingual field research discussed above will be forfeited. And the fieldworker will have to avoid monolingual communities. There is nothing new at all, though, in the idea that researchers cannot do everything but can only do what they have time to do and nothing more. Another reason to avoid working monolingually is to reduce the risk that the field research will fail to turn up anything useful. This is a legitimate concern. If your objective is detailed semantic analysis then, as Matthewson (2004) makes clear, the absence of a lingua franca could adversely affect your research or, at least, require much more time for the same level of analysis. The benefits of monolingual research in this case could be 'outranked' by the disadvantages of working without a lingua franca towards certain goals, especially semantic ones. There is a risk, then, that working monolingually with these goals could result in spending a lot of time and possibly coming away with nothing to show for it.

A final reason that might lead someone to avoid the monolingual method is when the field situation could require moral, ethical or political understanding from the outset of the field research. If you are working in an area where people are particularly suspicious of people from your home country, for example, it will likely be to your advantage to use a trade language, the national language, or some other language shared by you and the local community in order to more effectively explain your purposes and to understand the relationship that the community expects to have with you and the constraints that it expects you to operate under.

Choosing whether to work monolingually, therefore, is a complex decision that will have numerous implications for the fieldworker's research success, trust from the community, overall effectiveness and, also important, enjoyment of the field situation. There is no really 'correct' choice to make. Each person has to make the choice that they think best. The important thing is that people do field research.

Exercise 3.2

Think about how you would prepare for monolingual fieldwork in a possible fieldwork situation. Next, discuss whether one can carry out truly monolingual fieldwork in a contact study (like that on Somali in 2.2).

Jeanette Sakel

The Somali study – in the same way as other studies on language contact – has two target languages. Yet, the way in which speakers relate to the languages is different. The older generation have Somali as their L1, and most are clearly dominant in Somali. The younger generation may have Somali as their L1 at home (though many speak a good deal of English at home as well), but most have shifted to being dominant in English when starting school. Since both English and Somali are the target languages, we could argue that this is a form of 'monolingual fieldwork' in two languages! However, true monolingual fieldwork would involve the linguist speaking Somali when working on Somali and English when working on English!

The following anecdotes give further examples of monolingual and bilingual fieldwork.[1]

Dan Everett

[After arriving in the area by plane, badly motion sick, he entered the Pirahã village for the first time . . .]

Walking along the path to the village, overgrown with grass up to my knees and with river water up to my mid-calf, I smelled hair being singed. My head was throbbing, I was perspiring heavily, and I was thinking that in a few minutes the plane was going to leave me there. (One of the passengers who had visited the Pirahãs several times, but spoke none of the language, had offered to spend the next ten days – the length of this first, exploratory stay – with me. So I would not be completely alone.)

The Pirahãs were clearly asking me things, but I was paying little attention, just thinking that this language sounded like a greater challenge than my brains were up to. The fellow singeing the hair gestured for me to come over and have a look. He squatted by a fire, in the sun, with no shade, and had a large rodent (a paca, I later learned) that he had just thrown whole onto the fire. Blood was coming out of its mouth, dripping from its protruding tongue, and the smoke from its hair was, let us say, pungent. I just managed to control my gag reflex. But now I was beginning to recover. I remembered that I had a notebook and a pen. I pulled out my notebook and pointed to the animal. He looked at it and said something. I wrote it down and said it back. He smiled and everyone else seemed pleased. So then I tried to refer to the whole process, the smoke, the fire, the animal, in an effort to get 'singeing the hair'. He said something back. This time I didn't bother to try to write it. It exceeded my short-term memory's capacity for strange syllables. I stopped there in the hot sun and picked up a stick. I got the word for stick, repeated by six or so Pirahã onlookers. Then I let the stick drop to the ground and got that phrase. And so on. Within an hour after beginning my own private monolingual demonstration, I was pretty sure that the language had only three or four vowels and a small number of consonants, with some very strange sounds among the latter, and that it had two or three tones. I had also learnt about twenty words. Over the next ten days, I learned a number of expressions, none of them particularly useful for normal conversation, but was coming to think that this job might actually be doable. I had promised myself not to read anything about the Pirahã language until I tried to figure some things out for myself first (this was not a good move and I strongly recommend against this – you should read everything you can on the language before ever going to the community). When I emerged from these ten days and started to read what Arlo Heinrichs and Steven Sheldon had written on the Pirahã language, I was pleased to learn that my ideas formed in those ten days were not so bizarre. This was going to take a long time, but I could do it.

Dan Everett

[At a later stage, he went to work on another Amazonian language . . .]

When I first went to the village of the Banawa people (speaking an Arawan language), my expectations for the first day were based, naturally enough, on my previous experience with the Pirahãs. But when I got off the plane, I knew things were very different. The jungle, the heat, humidity and sounds were roughly the same. Yet men came up to me and addressed me in very good Portuguese. By the next morning, I was working with Sabatao Banawa, perhaps the best language teacher I have ever had. Though he had almost no formal schooling, he not only gave me very natural texts, but as we went through them to translate them together, his comments went something like this: 'This word means that the words here were spoken long ago, by a woman. This part of the word means that the one who is speaking is not sure. This part means that the pig was on a log, just above the ground.' And so forth. In other words, Sabatao was able to give me nearly morpheme-by-morpheme glosses. In my first three weeks among the Banawas, I felt I had learned more about their language than in my first six months with the Pirahãs. So even within a similar geographical area, field conditions can be radically different.

Let us turn to another part of the world now, for a final anecdote. This one comes from Loving (1975: 268) about her experience at the beginning of her career, working monolingually with the Awas of New Guinea.

Aretta Loving

We were especially on the lookout to learn to say 'What is this?' After two weeks we were tired of pointing and we wondered if the Awas were not equally tired of seeing us point. Evidently they were not, for they continued to be gracious enough to give us new words as we continued to point. One day, we were cooking some greens around an open fire. I pointed to the food, directing my 'question' to an elderly man standing around looking into the pot. He turned to the man next to him and said *anepomo*. I repeated this thinking this was the name of the greens. He and several others smiled and then leaning towards me, he said *tura* . . .   (1975: 268)

What Loving had learnt here was not what she had asked, but something much better – the precious phrase, 'what is this?'. It is difficult to over-emphasize how important this phrase is in learning a language. A companion phrase 'what is it/she/he doing?' is also extremely important to learn and Loving's anecdote provides a useful clue as to how both phrases could be learned in a monolingual field situation.

3.2   Learning the language(s)

If you do not speak the target language, it may be a good idea to study it prior to embarking on your fieldwork (note Dan Everett's anecdote above). The degree to which you are able to learn the language may stand in some relation to the length of your fieldwork, as well as the availability of materials on the language. In some cases there may be only a few materials, such as short wordlists, but even those can be good to study, as they give you a first glimpse of the target language.

Jeanette Sakel

On my first day in the Mosetén village, I sat under a tree, waiting for the village elders to meet me and discuss the conditions of my work. Various Mosetenes were around me, and we were chatting in Spanish. Behind me, I heard Mosetén spoken for the first time: two men sitting nearby discussed something and I understood the word *shiish* 'meat', which I had learnt studying wordlists prior to my trip to Bolivia. I addressed them in Spanish and said 'I understood that word, *shiish*, it means 'meat', right?' and the two were very surprised that I knew some of their language. They corrected me, however, as I had got it wrong: what they had said was *chhaesh* 'blood'. They had been – discreetly – talking about me in Mosetén, as I had a small cut on my finger, which was bleeding. This could possibly have been an embarrassing situation, but the men were keen to teach me how the two words differed in pronunciation, as well as other words in the language. I had gathered my first fieldwork data!

For languages with a wide variety of materials available, the question is how much to learn. In an ideal world, you would speak the language before embarking on your fieldwork, but that may take you years to accomplish, even with excellent teaching materials. How much preparation do you really need? There is no right or wrong answer to this, as it all depends on how much time you have got, and what type of fieldwork you want to do. It will be considerably easier for you to analyse the language if you have some prior knowledge, to save yourself 'reinventing the wheel'. Chances are that you will learn the language well while you are working on it – for example during transcribing, glossing and analysing your data (see chapter 6).

In the case of the Somali pilot study (see 2.2), Sakel spent a few weeks learning Somali before embarking on the study. This was just enough to understand how certain aspects of the grammar worked and to understand some simple utterances. When recording the picture stories, the same words and constructions came up again and again (e.g. the word for 'bird', as one of the picture stories was about a falcon), and after a while she was able to understand more of the picture stories.

If working bilingually, you may also have to learn the lingua franca if you do not speak it well. Again, your proficiency in the lingua franca will usually improve when using it on a day-to-day basis, but it may be a good idea to speak it reasonalby well already when embarking on your fieldwork, in order not to restrict your work on, and understanding of, the target language. If you do not have much time to learn the lingua franca, you may want to focus on learning a comfortable basic vocabulary and certain phrases (such as greetings or phrases you know will come up when, for example, negotiating payment). The initial goal is instant communication and understanding of what is said back. It is less important in the beginning, for example, to get all tenses right. So, don't be afraid of making 'mistakes'.

There are, of course, some other considerations. If you begin your first day of fieldwork saying 'I'm the linguist' in heavily accented Spanish, the speakers of the language may not take you seriously! It could be a good idea, prior to going to the field, to ask a native speaker to help you go through some of the phrases you will use most often and the answers you are likely to get.

If your aim is to work on particular grammatical structures, semantics or elaborate discourse systems, a very basic knowledge of the lingua franca may not be enough. For example, when eliciting complicated clauses it is a good idea to know how exactly these are expressed in the lingua franca, in order to avoid misunderstanding.

Exercise 3.3

Think about the languages you speak and the possible fieldwork you could carry out with your background. If you have a certain project in mind, think about the amount of preparation needed (e.g. if you wanted to work on an Amazonian language, you would probably need a working knowledge of Spanish or Portuguese, even if you intend to work monolingually).

3.3   Types of language data

There are various types of language data that you may come into contact with during your fieldwork. To begin with, there is the difference between spoken and written data. Spoken data can be innovative compared to the often more conservative written data. There are, however, genres of written language where innovation also happens, for example, online communication and text messaging, which can be argued to be closer to the spoken genre of language. Indeed, when looking at bilinguals' language use in these genres, we often encounter instances of code-switching that are generally associated with a spoken register. So while there is not necessarily a clear divide between spoken and written language, you may nonetheless find striking differences between spoken and written data. Written data can often be more complex in the grammatical structures found: for example, Karlsson (2007) and Laury & Ono (2010) found that in Finnish and in Japanese, written language is considerably more complex than spoken language.

Exercise 3.4

Collect some spoken data in your native language (or the language surrounding you while you are reading this); it could be from friends, neighbours or class mates. You do not need to record much, but try to get informal data, for example a discussion between two speakers. Transcribe (write down) your data and compare the language encountered to written data of the same language. The latter could be a newspaper article or a page from a novel or a formal letter. Then compare your findings to the language found in informal emails, text messages or posts from an (informal) online forum. Evaluate how the data differ.

Such linguistic differences are not just pertinent when comparing written and spoken language, but exist between the registers a person uses. A speaker may address his friends in a different manner from talking to his boss. But even when talking to his friends, his language may vary depending on whether he is tired, awake, drunk, sober, happy or sad. If we can find such differences in the language of one speaker, imagine how different speakers can vary in their language use! The differences may be very minor, for example when comparing the language use of two friends. However, when looking at the language use of people of different ages, social groups and regions, we may find significant differences between the varieties (e.g. Hudson 1996). Consider also the differences between types of written texts, such as instruction manuals, novels and short messages scribbled on 'post-it' notes.

Some linguists may say that the spoken word is the only important thing to study. While this is controversial, not least because sign languages would be excluded, there is a truth to it in that speaking is the primary function of language and all (non-signed) languages have a spoken form.[2] Should we therefore disregard written data altogether? There are clear advantages to working with written data. First of all, written data are generally easily accessible; we can, for example, look at other people's corpora without having to collect any data ourselves. Such corpora are often written, though oral corpora also exist. This brings us back to our definition of fieldwork (chapter 1): prototypical fieldwork would involve working with spoken data. Fieldworkers may choose to include the study of written materials alongside the collection of spoken (or signed) data. However, would working exclusively on written data be considered fieldwork? We could indeed say so, for example when the fieldworker is collecting written texts from speakers directly, rather than relying on already existing data.

Quite a few languages, of course, are not, or only rarely, written. These include indigenous languages such as Pirahã, which is only written by linguists, and Mosetén, which is written by linguists and a few community members. Other varieties used predominantly in the spoken domain, such as slang, will often be written in modern forms of communication, such as text messaging and online communication (see above).

Why is this relevant? It depends on what you are studying. If you want to document or describe a language as comprehensively as possible, it may be wise to collect data that reflect a wide range of linguistic usage. Even in other cases, for example when looking at specific features of language, it may be a good idea to be aware of differences in language use. For example, when conducting a language contact study seeking to investigate code-switching behaviour, studying formal written materials or recording spoken picture stories may not be appropriate to record the desired data. Rather, the fieldworker would aim to look at spoken registers, such as discussions between friends who are all bilingual.[3]

Finally, language use can also vary depending on other factors. Some people get very nervous when being recorded and resort to abrupt sentences and yes/no answers. Other speakers are good at telling stories, while less reliable in elicitation (see 4.1). All in all, when conducting fieldwork of any type, it is important to keep in mind the possible linguistic differences you may encounter.

3.4   Types of languages

Let us now briefly consider the different types of languages you could work on. What does it mean to work on languages with many speakers, as opposed endangered languages? If you have a choice of which language to work on, you may consider whether you value joining existing research networks on a language or language family, or whether you want to become the only 'expert' on a language, language family or language contact situation.

3.4.1   Major languages and languages with many speakers

Working on a major language has the advantage that you will have easier access to speakers. There is likely to be some material on the language already, and in that case it would be beneficial to become familiar with the materials before embarking on fieldwork (that is, if you have access to the materials, which may not always be the case). It would be a waste of time and resources to re-invent the wheel, so find out whether what you want to study has already been looked at.

Some languages with large numbers of speakers, in particular in Africa, have not been described in great detail. Access to the speakers of these languages may be limited due to their remote location or unrest in the area.

In general, even working on a major language can bring to light many new aspects, even in cases where a lot of work has already been done on the language. For example, going back to chapter 2.2, although there are a lot of materials on Somali, including grammars (Saeed 1999), there is very little on Somali in contact with other languages in the diaspora. Consider also our comment in the introduction (1.1) about English not being fully analysed.

Often, but certainly not in all cases, when studying language contact situations, one of the languages is a major language. This is due to the fact that often languages come into contact when a national language (e.g. Spanish in many South American countries) is used in conjunction with a traditional indigenous language.

3.4.2   'Small' languages and endangered languages

In the same way as there are many different major languages, the types of 'small' languages you will encounter vary considerably. Small languages can be very rewarding to work on. Chances are that there is less, if anything, written about them, which means you can become the main expert on that language. Often you work closely together with the people and your work can have real impact for their community.

However, you should be aware of some problems regarding work on small languages. First, you may lose access to the speakers. The reasons could be many, such as some speakers being unhappy with their payment and refusing to work with you in the future. Sometimes, personal conflicts can arise without your knowledge. For example, a speaker may not like you working with other members of the community. It can happen that by the time you are aware of such conflicts, the damage is already done and you may find yourself in a difficult situation (see more on this in 4.3.4). Other problems could be that access to the area where the language is spoken is denied due to war or other conflicts. In the cases mentioned so far, you may still find other ways to work on the language in question, but imagine the case where the number of speakers is diminishing to the degree that there are no speakers left to work with. Endangerment does not always coincide with numbers. Some languages with large numbers of speakers are heavily endangered, because the languages are not passed on to the next generation. This means that while there may be thousands of speakers today, there will be very few speakers in the future. This holds true for a number of African languages, for example. At the other end of the spectrum we find highly viable languages with only a few thousand speakers. An example is the Chimane language of Bolivia (which is related to the endangered Mosetén). Many Chimanes are monolingual, the language is passed on to the next generation, and attitudes among the Chimanes are very positive towards their language. This means that it is highly likely the language will survive, at least into the near future.

When studying an endangered language, you may find it difficult to find fluent speakers. In other cases, you may find a number of fluent speakers, but will be unable to collect different types of linguistic data because they only know one story in their language, or they refuse to meet up with the only other speaker left (maybe because they do not like them, which makes it impossible for you to record conversations). All or most of the speakers may die over the course of your fieldwork, and you may be left with many questions about the language and nobody to ask. These are extreme cases, but on the other hand imagine how important work on endangered languages is, nonetheless! You may be able to document a language (or aspects of a language) that could vanish in your lifetime, your data being the only materials available of that language. The same holds for fragile language contact situations, such as trade languages.

3.4.3   Well-described versus little-studied languages

Some people will see it as an advantage to work on issues that have seen considerable interest from other linguists, which means that there is already a research community to join. This will generally mean that the other linguists will be interested in your findings and that you can discuss your research with others. Likewise, working on a language that has not yet been analysed in great detail, but which belongs to a language family that other linguists are working on may also open up for collaboration. For example, working on an Austronesian language, you can be the world-leading expert on that particular language, but at the same time you have the advantage of being able to attend meetings of people interested in the language family. There will be workshops, journals, as well as books devoted to the subject and you may find it easier to disseminate your research.

Little-studied languages and language families, on the other hand, will give you a field in which you can excel. Your professional networks will probably be other linguists working on similar aspects to those you are interested in, such as specific grammatical structures, the history of the language, language contact or writing a grammar. It will probably also include other linguists working in the same region.

Jeanette Sakel

After working on Greenlandic – a fairly well-described language which attracts considerable interest from the linguistic community – I wanted my PhD research to be on something new. Ideally, I wanted to write a grammar of a little-described language. My motivation was to add to the knowledge linguists have of the language of this world. There was also a more selfish motivation, namely to become *the* expert of a language, rather than one of many studying similar phenomena. I think my wish to do so was borne out of the fact that I had wanted to do my MA (and potentially PhD) on a particular grammatical phenomenon of Greenlandic, but I found out at the last minute that someone I had never heard of before was just about to complete a PhD thesis on the exact topic! I was sure that something like this would not be likely to happen with a less well-described language. I was also very excited about the prospect of figuring out how the grammar of a language works. Before then, I had only investigated specific structures, but now I had the chance to look at a language from a lot of different perspectives. Structures are never unconnected – they are often linked together. Studying one structure will give you ideas about another or may cast questions on other structures.

3.4.4   Working on a language that you speak

You may wish to work on a language that you already speak, be it as a native speaker or proficient second language learner. Such a language could fall into any of the above categories. The last decades have seen an increasing number of speakers of less-described, endangered languages studying linguistics in order to work on their own languages. Similarly, many speakers of better-described languages (including English!) are working on their own languages, conducting fieldwork. Still, we may want to re-consider the issues discussed in chapter 1 as to how to define 'fieldwork': linguists who work on their own languages using introspection and grammaticality judgements would probably not be considered to be doing fieldwork.

Conducting fieldwork on a language that you speak can be rewarding, as you can start to work on the issues you are interested in (be it structures, language contact phenomena, etc.) straight away, without having to work up familiarity with the language first. Furthermore, you may already be part of the language community, which can be helpful when looking for suitable speakers. You may be able to judge which speakers would be appropriate for your study, carry out interviews in the language under scrutiny, and so on. For example, if you were studying code-switching among bilinguals, you could actively join in the recording and even try to trigger code-switching behaviour among the speakers. Indeed, you could do many of the things that linguists who do not speak the language would hire a main language teacher for (see 4.1.4).

On the other hand, there are a number of issues to be aware of when studying a language you already speak. First of all, it is important not to use introspection too much. You may have an idea how something works, but this may be very different from actual language use. Indeed, introspection is a type of 'reported language', and can be compared to elicitation. Second, you may have certain preconceptions of the language, and it is important to study the language as objectively as possible (the same applies to studying a language you do not speak (see 6.4.2

on elicitation). Furthermore, your role in the community may cause speakers to have certain prejudices towards you. For example, when working on dialects of a language, speakers may tend to speak a prestigious variety with you, as they may – consciously or unconsciously – think that this is expected of them when talking to a linguist. Again, this point could be a problem when working on a language you do not speak, and in that case it is even more difficult to control.

3.5   How to find a language to work on

Have you ever wondered how linguists find the languages they work on? To the outsider, this may seem complicated, but there are various ways of going about it. You may already have an idea of which language or languages to work on. If not, you can consider a number of aspects before making your choice. First of all, what is your prior experience? Which possible lingua francas, if any, do you speak or would you be interested in learning? You may have some travel experience and knowledge of particular areas of the world, so think about whether it would be important to you to be already familiar with a culture or environment, or whether you would want to get to know a certain culture better. For example, when choosing to work in the tropics, how will you react to the humid climate? Is the fieldwork area accessible, and how? You may want to work closer to home, but still a number of practical questions may arise, such as appropriate transport connections for you to reach the field site.

Some of these questions may be difficult to answer beforehand, such as how to deal with the tropical climate if you have never experienced it before. Don't despair. It is important to prepare and be aware of what could happen, but most fieldwork includes a degree of 'make it up along the way'.

If you want to find a language to work on, but are as yet unsure of where to go, it may be a good idea to look first at the areas of the world you would be prepared to work in (for example close to home, the tropics, a temperate climate, etc.). The next step would be to identify a language or languages that would be appropriate for the kind of study you want to conduct. The best way to find a language to work on is to look online for linguists working in similar areas, either geographically or on the topic you want to study. Ask them if they know of a language that would be appropriate, for example a language that is in need of documentation and description if this is your aim. Other linguists are often happy to help, and if they do not know a language to work on, they will probably be able to refer you to someone who does. Usually, you will find valuable contacts by talking to other fieldworkers (see 4.3.3).

There are also other ways of finding out more about languages. In general, a search on the internet will give you some idea as to what languages there are and whether any work has been done on them. A good place to start is the *Ethnologue* (www.ethnologue.org), set up by a Christian missionary organization. They aim to list all of the world's languages, the numbers of speakers and regions where they are spoken, additionally giving information on whether The Bible has been translated. This list may give you a first overview of the language of a region, and you can then do more detailed internet searches on languages that you like the sound of, or find other experts to help you in your quest.

Exercise 3.5

Have a look at the website of the Ethnologue and choose one country (exotic or familiar). Now go through the lists of languages given for that country. Which are the indigenous languages, meaning the languages originally spoken in this country before colonization or recent immigration?[4] Which other languages are listed, and why are they included in the list? Find out which languages are well-described and which ones are not, according to the Ethnologue. Then, find information about these languages elsewhere (e.g. the internet). How would you analyse the linguistic situation in this country?

Exercise 3.6

Similarly to exercise 3.3, try to think about yourself as a fieldworker and list a number of points important to you, such as where you would like to spend time and what matters to you. Then, think about how you could combine this with fieldwork, and what sort of project you could undertake.

3.6   Summary and further reading

This chapter has dealt with the languages of fieldwork, including the decision as to whether to work monolingually or bilingually. We discussed the advantages of learning the language(s) of the study, and highlighted the differences between spoken (or signed) and written data. We then moved on to diverse types of languages, as fieldwork on small endangered languages can be quite different from that on major languages. Finally, we discussed how you can find a language to work on.

For further reading on language endangerment, see, for example, Grenoble & Whaley (1998). On monolingual fieldwork, see a similar presentation by Everett (2001). Samarin (1967) discusses many issues concerning the languages of fieldwork. More recent books on fieldwork also have information on these aspects: for example, Crowley (2007) gives advice on how to choose a language to work on. On learning the languages of fieldwork, see Burling (1984).

4　The people

This chapter is about the people involved in fieldwork. You may think that these are the speakers and the linguist. They are indeed the main participants, to be discussed in detail in 4.1 and 4.2. Yet, there are other stakeholders to consider. For example, the (entire) language community, people associated with the language community – or area – in question, as well as third parties interested in your data or in the results of your study. When planning your fieldwork, it may be a good idea to consider which people could have an interest in your work, or what effect your work could have on the people involved. We will discuss these issues in section 4.3. Section 4.4 will be concerned with fieldwork ethics.

4.1　The speakers

One of the first tasks is to find speakers to work with. Not all speakers are equally suitable for fieldwork. While some speakers have intuitive linguistic knowledge, showing a great interest in your work, others find linguistic work challenging. At the same time, the latter may be great story tellers! Yet others have speech impediments such as missing front teeth, which can make it difficult to work on phonological issues. In general, working with a variety of speakers is usually a good idea, as different people are good at different things. Of course, the types of speakers you choose to work with greatly depend on the goals of your fieldwork project.

You may have noticed various terms used in the literature for the people who speak the language under investigation: speakers, informants, consultants, colleagues, collaborators, language-helpers, teachers, interlocutors, sources, sub-jects, assistants. As a general trend in this book, we adopted the term 'speakers', and 'teachers' (see below). 'Informants' is a term that many linguists use, but some consider it controversial, as it sounds as if these speakers are supplying illicit information, such as informers of a clandestine service. Due to these unfor-tunate connotations some linguists try to avoid the term altogether. Even worse than the implication of 'sinister', however, the term 'informant' is bad because it implies that the language community participants in the linguistic research are passive, with no goals of their own, little more than inert sources of information for the fieldworker. 'Consultants' is a term employed instead by some linguists, giving more power to the speakers: they are the ones being consulted about their knowledge. However, not all fieldwork situations involve this aspect of consulting, which could be understood as elicitation only. 'Speakers' and 'teachers' are far more neutral terms, hence our choice in this book (see Crowley 2007: 85–6 and Newman & Ratliff 2001: 2–4 for more of a discussion of the terms used).

We use the term 'speakers' to refer to all members of the language community, whether we work with them or not. Speakers we work with extensively over a longer period of time will also be referred to as 'teachers'. The teachers may help in ways other than merely supplying data, such as with setting up the fieldwork, finding speakers, or even collecting data from other speakers. They may carry out the transcription and translation of the materials collected. We will be going into detail on the different roles of speakers and teachers in 4.1.3, 4.1.4 and 4.1.5.

For now, we will look at what types of speakers you may encounter in general (4.1.1), and then how to contact them and choose people to work with (4.1.2).

4.1.1   Speakers' language use and proficiency

Speakers can differ considerably in their proficiency and language use. Speakers of different ages or social classes may use very distinct structures and lexical forms. Furthermore, there are slang and specialized vocabularies of certain professions. Indeed, finding two speakers with the exact same knowledge of a language will be a challenge. Even the same speaker will speak differently depending on the situation. For example, in a highly formal setting they may choose a variety closer to the standard dialect, but in a less formal situation they may speak a local variety (see 3.3). Think about the way you would, for example, address a potential new boss at a job interview compared to how you would speak to your close friends in the local pub (for most people, at least, there is a pronounced difference!).

If you want to draw conclusions about the language use of a community, it is necessary to include a diverse group of speakers in your study. If you only work with one speaker, you are analysing his idiolect, rather than the way in which the language is used in the community. Of course, you may work with just one or a few speakers, but in this case you have to be cautious with generalizations about the language in its entirety. There are situations when analysing an idiolect is a necessity, for example when there is only one speaker left of a language, or when you only have access to one speaker. You may also be doing a qualitative study (see 6.1), focusing on only one or a few speakers. In all of these cases, however, remember not to say 'language x works in the following way . . . ', but rather always be clear that you are studying one or various idiolect(s).

The other extreme is difficult to achieve as well. If you wanted to take into account every idiolect, it would mean that you would have to work with every single speaker, a task that is impossible for most viable languages (languages with a very restricted number of speakers would usually not be viable, and even in that case it could still be a difficult task to achieve).

If you want to draw conclusions about a population of speakers (for example when conducting a quantitative study, see 6.1), you may have to find ways to include a range of different, yet representative speakers. This is generally referred to as 'sampling'. An adequate sample can help you to draw conclusions about an overall population. You will have to make sure you include speakers representative of that overall population in proportion, including factors such as gender, age and occupation. There are different methods for sampling, such as probability sampling, which means selecting your sample randomly. In linguistic studies this is usually not feasible, as you may have a restricted number of people to work with. As long as you try to stay as close as possible in proportions to the overall population, using non-probability sampling can still lead to valid and generalizable results. Sakel tried to achieve this in the Somali pilot study (2.2), where speakers were selected from the main teachers' networks, trying reflect differences in age, gender, language use and proficiency, and so on.

It is important when presenting the results of your study to refer to your considerations and the ways in which you obtained your sample (see 7.3.3).

Exercise 4.1

Try to get a random sample among the people in your class or your social network. Your aim is to get as balanced a sample as possible, reflecting the different ages and genders present in your population. You can try different sampling techniques, for example, picking out ten people at random. Do those selected truly reflect the people in your overall population? You can also arrange the people according to their age and gender and choose ten subjects that would reflect a spread of characteristics.

Discuss how you could sample an appropriate group of speakers in different types of studies (e.g. a small-scale study such as the one you have just tried out with ten participants, as opposed to larger studies with 100 participants and surveys with 5,000 participants).

So far, we have looked at the individuals' use and knowledge of their language, and how it can differ from speaker to speaker. There is another aspect to consider when taking into account speaker knowledge, which complicates the picture somewhat: bilingualism and language endangerment.

According to Grosjean (2008), bilinguals (and multilinguals) are not two monolinguals in one person. This means that their knowledge of a language may vary significantly from that of a monolingual native speaker. Would a monolingual speaker's language necessarily have to be considered the 'pure' variety? In many parts of the world, bilingualism is the norm, and there may not be any monolingual speakers of certain languages. Depending on the nature of your study, you may have to be aware of the effects of bilingualism on language use.

Bilinguals may use their languages in different 'domains'. These are situations of language use, often divided up into categories such as home (language use with parents, siblings, children), friends, work and official situations. A bilingual may use one language in the home domain, such as with his family and close friends, and another in the official domain, such as at work. This type of bilingualism is common within a diglossic society such as in Switzerland, with Swiss German and High German spoken in different domains at a societal level. At the individual level, many immigrants experience similar divisions of domains, e.g. speaking Somali at home and with close friends, but English at work and in other official situations (as when filing a tax return). Other bilinguals may show less sharp distinctions in their language choice in different situations. For example, a child growing up bilingually may use one language with the mother and another language with the father. The distribution may appear quite equal. Still, there will be differences between the languages: the child may play certain games with dad, while doing other things with mum. This means that the child will probably be more comfortable speaking the mother's language in some situations, while the father's language may be preferred in others. Similarly, a bilingual person living in a multilingual area may use one language when visiting a market nearby, while using another one in a different part of town. Again, knowledge of the two languages may not be entirely the same, even though the domains may overlap.

Most bilingual speakers, even when equally proficient in both languages, have a dominant language at any one time. The dominant language can sometimes surface when speaking the other language. A German-English bilingual, with German being dominant at the time of speaking, may utter (1):

(1)   *I really want to help you, **aber** you should help me, too, **ne**?*
                                  but   TAG
         'I really want to help you, but you should help me, too, alright?'

In this example, two elements from German are used: *aber* 'but' and the tag question *ne?*, translatable as 'alright?, right?'. Indeed, in situations of bilingualism, where one language is dominant at a time, these things tend to surface (especially functional elements such as conjunctions – *but* – and discourse markers – *alright*; see, for example, Matras & Sakel 2007; Matras 2009).

The same bilingual may also utter (2):

(2)   *Tomorrow I go to London ...*
         'I'll go to London tomorrow ...'

In this example the influence from German is more subtle: there are no overt words from German. However, two things are different from how they would be said in English. First, we find that the constituent order is different in the placement of the temporal adverb *tomorrow*. The speaker is following the German constituent order, and German grammatical rules, which influence the English spoken by this person in this situation. Second, we find that the present tense is used instead of the future tense in expressing an action in the future: although this may be considered correct in English, English speakers generally prefer to use the future tense to express future events, while German speakers generally express the future using the present tense as in example (2). Even though it is not wrong to use the present tense in English, such usage is not very frequent. The German bilingual may overuse the strategy acceptable in both languages, while avoiding a strategy that is different in his non-dominant language.[1]

Hence, the language of bilinguals is likely to be different from the language of monolinguals. When dealing with bilingual speakers we will have to take this influence into account.

Apart from speaking their languages in different domains, bilingual speakers may not always be fully proficient in both languages. Indeed, in some cases bilinguals may use one language less and less and start to lose it. You will probably encounter such language attrition when working with immigrant communities or with speakers of endangered languages. There can be various reasons for attrition, such as economic pressures, mixed marriages and language attitudes. The original language is given up in favour of the dominant language in the environment.

Language contact and attrition are fascinating subjects to study, and you may wish to find speakers that are undergoing such changes. However, if your aim is to document a language, write a grammar, or generally study particular aspects of the structure or lexicon, it is best to be aware of these influences and find speakers with a high level of proficiency in their language.

Those speakers who are less proficient than fluent speakers – be it in their grammar use, in using elements from another language much more frequently, or indeed not being able to use the native language without major influence from the contact language – are generally referred to as *semi-speakers*. This term goes back to Dorian's (1973) study of Scottish Gaelic from East Sutherland. She found that some speakers were very fluent, while others had clearly reduced repertoires in Gaelic but were dominant in English. The term has since become common-place in linguistics, particularly in the fields of language endangerment and death.

Since Dorian's study, various linguists have suggested further terms to classify different types of speakers. Grinevald (1997) uses the terms *fluent speakers*, *semi-speakers*, *terminal speakers* and *rememberers*. Terminal speakers, while belonging to the language community, may only be able to express very few phrases in the language. These differ from rememberers, who may have spoken the language in the past but have lost most of their command. The reasons are many: they could have been forced to give up the language, or not had any contact with the language for many decades. The latter category generally also includes speakers who have only passive knowledge of the language.

When it comes to finding teachers, the linguist should be aware of these differences. In some cases there is a decreasing number of speakers left to work with, some of whom are likely to be rememberers rather than fluent speakers

(Evans 2001). In situations where different ranges of speakers are available, however, it seems to be a good idea to work with those with a high command of the language, if it is the traditional language you want to study. If you are interested in contact phenomena, or in language revitalization, on the other hand, semi-speakers or even rememberers may be interesting to work with (Evans 2001).

High proficiency is not everything when it comes to working with speakers. Some speakers are good at giving out linguistic information, such as readily presenting you with different forms of a verb paradigm. Others may be better at telling stories. Some are very intuitive about the structure of their languages, being able to compare languages or point out differences in usage between people of different ages or between villages (to keep things in perspective, it is worth adding that linguists have similar individual differences, which means you may be good at a particular study, while not so good at something else).

There are even a number of reasons why linguists may prefer to work with semi-speakers. Some semi-speakers have a pronounced interest in keeping the language alive, realizing what has happened to their own language use and knowledge. These individuals are often keen to set up language programmes, and invest a lot of time and effort in the study of the language. They may have a great interest in your work, are eager to learn and to help out. Another attribute of semi-speakers is that they are dominant in another language, often the language the linguist is using as a lingua franca (for bilingual fieldwork, see chapter 3). This can be useful if you plan to work bilingually.

While semi-speakers are often easy to access (culturally and linguistically), they are generally fully fledged members of the language community and have access to fluent speakers the linguist may wish to interview. Semi-speakers may even conduct such interviews. Due to this access, they are often ideal assistants when it comes to data-collection. But not just collection, also transcription and analysis of the data can be carried out very well through the help of a semi-speaker. The authors of this book have worked in a number of fieldwork situations where some semi-speakers were able to read and write, while most fluent speakers were not.

Exercise 4.2

Imagine the 'perfect' speaker in a fieldwork project (you can make up a possible project or use one of the examples from chapter 2). What would he or she look like? Which attributes would you judge as the most important ones, which others are less essential? How could the strengths of different speakers be used in your study?

4.1.2   Contacting a language community

There are various ways of contacting a language community. For example, in the Somali study, Sakel contacted other researchers working with members of the community. She also attended events organized by or for members of the Somali community. In this way, she got to know people with key roles, as well as those working with Somali speakers in Bristol.

Jeanette Sakel

In the Mosetén project, establishing contact with the community was far more complicated. I knew of two different 'outsiders' who had been in contact with the community, one of whom was not contactable at the time, while the other was not willing to help me. As I had a restricted amount of time for my PhD project, I decided to go to Bolivia myself to establish contacts and to find out if the language community were willing to work with me. I decided to go to the village of Covendo first, which became the centre of my studies in the end. Once in the village, I arranged a meeting with the village leaders and negotiated my work conditions with them.

This way of contacting a community is possible, though not always the easiest way forward. What would it be like? You would not be associated with any particular interest group, such as missionaries or geologists who happen to work in the area. This can be an advantage, as you will be judged on your own terms and not through someone who could, potentially, be in conflict with members of the community. On the other hand, the people may not be able to 'place' you, may be suspicious of you, and may not be willing to work with you as they do not know if they can trust you. In the grand scheme of things, it is a good idea to find someone who can introduce you to the community, if at all possible, as it generally makes the beginning of fieldwork a lot easier for you.

Once you have been introduced to the community - in one way or another – you can try to find language teachers.

Exercise 4.3

Think about ways of finding speakers. For example, if you were to work on an immigrant language or linguistic minority language in your local community, where could you go to find speakers?

4.1.3   Selecting the speakers

When you start working on a language, there may be a range of people with different backgrounds to choose from. Ideally, you would choose to work with a range of speakers, potentially a representative sample of speakers (see 4.1.1). There are various reasons for this. As discussed above, linguistically, you want diversity and statistical significance (sometimes these conflict) in your sample. But another reason for not working with a single teacher is that the linguist should avoid becoming a *patron* (in the Latin sense), i.e. an employer responsible for the employee's overall well-being. In some types of fieldwork it may be advisable to work with a number of women and men over time, from a variety of ages. At the same time, the fieldworker must guard against confusing data from different dialects and should offer suggestions on how to keep dialects separate.

Dan Everett

There are situations in which, initially at least, you may have little or no choice as to who your teacher is going to be. When I first began research on the Kisedje (Suyá) language, I saw several potentially good teachers. The best, it seemed to me, was a man who was the community's official translator. He was bilingual in Portuguese and Kisedje. But when I approached him, he said that he had no time for such work. Moreover, he said, it had already been decided by the chief that my teacher was to be his daughter. Faced with a community-based decision of this type, it may be acceptable to explain why you'd prefer someone else. But that can be risky at the outset of field research, when you do not know the people or the culture well. By and large, the safest course of action is to make the best of the community's selected teacher(s) and later, when you are better attuned to values, decision-making, persons, and consequences in the cultural context, you can ask for a change in, or additional, teachers if you think it would work better. Once again, however, linguistic field research generally requires multiple teachers. This is because the conclusions are based on the assumption that they have inter-speaker validity. You cannot make this assumption if you work with only a single language teacher. (So don't worry too much about who you get as your first teacher if this person is selected for you.)

Let us assume that the linguist can work with anyone they please. How do they go about selecting a language teacher? Some qualities to look for in a language teacher are given below, although none of these is ultimately necessary or sufficient to guarantee a good teacher. Of course the attributes you are looking for in teachers will greatly depend on the nature of your study, so not all of the following points will apply. Still, they may all be helpful.

1. *Good story teller*: This is important because it will affect the quality of the texts you collect. Especially when collecting oral literature, you should attempt to work with someone respected in the community for telling stories of this sort well and appropriately.

2. *Friendly*: Other things being equal, it would be nice to work with someone that you have a good chemistry with, someone you consider friendly, for example.

3. *Speaker of the correct dialect*: It would be unfortunate if you concluded a significant portion of your field time only to discover that one of the speakers you had worked with in fact spoke another dialect or had given you a very different register than what you thought you were getting. So you must check out from the outset whether your teachers are representative of the dialect you are studying.

4.   *Mother-tongue speaker*: This sounds obvious, but if you have not worked on a language previously, you might mistake someone for a native speaker of the language when in fact it is their second or third language. You must find out what language their parents spoke to them and what language they now speak in their homes (see also our discussion in section 4.1.1, above).

5.   *Patient*: The fieldworker is continually asking questions that a child should know, from the perspective of the native speakers. And they ask questions about details that are extremely uninteresting, asking one to repeat the same word over and over. Thus, working as a teacher for a linguist can be extremely tiring. A good teacher should be patient.

6.   *Reliable*: The linguist's time in the community and the success of the entire field research programme depends on the ability to plan. If a language teacher cannot be relied on to show up sometime near the pre-arranged time and if this goes on for too long (the 'too' to be determined by the linguist), then the teacher is not reliable and should therefore be switched, however delicately – to avoid offence, etc.

7.   *Unintimidated by linguists*: Some language teachers are intimidated by the linguist's education, nationality, money, big words, cushy job, and so forth. Some of these teachers therefore do not like to correct the linguist's pronunciation, or his or her conclusions, data, etc.

8.   *No speech impediment*: If you study the sounds of a language, you need to be sure that the pronunciation you are hearing is a standard one in the dialect/language under study. If someone has an obvious speech impediment, you cannot be sure you are getting standard pronunciations. This can lead to faulty generalizations about the language's phonetics or phonology. Hence, at least for sound-system analysis, language teachers should be free from any speech impediment.

9.   *Shows ability to reflect on language as a formal system*: For some language teachers, the linguist's structural investigations will have little interest or meaning (moving stress around in the word, building and testing sentence paradigms, etc.). But there are rare teachers who turn out to be talented, natural linguists and show an ability to reflect metalinguistically on their own grammar. Such speakers can suggest paradigms, find regularities before the fieldworker sees them, provide transcribed, translated data, etc. They are marvellous linguistic resources and should be looked for, cultivated and trained. Where appropriate, the fieldworker should attempt to give linguistically talented teachers more formal training if they desire it (see also the anecdote below).

10.   *Well-respected in the community (at least not marginalized)*: Occasionally someone available to work as a language teacher is ostracized from the community or seen as marginal (in fact they may be trying to get work as a teacher because they have no other employment).

This can be detrimental to the research if when you proceed to check examples with other language teachers they reject all examples given to you by your 'marginal' teacher, simply because of that person's social status rather than because of their linguistic ability. But you will not be able to tell the difference easily, affecting the research in ways that may not be easy to predict.

Exercise 4.4

Think about your own abilities as a language teacher, if someone should ask you to do such work: would you be good at telling stories, analysing language data or other activities? How about your friends and other people in your network? Compile a list of people you know appropriate for different types of fieldwork (telling stories, etc.).

Regardless of how many or how few teachers you actually work with, it is important to know how to select them. As you select your teachers, you should also give thought to how you present your linguistic objectives, the nature of your job and the nature of your teacher's job to the community. If your fieldwork is on an indigenous language, perhaps the community will have had previous experience with anthropologists. In this case, it is important that you distinguish your objectives, because the linguist will work quite differently from the anthropologist, with objectives that are perhaps harder at times for the people to grasp or sympathize with. In any case it is advisable to avoid claiming that your objective is to learn their language unless you in fact intend to learn it. It can cause misunderstandings if you are cheerfully working away but with no marked progress in your ability to speak the language. If the teachers saw that as their primary goal yet you have not progressed much, this could lead them to conclude that they are bad teachers, you are a bad student, or both. This can lead in turn to a lack of interest in helping you.[2]

Alan Vogel

[A missionary among the Jarawara, he offers the following suggestions on training native speakers, based on his Jarawara experiences . . .]

I think two kinds of training may be relevant here. First, I trained Jarawaras to transcribe tapes of recorded stories. These transcriptions are not perfect by any means, but they are a huge help to me. For one thing, they hear a lot of things that I would not. They gladly spend eight hours a day transcribing tapes. Secondly, I made up a questionnaire on plants with about ten questions. I gave the younger Jarawaras, who write well, the questions, along with sheets of paper, each with a name of a plant that I had gotten, and asked them to get the answers to the questions from the old men who know all about the plants. It produced volumes of information on hundreds of plants. It's important to realize, of course, that when we started with the Jarawaras, no one knew how to read or write in Portuguese or their own language. We had to devise the orthography (adapting the Jamamadi orthography), and after members of another missionary organization made up a primer, my wife taught several young men how to read and write Jarawara. She taught them how to teach others, and they did. The other missionaries among the Jarawara did the same thing in Agua Branca, and today the Jarawaras are basically literate in their own language.   (personal communication)

4.1.4   The main teachers

The main teachers are the people you work with a great deal. They may help you in your study by providing direct access to the language community you are studying. The exact roles of the main teachers can vary and will depend on each field situation, as well as the qualities of the persons in question.

A main teacher is often someone you will find after contacting the community, someone who is either recommended to you (such as the two speakers in the case of the Somali fieldwork, see 2.2), someone pointed out by the community as their natural 'linguist', or someone who approaches you with an interest in your work (not just an interest in the potential payment – even though that may play an important role as well; see below for fieldwork ethics).

It is good to get to know the speakers in question, and to negotiate what you expect from them, as well as what they can expect from you. They may be able to help with the gathering of data, such as going out to record other speakers. They may be in a position to help with the transcription and translation of the data, in particular if they are literate and bilingual.

Depending on your study and what type of speaker you are working with (fluent speaker, semi-speaker, etc.) you may be able to do elicitation (see 6.4) with your main teacher, or they may be able to help you translate or analyse your data. It can be very helpful to have good access to this speaker to sort out any minor problems of analysis and interpretation. In general, it is useful to have a number of teachers who are able to help in different ways. If the situation permits, it would be ideal to have more than one main teacher, so that if one is not available for a while, the other one is still around and the project does not have to be put on hold. Or, you may have different (main) teachers for different tasks: some people are excellent at gathering data, but less proficient in their language so that they are not ideal for elicitation. Others are good at story telling, but do not have the intuitive abilities desirable for elicitation, while yet others are excellent at transcribing and translating the data.

4.1.5   Other speakers

Unless your study focuses on the speech of very few people, you will work with a broader range of teachers and speakers. You may work with these teachers over a short period of time, or revisit them at various times during your fieldwork. Other speakers may contribute only once to the project.

In the Somali project (see 2.2), those people taking part in the picture stories and interviews would be considered 'other' speakers. Sakel only worked with these speakers once. The two research assistants, on the other hand, would be the main teachers – those organizing the study and being at hand for the linguist to work with. When collecting data from a wide variety of speakers, as in the Somali study, such a distribution of speakers and main teachers is typical. In studies of a more qualitative nature, such as the documentation and description of a language, other teachers' contribution to the fieldwork can be varied. For example, in the Mosetén project (2.1), some of these additional teachers were interviewed by the linguist, and some were interviewed by the main teacher, yet others were recorded when giving public speeches, telling stories, participating in (minor) sessions of elicitation and grammatical judgements, or simply observed by the linguist (participant observation).

How do you go about finding these speakers? Often the main teachers will be able to help. In the Somali study, Sakel wanted to find speakers of different backgrounds, ages and immigration histories. The main teachers looked for suitable speakers among their acquaintances, organizing the fieldwork sessions around the availability of these speakers. In the Mosetén fieldwork, the main teachers similarly helped to find other speakers. Once the linguist was known in the community, many other opportunities to find speakers opened up, and many speakers who were available and interested were recorded.

Altogether, it is a good idea to have access to the community via one or more main teachers. Once that is achieved, it is usually no problem to get access to other speakers of the language. Yet, the following anecdote shows that finding other speakers can prove difficult when language attitudes come into the picture.

Magnus Huber

When working with speakers of Ghanaian Pidgin English, he was made aware of a man who 'really speaks pidgin' and 'whose pidgin is so strong that few people understand what he is saying'. However, when he met the man, it turned out that he merely had a speech impediment. The other speakers had associated 'incomprehensible' with 'pidgin', showing that whatever is unclear and diverges from the norm is stigmatized and regarded as a 'pidgin'.
(personal communication)

4.2   The linguist

Apart from the teachers, the other main participant is the linguist, or the team of linguists (see 4.2.3 for individual versus group fieldwork). Ideally, the researcher has received some training in linguistics and fieldwork prior to embarking on the study. Such training differs depending on what the focus of the study is. Someone wanting to write a grammar of a language should have a general understanding of phonology, morphology and syntax, as well as a broad knowledge of different linguistic theories and directions. For example to write a descriptive grammar which will still be readable in twenty years from now, it may not be a good idea to follow the latest theoretical framework, which may be out of date at that time. Someone embarking on a study on language contact phenomena will need a general idea as to what to look for and which aspects would be worth studying in order to arrive at new insights in the field.

Altogether, good preparation is important and should be prioritized, even when there is little time. There is no reason to re-invent the wheel by studying something that is not relevant or that has already been much studied.

Exercise 4.5

Use self-reflection to list your strengths and weaknesses. Include your professional background (such as training in different fields of linguistics), as well as your personal background (patience, etc.). How can you take advantage of your strengths in a fieldwork project? How could you overcome your weaknesses?

Dan Everett

In early 1977, I began a four-month 'Field training course' offered by the Summer Institute of Linguistics (SIL, a missionary organization) in Chiapas, Mexico. To all participants, however, it was known informally as 'Jungle Camp'. Jungle Camp had five phases. First, there was an orientation to Mexico, cross-cultural relations and equipment purchasing in Dallas, Texas. Next, there were several days of adaptation to Mexico, including visits to the Ballet Folklórico, Tenocticlan, Basílica de San Guadalupe, etc. After this general orientation to the country, we proceeded south to Chiapas, to SIL's initial training base, Yaxmiquilpan, where we learned to butcher beef, preserve meat, give injections, provide first aid care, travel in dugout canoes over rapids, repair kerosene lamps, live under primitive conditions, learn how not to get lost in the jungle, which jungle plants can be eaten, how to hang a hammock with mosquito net, etc. We also began physical conditioning, involving multiple day-long hikes of up to thirty miles through the jungle, in very hard conditions (90% + humidity, knee-deep mud, mosquitoes, and so on), including one fifty-mile hike to the village of the Lacandon people. The training's principal highlight was a 'survival hike', when people were pulled out of the group at random and taken into the jungle to spend three to six days alone, with no food, no water, and only what they were wearing – no change of clothes. This meant that everyone walked around with rope, matches, a machete and a few other tools that could be carried, in anticipation of the survival hike. The lesson learned was very simple indeed – be prepared (and all that preparation did help when I was called out and spent five days alone in the jungle, foraging and fishing and other things that linguists don't normally expect to do).

The Lacandon village was the first completely new cultural experience for me. All other trips I had made, I could at least identify a few points of similarity with my previous experiences. Not with the Lacandones, however. Everything seemed so different from anything I had ever experienced before, that I felt somewhat overwhelmed. Unfortunately, I was unaware of what to observe or how to observe in such circumstances, having no background on the Lacandones, no linguistic orientation to them, etc. I arrived in utter ignorance and left no less ignorant and shocked at how different things were from what I had expected to find. It is never excusable for a student of culture or language to enter another group without preparing themselves carefully first with good questions to answer.

So many things could have commanded my attention. For example, how was the village located in relation to the jungle, bodies of water, other villages or settlements? Who lived in each house and what were their kinship or other relations to people in other houses? What were the kinship constraints on spatial distance or proximity of dwellings? What greetings were used? (By the people for foreigners? Between men and women?, etc.). How were people dressed? (Were there, for example, differences by age? By gender? By village prestige?) What were the dimensions of the houses? Of the open spaces between them? What were the terms for basic vocabulary (e.g. the Swadesh wordlist)? And on and on. I measured nothing. My photography had no real scientific objectives. My first day among the Lacandons was largely a day lost, a precious opportunity squandered. The first day in a new environment is the only time you will ever see the culture without previous experience of it. At the same time, from that first day, the sensory meter starts running. And this flow of sensory experience biases the mind, by accustoming it, by making the new old, by dulling curiosity. This in turn means that it is unlikely that you will ever be as acutely alert to the newness and strangeness of this culture and language as on the first day. It is your responsibility, therefore, to arm yourself with questions and to begin asking and trying to answer them within your first hour in the community.[3]

4.2.1   The significance of the first day

When you are new to the community you are studying – be it in a remote setting, such as Dan Everett's experience recorded in the anecdote above, or in the town where you live, with people you have not previously met – the first day is crucial. You will get to know people and they will get to know you. To make this first encounter as enjoyable and as successful as possible, there are a few things you can do.

First of all: be prepared! We cannot repeat this often enough: read about the people you are working with; find out about their language and linguistic situation.

This first day is the day when the speakers will form their opinions about you. Are you a trustworthy person? A nice person? What are your purposes there? How approachable are you? Will you give them things 'for free'? Are you someone people want to know better? Linguistically, you are more likely to impress positively by accurate mimicry and quick learning and use of phrases. As you unpack your bags, you should listen for question-like intonation and try to mimic it. Don't worry about mimicking things you do not understand. Of course you will embarrass yourself. Just do not take yourself too seriously and you will be fine. Have a good time.

This is also when you begin to form your working and personal relationships within the community. First impressions are very important. The consequences of a bad first impression are difficult to gauge. So it is better to give a good first impression and to make an effort to receive one. Yet, that can be tricky. If someone asks you for something, will giving it to them make you seem like a pushover, forever dooming you to nagging about giving away your possessions, or will it be seen as a sign of generosity, not necessarily inviting more requests? A way to deal with this is by watching others, asking others, reading and learning from others' experiences.

On this initial day of newness, you should be learning more than linguistics. For example, this is the time to draw maps of the community, learn who the community leadership is – if there is one – and where they are located. If possible, contact the community leadership before you set off. This might be by phone or email, possibly by radio in more remote areas. Explain your objectives, your aspirations and find out about theirs. Begin negotiating the understandings necessary for all to benefit from the research (see 4.4.4). If you are living with the community, learn how take care of your rubbish and other waste, where and how to get water, and so on. Find out about proper relations between strangers (you!) and the community. Photographs are best taken at this stage, before jadedness sets in. This is also a vital time for gathering metalinguistic phrases, e.g. 'what is this?', 'what is she doing?', 'when are you going?', etc. Use this day to the fullest. It will never come again. And no other days will be remotely similar.

4.2.2   The role of the linguist among the speakers

In a field situation, the linguist may become a person of authority: you are an employer, having certain responsibilities within the community. This role may not come naturally to everybody and initially it may be a bit of a shock. Even in a non-prototypical fieldwork situation, your speakers may look to you to help with the different aspects arising from the project, for example how to fill in an income tax return (following the payment of their work), or how to get the permission to work in the first place, if they are an asylum seeker.

When carrying out fieldwork in a poorer country, you may be incredibly rich compared to the people you work with, even if you survive on very little in your home country. When working with isolated communities, you are likely to be in demand for your outside knowledge or access to goods such as medicine. This is a role some fieldworkers prepare for by reading classics such as Werner (1993/2010) *Where there is no doctor* (see 5.2.4). If you are carrying out a questionnaire study or linguistic experiments, the way you are viewed by the speakers may greatly influence the data you are presented with.

Many speakers get great satisfaction out of working with linguists. Either, they are naturally interested in how their language works, or they find it exciting to work on a valuable project for their community. It is worth keeping this in mind when doing fieldwork: the speakers are interested in what is going on, even if they may be shy and not say so.

In all situations, the linguist has to be patient and acknowledge the efforts of the speakers. There is no place to say 'what you're telling me is wrong'. You may not have understood the language fully, and what the speaker comes up with should be taken into account. Even if you have the suspicion that what they say is misunderstood, remain polite and accept the judgement of the speaker. You may then check the data with others and if your suspicions are well-founded you can avoid working with this particular speaker in the future.

Dan Everett

Occasionally I meet linguists or anthropologists with the quaint idea that they can become just like any other member of the community. So if they see the people going nude to take their baths, for example, these people cheerfully skip to the river with the rest of the community, in all their European nakedness. Most communities are puzzled by such behaviour. The fieldworker should show respect and not give offence. And they should adapt *to an appropriate degree* to the culture and behaviour of the community, but they are usually expected to respect the simple fact that they are not one of the community and will never be exactly like them. There can be exceptions, of course, but it is important that the fieldworker enter the community aware that 'going native' can be and usually is both silly and offensive.

The chief of the Kisedje people, Kuiussi, raised this issue with me at the beginning of my project to study their language. He said, 'I don't want to see you or any of your people naked in our village. We go naked, this is our custom. But it is not your custom and it means something different to you than it does to us. And I don't want any of your group having sex with any of our group because you are not part of our group and we are trying to preserve our language, our culture, and our identity.'

All the same ethical standards that would apply to the fieldworker at other times, for example at their university or if conducting fieldwork in their home country, apply to them in the language community. Moreover, to these can be added the standards of the language community and the laws and expectations of the country in which the community is located. 'Sex, drugs, and rock n' roll' are not what the fieldworker has gone to the community for. Most communities have extremely conservative values concerning personal dignity and morality. Some have more liberal standards. The general rule that we would like to suggest in this regard is that the fieldworker figure out the moral standards of the community and follow them closely, even if some members of the community appear not to do so.

A final issue has to do with the fieldworker's potential 'temptation' to interfere in moral actions of the community. For example in a recent well-known case in Brazil, a missionary couple interfered with a community's practice of infanticide, by taking the baby that was about to be killed out of the village by emergency flight, causing some offence among some in the community (even though in this particular case the parents of the baby wanted it taken out of the community). This is roughly like an anthropologist studying US culture blocking access to abortion clinics. It may be a deeply felt moral conviction on the part of the fieldworker but it will always have extreme consequences.

Dan Everett

I have seen Amazonian Indians torture animals, roasting them alive, plucking out their feathers and chasing them around, giving them to little children to pull apart while they are still alive. I have never interfered. I have been bothered by this many times and deeply. Perhaps another person would have interfered. I did interfere once when a group of men were about to sexually harass a young girl in the village. Should I have done that? I felt that I should have at the time. And there were no bad consequences to anyone, though I had no way of knowing what the outcome would be.

4.2.3   Teamwork among linguists

Fieldwork – in particular prototypical fieldwork – has long been considered the domain of the individualist, the strong personality who is self-motivating, able to withstand loneliness, well-rounded – a sort of Indiana Jones. That is, it is not normally thought of as an environment for teamwork (at least not with members of one's own culture). Still, we are not just looking at prototypical fieldwork here. Furthermore, even the most prototypical of fieldwork situations can benefit from group fieldwork.

Exercise 4.6

How could fieldwork in a group be advantageous to individual fieldwork? Think about fieldwork in remote settings, as well as non-prototypical fieldwork, such as on immigrant languages in your home environment.

Working in a team of linguists, you can take advantage of a larger knowledge base. If your team is balanced in terms of specialities and experiences, you could have solid coverage of most of the fields studied. You can review data together and discuss methodologies. You can also make use of the individuals' strengths. For example, if one person in your team is very outgoing and good at interviewing, this may be the person to choose to do elicitation or carry out stimulus tests (see 6.6).

Some studies, for example documenting and describing a language, draw on a number of specialized skills that may go beyond those of individual linguists. Just as there are more specialities available, a team can achieve more. The task of, say, writing a grammar, can be distributed and each member of the team can work on a section of the grammar. To be sure, everyone should read everyone else's work and comment on it, but there is no way that a single individual can do the same amount of work in the same amount of time as a well-organized, well-selected team. One member could take primary responsibility for a dictionary, another for a pedagogical grammar, another for the reference grammar. There are many ways the tasks could be divided so as to increase both their scope and quality.

Another important advantage of team research is that it can help make results more replicable for non-team members, as well as facilitating replication of results prior to publication. This is so because working as a team enables all results, methodologies and analytical decisions to be subjected to discussion, criticism, testing, refinement and development by the group as a whole. If the research team is well-managed, with each team member contributing a needed speciality, then each member will teach the other members, challenge the other members, and strengthen the project as a whole, beyond what any single field researcher could accomplish working alone.

4.3   Other parties

Apart from the speakers and the linguist, a number of other parties can be directly or indirectly involved in your fieldwork. They may have an interest in your work and its results. These parties include the general language community, organizations working in the area or in related fields and other researchers. We will discuss these one by one, followed by how to deal with conflicting interests.

4.3.1   The language community

The first group of people interested in your research will often be the wider community of speakers of the language (see also the ethics section, 4.4.1). It is important to keep in mind that these people have a close and often emotional relationship with their language. Be kind. Linguistic expressions such as 'this language isn't ergative, while all the surrounding languages are' may not be perceived too well by the community, as they may think they are 'less' in some way than the others around them. Rather, saying 'this language is special in displaying accusative alignment, while all surrounding languages are ergative' may give the speakers something to be proud of.

Often, fieldwork leads to a change in language attitudes within the community. By your sheer presence, the speakers may find that their language is worth something: 'At least this linguist is interested in it!'

Jeanette Sakel

When I first started my fieldwork among the Mosetenes, I found they were proud of their heritage, yet I had the impression that they tried to keep their language and culture separate from life outside the community. Most Mosetenes would only be seen speaking Spanish in the local market town, inhabited by mostly Spanish-speaking migrants from the Andean highlands (many of Aymara origin). It turned out that the latter group had quite negative attitudes towards the Mosetenes and their language. I overheard opinions like 'they don't wear shoes, they're wild natives living in the forest'. Funnily, the Mosetenes dressed in a much more Western way than the Aymaras, many of whom were clearly showing their ethnicity in their dress. I had the impression that the negative attitudes towards the Mosetenes and their language were among the main reasons for the language being endangered.

When I conducted fieldwork on Mosetén, some people became aware that their language could be used for something. The language became a source of income for a wide range of speakers, in particular the main language teachers. In the course of the fieldwork, we put together booklets in the language and distributed these among the speakers. People in the community saw that their language could be written down. It was no longer merely perceived as a 'dialect' (a common way for people to mis-name small languages), but as a language in its own right.

Usually the language community has an interest in your research results, and sometimes they do not like your findings. You have to keep in mind that you have a responsibility as to how the community is portrayed to the outside world: make sure you depict things as accurately and non-offensively as you can. Remember that the speakers helped you and have the right to have their data discussed fairly. In some cases, 'bad' behaviour on behalf of linguists can lead to all sorts of repercussions, not just for the linguists themselves but also for coming generations of researchers from any other fields (see also Crowley 2007: 172).

4.3.2   Organizations in the area or in related fields

This heading encompasses a wide variety of organizations with a potential interest in – or even impact on – your work.

Some organizations have been set up directly by members of the community you are working with. It is often a good idea to be in contact with these groups, while keeping in mind the goals of your own study. It can sometimes be easy to get overwhelmed by other agendas.

There may also be governmental organizations working in the community, and they may have a pronounced interest in what you are doing. In Brazil, the Indian Agency (FUNAI) as well as several other governmental agencies are often directly involved in work in the language communities, and contact with them is unavoidable (for example FUNAI controls access to language communities). In the Somali community in the diaspora, you may come into contact with officials from the immigration service and similar organizations. In all cases these organizations may be valuable sources of information and collaboration and they will most likely be interested in your research results as well. Be aware that the data you have collected could, in principle, have negative effects on the language community or on individual speakers. It is best to make sure that ethical guidelines are closely followed, and that the speakers' anonymity is maintained at all times, unless you have been given permission to use their names.

Other organizations you may encounter in a fieldwork situation are funded projects, often associated with an NGO (non-governmental organization). These could be development agencies in Third World countries, projects working on the integration of immigrants, or projects working with bilingual education. Again, it may be a good idea to network with these organizations and find synergies.

In a remote fieldwork setting, but also in other situations, you may work alongside missionaries or other religious organizations, who – like you – will have their own agendas. In most cases, missionaries aim to understand the languages of the peoples they study, and you may be able to share you linguistic findings.

Jeanette Sakel

When carrying out fieldwork on Mosetén, I contacted the North American missionaries working on the only related language, Chimane. One of the missionaries, Wayne Gill, was a keen amateur linguist, and had put together a substantial dictionary of the language. He had also written a pedagogical grammar for new missionaries, as well as a variety of school books and materials of a religious nature. His linguistic work was very valuable to me and the dictionary in particular was helpful many a time when analysing my data.

During my second fieldtrip to the Mosetenes, I decided to travel to the adjoining Chimane region in order to meet up with Wayne Gill. I found people who were willing to take me downstream – deep into the Amazonian jungle – by boat, and who dropped me off at the best mooring place and pointed me in the approximate direction of the mission. I followed their directions, walking along a footpath that forked occasionally.

I had to cross small streams, and some of the paths were very muddy, so I decided to take my shoes off. After about 45 minutes, by which time I should have reached the mission, I was still in deep wilderness and started to worry. Soon after, I was met with an extraordinary sight on my jungle path: there was a group of cows, led by a scary-looking bull. And there was me, barefoot, on a very narrow path flanked by dense vegetation, forearmed with warnings about snakes and spiders, trained in techniques of how to minimize their dangers. I would never have expected that cows would be my most dangerous wildlife encounter! I stayed back, unsure of what to do. Not wanting to look the bull in the eyes, I slowly started to put on my shoes. Luckily the majority of the cows lost interest in me. However the leading bull stayed rooted to the spot looking right through me. There was nothing I could do but stand still and hope for the best – there was no route around the cows as this would take me into the dense undergrowth. After another few minutes in this 'Bolivian stand-off' the bull eventually decided to take off into the undergrowth, as did the rest of the herd.

Visibly shaken, I continued on the path and soon came to a smallholding (hence the cows!). There was an indigenous-looking man in the yard. Knowing that many Chimane speakers are monolingual – especially in remote locations like these – I greeted him in Chimane and proceeded to ask him in Mosetén (with as good a Chimane impression as I could master) where the house of the missionary was. He smiled and pointed me in the right direction, replying in Chimane that I was almost there. Then he left, not surprised at all that I spoke his language. I set off along the path again. I don't know what had surprised me more: the cows on the jungle path, or the fact that I had just had my first conversation in Chimane without the interlocutor being the least surprised that I spoke his language!

Apart from the organizations mentioned so far, you may also get into contact with other groups living in the area. Examples of these could be the Aymara settlers living in the Mosetén region, or other immigrant communities in Bristol. These people may be interested in your work, maybe because they want you to work with them instead, because they fear that they would be portrayed badly in your research or because they have a genuine interest in the people they share an area with. Often, speaking to these locals can give you a different insight into the linguistic situation. For example, settlers in the Mosetén region may give new insights into the linguistic attitudes leading to the endangerment of Mosetén. Speaking to other immigrants in Bristol about speakers of Somali, we may gain more insights into potential conflicts. For example, time of immigration may be related to status within the area, and the Somalis, being one of the newest waves of immigration into the city, may have a low status among others, which could have an impact on their language use.

Exercise 4.7

Take a community of immigrants or language minorities in your home environment. Find out which organizations (e.g. governmental, non-governmental) work with the community. If you carry out a thorough search you will probably end up with quite a long list.

4.3.3   Other researchers

Consulting libraries or archives specializing in the area or located in the area where your study takes place, you will learn about other research that has been carried out in your field. This could be other linguistic research or studies of a different nature conducted in the same field situation. For example, various other researchers have been in contact with the Mosetenes, including anthropologists, geographers and geneticists. The Somali community in Bristol was studied by historians and educationalists.

Depending on your interests, timeframe and involvement in the community, it is usually a good idea to establish contacts with the other researchers: it can lead to collaboration, you can use the same pool of resources, such as access to speakers, and you may find common interests that could lead to future grant applications.

When conducting fieldwork in a different country, you may encounter national scholars working in similar fields. The fieldworker should (and may be obliged to) develop close relationships with them. It is important that the local scientific community know about the linguist, about the research being conducted, about the community's response and so on. There may be legal requirements to this effect in the country in question (as there are in South American countries, for example), but beyond the legal requirements it is simple professional courtesy to develop and cultivate relationships with linguists or related disciplines in the country of research.

You may also come across researchers who have studied the language or linguistic situation you are looking at. You will probably come across these as part of your fieldwork preparation. Unless you are working on a well-described language or linguistic situation, it is a matter of courtesy to contact them and tell them about your work. Chances are they will be happy to welcome someone else into their community. They may have unpublished materials that they can share with you, or ideas on how to proceed and where to start; or they may be available for collaboration in the future. On the odd occasion, other researchers may be 'territorial' and conflicts may arise.

4.3.4   Conflicting interests

Without trying to be pessimistic, we will have to mention the scenario of conflicting interests which field linguists may encounter from time to time. The people you work with may have conflicts with other groups that you may be dragged into by working with them. Sometimes, conflicts arise within a community, for example individual speakers not liking each other. There are cases of linguists not being able to record conversations because the last remaining speakers of a moribund language have refused to meet up and talk to one another. You may come across conflicts of various types, and will have to find ways of dealing with them, or at least accommodating to them, in your fieldwork.

We will look at four common types of conflicts in this section: **1.** problems with the speakers; **2.** problems with the community; **3.** problems with organizations; and **4.** problems with other researchers.

1.　　*Problems with the teachers*: You may, at one point, run into problems with one or more of your teachers. These could be problems such as money-related issues or problems based on misunderstandings. The best advice is to adhere to the ethical guidelines (4.4). Make sure that you are fair to the speakers and teachers and portray them fairly. If there are still unresolved issues, you may have to consider how to either tackle the problem directly or find new teachers. The latter can – in some situations – be difficult, so it is always best to evaluate the situation. What led to the problem arising in the first place? What could you have done differently? Can it be mended – or could it be mended in a subsequent situation (i.e. with other teachers)?

2.   *Problems with the community*: In a number of cases, linguists have encountered problems with the language community during or after their fieldwork. In some cases, the community does not support the work and wants the linguist to stop – or refuses the linguist permission to disseminate the data. For example, some indigenous communities are reluctant to 'give away their language' and community leaders may have very clear ideas as to what you are allowed to publish and what not. In some cases, community leaders or important members of the community may block your work for political or other reasons. Ethically, the data belong to the language community and they may refuse you permission to publish the data. It may be advisable prior to starting work on a language to check out whether such a scenario is likely to happen and how, if possible, you could avoid it. Questions you could ask are whether the community needs to come to a consensus, if one person can block your work, or whether you will get general consent from the community leaders or teachers prior to your fieldwork. Talk to other linguists who work on the same language or in surrounding areas and ask them about their experiences. This may prevent serious problems later.

3.   *Problems with organizations*: You may not be the only person working with the speakers. There may be other organizations with an interest in the people. Keep in mind that in the same way as your research has a goal, the other people are working towards their own agendas. While it is good to be open and offer to collaborate or help, it is important not to lose sight of your agenda. It may sometimes be difficult to deal with people who do not want you to work in the area. Make sure you stay safe.

4.   *Problems with other linguists*: In some cases, other linguists working in the same or related areas may react negatively to your research. A way to ease this from the start is to contact all, or as many researchers as you can, involved in the area and tell them about your research. You could involve them in some of your work. Collaboration can teach you a lot and make friends of potential competitors. Unfortunately this does not always work out. Many linguists have been in situations where other linguists have reacted very negatively to their research. There is no real solution to this, other than saying that no one 'owns' data, other than the language community itself. However, make sure you are not the cause of the real problem: be ethical in your choice of what you study. If you know someone else is doing a similar study,

choose a different topic or if that is not possible, try to collaborate with them. Find a way in which both of you can get something out of the research, without treading on each other's toes.

4.4   Fieldwork ethics

As will have become clear from the chapter so far, ethics should be at the very forefront of your mind when conducting fieldwork. Establishing a 'best practice' for ethics cross-culturally can be complex. On the one hand, there are universals or near universals of conscience and you can go a long way towards establishing a sound ethical basis for your fieldwork by following your conscience and 'doing what seems right'. But regardless of how well-developed your conscience is, this subjective rule of thumb is far from an adequate basis for governing the ethical aspects of any given fieldwork project. Ethical fieldwork is not simply avoiding gaffes or the giving or taking of offence, or failure to commit criminal acts. Just as peace is more than the absence of war, so ethics involves a positive, pro-active code of behaviour and right-thinking intended to leave the field situation and language community better off than when the linguist first 'found' them. Moreover, no researcher can avoid explicit consideration of ethical issues, because all major universities and funding agencies in the Western world require that all research projects associated with them pass a rigorous ethical review that requires that the researcher(s) deal with the issues discussed in this chapter. Furthermore, many *countries* have protocols for ethical fieldwork that the researcher needs to be aware of prior to conducting their study. It is best not to assume that you will be told about these. Rather, you may have to actively seek advice on these issues at your university, as well as the requirements of the country in which you want to carry out your research.

In what follows we will distinguish between 'language communities' and 'individuals'. When possible, both should be involved in the ethics considerations. However, in some cases this is difficult or even impossible. When talking about a 'language community', this can be the entirety of speakers of a language, such as the Pirahã language community (approx. 450 speakers); it could also refer to the language community within a certain area, e.g. Somalis living in Bristol (approx. 30,000 speakers).

4.4.1   Information and consent

The first issue that arises in any fieldwork is to get the consent of the speakers and, if feasible, of the language community.

Who do you approach in order to ask for consent from a community for carrying out your fieldwork? It may be possible to find community leaders or highly regarded members of the community. The Mosetén project (2.1) proceeded this way, while it was initially more difficult to contact community leaders of the Somali community (2.2). The latter is not only very large and diverse, but also very new. While a range of community institutions exist, others are still only emerging. In some cases, however, contacting a community is difficult or impossible. Consider a small-scale study of the code-switching in one particular bilingual family. The relevant people to seek consent from would be the family, of course, and there may not be any other community involvement.

Altogether, when it is feasible, contact with community leaders is a good idea and it is established practice in ethical fieldwork. Not only does it make your research 'official', but you are likely to benefit in getting new suggestions or making new contacts.

More important than contacting the community, however, is the *informed consent* given by each individual participating in the research. This consent should be registered in such a way that it is accessible and clear to all that the consent was voluntary and informed. One way of doing this, when working with a literate society, would be to spell out the details of the research in writing and ask the participants to sign an agreement to work on this project. The agreement should include the details of the research, as outlined in the following list.

1.   *The objectives of the research*: What are your scientific reasons for working with these speakers or the community? How did you make this clear to whoever is funding you? Work hard to ensure that the community really understands why you are there. Do not be satisfied with giving them vague ideas about 'studying your language' or some such. When asking for consent to use the materials, it may be a good idea to make clear that you want to use the data not only in your current project, but possibly in future projects. For example, if your aim is to write a grammar, you may later want to publish articles on aspects of the language. In the strict sense, if you have not asked for consent to use the data for other than the grammar, you would act unethically publishing the data in another way.

2.   *The methodology of the research*: How do you plan to go about finding out the things you want to know? How do you expect the members of the community to be involved? What will they do? What are the possible risks to them in terms of physical safety, group or individual prestige or loss of face? Will the data be anonymized? Make it clear that recordings will never be done without the speaker's knowledge, nor will recordings be used in your research without the permission of the speaker (see 6.3 on ways of recording naturalistic data).

3.   *The funding of the research*: Who is funding it? What are the categories of expenses? For how long is it funded? What percentage of the funding is for the community? People are rightly suspicious about where the money is coming from. And they may have heard all sorts of rumours about the linguist's nationality and that country's activities

in the world. This has the potential downside of confusing people.[4] Why, for example, might the linguist have a grant for £100,000 if their share is only £8,000? Why is the linguist staying in a hotel, spending *their* money instead of staying with a community member and paying the savings to the community? This is a very sensitive issue. It is not always a good idea to tell everyone everything about the finances. On the other hand, it is not a good idea to ignore the issue either.

Dan Everett

An interesting example of the kinds of unexpected issues that can arise in this regard comes from a recent research project of mine. As is common nowadays, the funding agencies listed my projects along with the total amount of funding in each on their public web pages. The language community found these pages and read about the projects. During my next visit, the people were all concerned that I was profiting from the research because the total funds listed by the funding agencies greatly exceeded the amount to be received by the community. I had thought before this that it made little sense to explain to the community things like indirect costs, overheads, postdoc salaries, secretaries, and university office supplies. But suddenly, I needed to do this. So I did. Along the way, I explained to the community that I received nothing in salary at all for the research and that I would earn exactly the same if I never returned to their community or indeed if I never did field research again. This was important news to them, because they thought that I was able to make a living only because of their consent to work with me and that therefore they should be seen as my employers. This was a very new experience for me, because previous groups I had conducted research on, in the Amazon, would never have looked at the internet or questioned me in this way. This is why it is essential to consider each group anew and not to lecture the community but to have a dialogue with it, giving plenty of time and opportunity to discuss issues of finance and so on.

---

4.   *The outside participants in the research*: The community will want to know if there are any 'silent' partners in the research, i.e. postdoctoral research associates, professorial colleagues, graduate students, etc. who are involved in the research, but who never come to the community.

5.   *The potential for profit of the research*: Any profit you make from the research will be of interest to the community. Many linguists find it appropriate to inform the language community of their profits, and to share some or all with the speakers.

Dan Everett

Some anthropological studies make a profit. Anthony Seeger's book, *Why Suyá sing*, (Seeger 2004) has sold thousands of copies and makes a reasonable profit. A large part of it (perhaps all) goes to the Suyá community. As we discussed my linguistics research and the publication of a grammar and dictionary on Suyá, I assured them that any profits at all would go to the community but that it was unlikely that this would amount to much (ergativity is a less likely marketing tool than exotic music). Likewise, Barbara Kern and I gave all the profits of Everett & Kern (1997) to the Wari' community. I think that this amounted to a few thousand dollars. Not a lot, but at least something.

6.   *Payment to the community and to individual language teachers*: It is crucial that everyone involved in the research understands how much they can be paid and what the parameters are, if any, for salary increments, non-budgeted requests, etc. Once agreements are made they should be put in writing (or on video) in order to document the financial arrangements. There is a serious issue that occasionally arises when a community wants to renegotiate financial terms as the project goes along, but that is an issue that each fieldworker will have to confront on their own. The only solution to that is to reason with people and stand firm within the parameters of the research budget.

Dan Everett

On the DVD of the film 'The Mission', one of the special features includes the documentation of a dispute over pay and working conditions between the production company of the film and the Waurani people who played the part of the Guarani in the movie. The people refused to work at a crucial juncture for the movie, in the last days of production, because they believed that they had been lied to. Apparently, what had happened with regard to the payment was that the production company had thought that it could pay the community a lump sum which could then be used or divided as the community saw fit. However, the community had not understood things quite this way and individual Waurana were expecting to be paid at the proportionate amount that had been promised to the community. Moreover, the production company seems to have thought that the Waurana were committed to the making of the film, as something benefiting indigenous peoples, when in fact the Waurana were concerned about getting back to their villages, to their fields, etc., all of which were much more important to them than the goals of the movie. Eventually an understanding was reached. Part of the problem was that no one in the production company spoke Waurana. As someone who simply watched the DVD, I had the impression that the production company, like many Westerners, assumed that the community had a socialist rather than individualist view of economy and wealth. Whatever the reasons, it is an excellent example of why it is vital to explain all financial arrangements with the people before more serious problems develop.

7.   *Personal gain of the linguist*: The linguist will get something out of the research, e.g. tenure, a job, promotion, a pay rise, fame, a book, etc. It is important for the community to understand these advantages

to the linguist as well as possible. But it is equally important that no one should have the idea that the linguist is going to get rich from the research or that the linguist's higher standard of living is a result of his or her work with this particular language community. As said earlier, we have made the effort to explain to groups that we work with that our salaries, incomes, job security, etc. do not depend on our fieldwork, at least not on fieldwork in their specific community. It is important to explain this at times so that the people do not get the mistaken impression, as some people have said about linguists, that 'you live on their backs', i.e. that the linguist is exploiting the people since they live relatively well and can travel, whereas the community that is perceived as paying his or her salary does not.

It is also important that the form of consent from the community to work on the project with the linguist is a form that they have access to. For example, when working with languages where there have been few previous studies and where the people are pre-literate, there is little point in getting a headman to 'make his mark' on a contract that no one in the community can read.

Dan Everett

What I usually do in pre-literate communities is to record their consent on video and then let them edit it and re-record it until they have explained the conditions as they see fit. I then leave a copy of this with them, whether or not they have the means to play it. At least then they can find someone with the means to play the tape or DVD and make sure that it says what they think it says. And these recordings should include the linguist explaining the goals of the project to the community prior to their giving consent.

If you are working with children, you will need to get additional permission from their parents. You may also need to apply for police clearance prior to embarking on your study.

Exercise 4.8

Find out about your university's ethics guidelines. If you are not based at a university, try to find out about the ethics guidelines of a funding agency (such as the ESRC in the UK, the DFG in Germany, the NSF in the USA, or the ESF in the European Union). What kinds of information do you have to include?

4.4.2   Payment and working conditions

Once consent is established, it is important to make sure that the working conditions and potential payment are clearly marked out. It may be a good idea to start working with speakers a few times, before committing to them by putting them on the pay-roll. It gives you an idea as to how fast they work, what they do, and if you get on with them. You may also want to consider training the teachers (see 4.4.3 below).

The community and all language teachers must understand the conditions under which they are employed. When and for how long are they to work? How much will they be paid? Will this pay exceed the national minimum wage? Do they have to leave their community? What rights for return do they have if they fail to honour the agreement on time outside the village? Other questions will arise in different local contexts, of course. Much care must be taken to avoid misunderstandings, and all understandings and agreements should be recorded in a community-accessible fashion.

When it comes to payments, paying your speakers as much as a qualified teacher would earn in the country or area in question is a good guide – a teacher's job is comparable to what your speakers do for you: they teach you their language. Thus, before embarking on fieldwork, it may be a good idea to find out how much a teacher earns. Having said this, in many fieldwork settings you have to consider tax systems and so on, or you may be bound by university rules as to how much you pay your speakers. For example, in Britain, there may be clear guidelines as to when someone has to be employed on the university pay-roll, and how much they are paid according to their qualifications and their job-description. It is a good idea to check this with your funding agency and university at an early stage.

You may ask what to do when working in a community that does not use money. A solution favoured by many fieldworkers is to buy useful goods instead. Depending on the setting, you can buy items for the community and/or for the individuals who work with you. From our experience, the teachers will probably let you know what they need in exchange for your work.

Jeanette Sakel

When conducting fieldwork on Pirahã in a small research group in 2007, we bought a range of items as presents and payment. We distributed most of the presents upon arrival. These included different foods, useful household items and tobacco. The latter is a highly desirable commodity among the Pirahã and was received with great delight. In the same way as distributing gifts among the Pirahã, we received game and fish from the speakers.

The evening before we left the field site we distributed the remaining goods among the speakers as our final payments. All adult members of the local village had worked with us, but some had helped us far more than others. In order to be fair, we noted down how much we worked with each speaker. We made sure that our teachers were rewarded in a way that was perceived as fair within the community. Gifts included cloth for dressmaking, fish-hooks and equipment we had brought to the village, such as hammocks, and even some of our clothes.

While paying your main teachers may be relatively straightforward, how would you proceed with speakers who work with you only sporadically or just once? Our suggestion is to make it clear what the speaker will expect from you. If you work with someone for a number of hours, they may appreciate a payment. You could pay them a one-off consultancy fee. For shorter sessions, such as in the Somali study (2.2), small presents may be more appropriate than payment. Such presents can be anything valued by the speakers, and gift boxes of chocolates are often well-received.

4.4.3 Training language teachers

Why would the linguist, whose time is already far too limited, want to take any extra time away from his or her linguistic investigations to train language teachers in any skill not directly related to the linguist's own goals? The answer is primarily that this is an ethical responsibility. Just as the linguistic research is ultimately intended to enhance the linguist's career and improve the linguist's quality of life, so the research should enhance the teacher's quality of life. This is *empowering* fieldwork and it is not an option. Linguists and anthropologists, like missionaries, have the skeleton in the early histories of their disciplines of following in the wake of and contributing to attitudes of colonialism (it would be a good idea for every fieldworker to read Said's (1978) *Orientalism*). Passing on skills and knowledge in mutual exchange and respect should be the hallmark of modern fieldwork. The linguist takes and must give back. And money is not enough.

When teachers are trained and interested in the research on their language, they can become pro-active co-researchers. As they come to understand and identify with the research on their language, they can gather a good deal of the data, record them and transcribe them. They can also translate them themselves. The linguist can then review all the data they have collected and verify them against the developing analysis and check them with other speakers for relevance, naturalness, accuracy, etc. We found that this method worked reasonably well in various field situations, such as with the Banawá (Dan Everett) and the Mosetenes (Jeanette Sakel). Alan Vogel (personal communication) reports that this worked well with the Jarawara people of Brazil.

In some fieldwork settings there may also be additional ways in which teachers can be trained, as the linguist may possess knowledge that the individuals or the community find important. This could, for example, be teaching children to read and write, either in the target language or in a contact language.

Dan Everett

I have trained Pirahãs in the operation of my motorboat. We have had lots of fun driving this National Science Foundation-purchased boat and 40-horsepower engine around the Maici river. Pirahã men have piloted us right into jungle growth on the river bank and onto beaches. But we had a blast. And now when I am in the village, I know that if I am injured or ill, the Pirahãs themselves can pilot me out. So I get a direct return on this investment of time. And the Pirahãs now have a skill. They do not have motorboats, but they enjoy showing outsiders how they can pilot mine. The Kisedje people of the Xingu regions of Brazil already know how to drive cars, pilot motorboats, and handle other types of Western equipment. However, they need computers for some of the activities of their tribal association and want their people trained to use these computers. So my project provided them with a laptop computer and training in its use. We are on regular email contact now, no matter where I am in the world. I have also trained people in giving injections of anti-venom and in the use of anti-malarial pills. I regularly take in National Geographic and other movies about other regions of the world so that they can learn about other peoples, regions, animals, etc. The resulting discussions are enjoyable activities for all of us.

How does one go about training language teachers? This will depend tremendously on the level of familiarity the people have with the things that the linguist brings to the field, such as education, equipment, medicine and so on. The more familiar they are, the more likely they are to have specific objectives in training in one or more of these areas. For linguistics, the linguist should discuss his or her objectives and the methodology of linguistics. And they must always be careful to explain global and local goals. Why did they come to the community? What are they trying to learn about in today's session? Why is the linguist asking this or that question? Training can also be facilitated by asking the teacher for his or her advice and insights. This type of reflection helps the teacher to think like a linguist about the language. Different approaches are required by different cultural contexts.

4.4.4   Helping the community

The researcher will often be associated with community aspirations, at least in the minds of the community if not in their own mind. The community may want the linguist to help them raise funds for community projects, speak to the government about encroachments on their rights, travel with them to negotiate with people or groups that impinge on the community's well-being in some way, and so on. Pro-active application of ethics will motivate the fieldworker to serve as an advocate for the group. This can be a very important service, as the linguist, a prestigious intellectual, can offer what will be deeply valuable to and appreciated by the community.

Any fieldwork these days is bidirectional in that the linguist gets data from the speakers, but the speakers get something in return. Apart from payment and training, the linguist can provide materials related to the fieldwork for the community. These could be booklets of stories in the language or short grammar books for school use.

> ## Jeanette Sakel
>
> Upon my arrival in the field, Mosetén had at least three different orthographies, suggested by missionaries and linguists. Still, there was no written tradition, and apart from very few Mosetenes who had taken part in an orthography project a number of years prior to my fieldwork, nobody was able to write. The speakers of Mosetén got together and decided which orthography they wanted me to use in my linguistic work, as well as in a number of booklets for the community that I worked on with a range of teachers during the course of the project. The first booklet consisted of a number of short stories, jokes and songs. The next one was an illustrated story. Another was a primer with names of animals, geographical features of the area and culturally specific items, designed for the local school.
>
> I produced these booklets cheaply, by photocopying the pages and by having the covers printed at a local printing shop. The main teachers then handed them out to the speakers of the language.
>
> Finding linguistic materials to provide for languages like Mosetén may be straightforward, but what can we do in cases of well-studied languages? I broached this subject with my Somali teachers and an issue that was mentioned again and again was bilingual education. There are already a number of initiatives in secondary schools and Saturday supplementary schools. Some of the speakers found that these initiatives target only some members of the community. Many parents are worried that their children could lose the language, making a return to Somalia in a more peaceful future difficult. For this reason, I and my main teachers decided that our project should aim at informing bilingual education, for example by writing reports of findings for policymakers and parents.

Not all linguists are comfortable with working as advocates of the community they study. For example, Bowern (2008: 161) advises not to get too involved in community issues, as this may lead to problems in the long run. In principle, it depends on what you find appropriate, though it may be a good idea to discuss these issues with an ethics committee.

4.4.5   Ethics for the dissemination of the data and the results

One issue that is becoming more and more important for all indigenous communities is ensuring that they control the applications of their knowledge and community outputs. Who owns the linguistic data in a text for example? Who has the right to prohibit or constrain the use of all data? The answer is that the speakers control all data. The linguist must not use any text or examples without the permission of the speakers. While language data may merely interest you from the perspective of phonological or grammatical structures, for the speaker it is much more: the data contain personal information, as well as other issues that the speaker may not be prepared to share with the world.

The community has the right to demand the return of all tapes, videos, transcriptions, and so on – all forms of their language gathered by the linguist – at any time. They must be apprised of this right and this understanding must enter the written or videoed record of agreement between the fieldworker and the community.

Not all speakers choose to be anonymous, however. Some speakers explicitly seek to be acknowledged for their input. It is therefore important to give the speakers a choice as to whether or not they want to remain anonymous. If a language teacher has given considerable input to your study, you may want to consider co-authorship.

The primary results of scientific research are publications, web pages, or other forms of public dissemination of one's findings. The decision as to who should share co-authorship (and thus blame or fame) for a particular article, book, report, etc. is a very important one. Should all language teachers automatically be entitled to co-authorship? Or if the linguist is helped in their living in the village, introduction to the people, or data-gathering by a third party, is this third party (e.g. local missionary, government official, non-indigenous citizen of the country) entitled to co-authorship? This is a thorny issue. But we suggest the following rules of thumb.

1.   Was the person essential to the research in whole or in part?
2.   Did the person make a major intellectual contribution to the research?
3.   Was the person actively involved in the writing of the piece?
4.   Was the person responsible for obtaining funding or the principal investigator of the grant?
5.   Does the person want co-authorship?
6.   Does the person believe that they have earned co-authorship?
7.   Would it be intellectually dishonest to award or deny co-authorship?
8.   Did the person collect the data for your study?

Let us say that your entry to a community, your having a place to live in the community, and the people's willingness to help you learn their language, are all the results of someone else's efforts. This would be deserving of credit in the acknowledgements to the research, but by itself does not entitle the person to co-authorship. However, there could be additional factors, e.g. if they spoke the language and ran your experiments for you, served as third-party interpreters, or otherwise became essential to your data-gathering. Further, if during the course of data-gathering they offered suggestions that were crucial to the final shape of the research, then this would also cause re-thinking of whether or not they deserved co-authorship. Did this person give you ideas, suggestions, and intellectual help without which the research could not have been conceived or carried out or had anything like its final form? Then co-authorship seems appropriate. If the person was actively involved in the writing up of the research, either by actually contributing original sections or by consulting with the linguist on many major or subsidiary points, then this person should be considered for co-authorship. If the person advising the linguist is the actual principal investigator of the grant then, for some people, this would automatically entitle this person to co-authorship. In some of the natural sciences, this is common. However, although we believe that principal investigators rightfully demand veto power over any research coming out of their funded projects, we do not believe that they are automatically entitled to co-authorship if this would violate (7), e.g. if they made no intellectual contribution to the particular research of the report.

It is also important for the fieldworker to know what a person wants with respect to co-authorship. Do they believe that they have earned it and do they want it? Then, subject to (7), they should receive it. If it would be intellectually dishonest in the eyes of the fieldworker to award co-authorship, then perhaps it should not be offered. We suggest that in such a case the linguist should contact someone from their home institution or at the journal or other outlet they plan to submit their research to for publication, to get advice. On the other hand, such a decision could have long-term effects on the researchers, the research, and feelings of exploitation. For this reason, we believe that co-authorship should be offered when the person feels they have earned it and they want it.

Occasionally it arises that one researcher collects data and does not analyse the collection. Then another linguist may find the data (openly and honestly with no violations of any ethical standards), analyse them, and publish the results. In such cases, does the original gatherer of the data deserve co-authorship? Not if the data are published. However, if the data are unpublished, then the linguist should contact them, ask them about the analysis that the linguist is proposing, asking if the collector of the data knows of any counter-examples or other problems in the linguist's analysis and then offer co-authorship if the original collector of the data feels that they have earned it and if they want it.

4.5   Summary and further reading

In this chapter we discussed the participants of fieldwork, including the speakers, the linguist and other stakeholders. We looked at individual differences and talents of speakers (and linguists) and how to make use of these in fieldwork. We furthermore discussed the role of the linguist, as well as fieldwork ethics – something every fieldworker will have to adhere to.

Further reading includes Mithun (2001) on the roles of the speaker and the linguist. For selecting speakers, see Lanza (2008), who focuses on language contact studies – but some of the aspects can be applied to other types of fieldwork. Additional considerations for working with bilinguals can be found in Grosjean (2008: ch. 14). For more information on sampling, see Dörnyei (2007: ch. 5).

It is advisable also to find actual studies similar to the one(s) you intend to do, in order to gain information on how other researchers have chosen participants.

For fieldwork ethics, see the overview on the website of the Max Planck Institute for Evolutionary Anthropology: www.eva.mpg.de/lingua/resources/ethics.php. You can get valuable information on anthropological fieldwork from www.aaanet.org/committees/ethics/ch1.htm. For the ethics guidelines of a university, as well as additional information, you may want to look at the following website of the University of Toronto: http://individual.utoronto.ca/ngn.ethics_overview.htm.

5   Fieldwork preparation

In the present chapter, we want to address the issues that come up when preparing for different types of fieldwork. As this preparation is highly dependent on the setting of your work, some sections in this chapter will be more relevant to your particular situation than others.

The theme of this book is that fieldwork can be carried out in many different ways, ranging from prototypical fieldwork to less classical methods. Fieldwork settings can differ considerably, between going far away to staying close to home; conducting fieldwork on your own, with your family or in a group of researchers; working for long or short periods of time, and so on.

Yet, a considerable part of the chapter is concerned with preparing fieldwork in a remote place, because this type of fieldwork generally requires an additional layer of preparation.[1] The first sections are concerned with preparation for any type of fieldwork, and it is important to consider whether you want to go far away, stay close to home, document a language or work on a specific structure. Altogether, careful preparation is the backbone of any type of fieldwork: it will help you to have strategies in place to deal with unexpected situations; make sure you cover the various aspects you are setting out to study; and will help you to avoid wasting your own, as well as the speakers', time.

5.1   Linguistic prefield preparation

There are various ways to prepare for the linguistic aspects of your field experience. These include defining your research focus, learning to use your recording equipment, reading up on the topic of study, and so on. Other preparations, such as learning the languages and lingua francas, have been discussed in chapter 3.

Exercise 5.1

From now on, a range of exercises will relate to a particular research project. By now you probably have a good idea what fieldwork entails, and may have found your own preferences for types of fieldwork (see exercises 3.3 and 3.6). Think about a fieldwork project that you could imagine carrying out in the future.[2] How would you prepare for such a project? Make a list of the different aspects involved.

We will get back to your fieldwork situation in subsequent exercises below.

5.1.1   Research questions

You are going to the 'field' to study aspects of some language. You probably have a general idea of what you plan to study, but it is always useful to bring your research questions into ever sharper focus as your journey into the unknown takes shape. So, before you apply for a research grant or go to your field location, ask yourself this: am I clear on what I want to study? Can I explain it to others without being too wordy or abstruse? Can I explain it convincingly to the mirror? What is the exact object of my investigation?

Part of getting an answer to these questions is to consider whether the object is to study something directly observable or something only inferable. An example of the former would be the measurements of formant frequencies of consonants and vowels across a wide range of speakers. An example of the latter would be constraint rankings proposed to account for the morphological structure of the verb of language 'x'. This type of object clarification will affect your preparation, including your budget and your need for skills (e.g. in sound analysis software or constraint ranking evaluation).

Another issue to consider in this regard is whether you are ultimately more interested in the explanation of similarities between languages or in the documentation of their differences (contrary to some opinions, the former is not necessarily a better goal than the latter!). Are you interested in corpus-based studies or speaker intuitions? Are you interested more in qualitative studies or quantitative studies, or a combination of both (see 6.1)?

A less obvious, but perhaps equally important, way to clarify your research objectives, once you have decided on your main question, is to carefully consider the ancillary questions implied by your 'big research question(s)'. For example, you may decide that your big theoretical research objective could benefit from some statistical analysis. How much time should you therefore give to the study of statistics? Or to learning about questionnaire preparation?

It is common for students, and PhD students in particular, to specialize, to deliberately focus on a narrower range of questions, to the exclusion of many other interesting, but not directly relevant issues. This is quite reasonable in most contexts. But it can be unreasonable and counter-productive in fieldwork, at least in an extreme form. A fieldworker not only needs to *know* more, because they will be faced with more information that requires knowledge to sort through, but they need more *reflection*, because they cannot always leave the field to get additional training if ancillary issues require it. This limitation has the corollary that very careful and detailed thought needs to go into the formulation of research questions to be asked in the field and that these questions and related issues should influence prefield training.

We suggest the following as a potential method of prefield research preparation. First, develop a list of the research questions you want to ask. The first version of this list should be done hastily, just jotting down questions as they occur to you, things you *might* be interested in researching in the field. These questions should be formulated before, during, and after reading all you can about the field language and theoretical issues you expect to research. Second, narrow this list down to those questions that are most vital to your research and career objectives. Third, organize the questions (e.g. What are the main, as opposed to ancillary, questions? Which ancillary questions accompany which main questions, etc.?). Fourth, *operationalize* each question – how can it be made 'behavioural', i.e. into something you need to *do* in order to investigate it? It's a good idea never to stray from the empirical core of your research at any stage of planning or execution. Refine and add to this list as you feel necessary. Next, build an initial plan. How might you ask and answer these questions in the field? The following chapter will deal with the methodologies concerned with this.

Exercise 5.2

In your hypothetical fieldwork situation, try to think about possible research questions, operationalizing your questions and building an initial fieldwork plan.

5.1.2   Choose a mentor

It may be a good idea to get an advisor or a mentor – a senior academic or a colleague whom you trust – to ask you useful questions and offer suggestions. The exact role of this person will depend on your career stage. For graduate and undergraduate students, of course, an advisor is vital. You need someone who is willing to answer your formal, informal and personal questions. There may not be such a person at your home institution. It could well be the case that your mentor is across the hall; but it is equally possible that he or she is in another country, especially if your advisor and your mentor are different people (the former playing a formal, institutional role, the latter a more personal, intellectual role).

Ideally, you want someone with field experience, preferably in the geographical and linguistic area where you will be working or with in-depth knowledge of the topic you are studying. You want someone successful in getting data and publishing. Maybe they can even put you in contact with the local community of scholars where you'll be doing research. You should have someone who can advise you on the bureaucratic, mundane aspects of fieldwork (e.g. how to fill out forms in another language and culture, whether to buy a pressure cooker, how many kilos of books are worth taking, when is the best time to be in a particular field location, what the best local transport is, how to stay in touch with the 'outside world', etc.). You also want someone who can read your work in progress and tell you how to get data, ask questions and read more to make that work better. In fact, it is not inconceivable that you could benefit from multiple mentors. And these need not, again, correspond to an actual academic advisor if your research is not for a thesis.

5.1.3   Prefield literature review

One of the most important aspects of fieldwork preparation is to read as much as possible on the language and people you are going to study. If possible, also gain insights into the greater context in which the language and people are located. Find out about the politics, such as the speakers' relations with other groups and their reaction towards outsiders (e.g. fieldworkers). If you are working with speakers of a culture very different from your own, find out about their customs.

Next, read all the linguistics you can find on the language you plan to work on, as well as on surrounding languages (or languages in contact with the one you want to work on). As you read – *think*. How could this study have been improved? What kind of data are necessary to write a paper like this? How much time did the author spend with the people to collect the data upon which his or her studies are based?[3] What has been written already about the structure of the language? How much has been written about the ways in which that structure is put to use or acquired? How much is there on the history of the language?

For all projects, it is important to get an overview of the language you want to study. In particular, when you want to document the language or write a grammar. Also, if you expect to continue your fieldwork with this group for a long time, take time to compile an exhaustive bibliography on the language, the language family and the area. If possible, read it all, which can be easy for some languages, where there is very little. Other languages are well-studied and you will not be able to read it all or even list it all, but will need to be selective, with exhaustive reading and compiling for some categories, very little for others. Your own research questions will have to guide you in your efforts. Classify the works you have read. Know which are most useful. You may want to take these with you to the field.

If your literature review reveals that there is no extant sociolinguistic survey of dialects, language attitudes, demographics or geographical distribution of the language, then note this down. This should be undertaken at some point during the first field research trip.

Exercise 5.3

For your own fieldwork situation, try to find publications that deal with what you want to study. You can combine searching the internet for the language(s) you are interested in, looking through your library and searching library databases (your university librarian will be able to help with this) to find literature on the topic. Often you can find further sources by looking through the references given in the publications you have found.

5.1.4   Computers and tools

Any discussion of equipment or technology will date a study quickly. So we do not intend to spend much time on this. However, there are a couple of things to say in this regard that will be somewhat impervious to time.

First, technology is vital in field research. Even though you may believe that you have very good 'ears', machines can be invaluable in helping you to notice sounds and patterns which unaided ears may miss.

And technology provides a record for the future, however outdated it eventually becomes. Consider, for example, the significance of the portable cassette tape-recorder for the history of field research. It is true, trivially, that early fieldworkers got by without this, now outdated, device, just as everyone gets by without inventions yet to come. But wouldn't it now be priceless to listen to audio-tapes or watch video-tapes made by Sapir, Boas, Newman and others, checking their facts and interpretations more carefully, or possessing a more complete record of the languages they studied? As we recognize the need to study, for example, endangered languages, technology capable of accurately preserving and measuring the sights and sounds of these languages becomes ever more important.

Some questions to ask with regard to field-equipment are:

1.   Who will be able to use the output of your equipment now and in the future?
2.   Is the equipment portable?
3.   Does the equipment provide state-of-the-art accuracy, or as close to it as the fieldworker can afford?
4.   Will the equipment help to record both the grammar and its cultural matrix?
5.   Does the equipment use a practical power source for the location in which it will be used (such as long-life batteries or solar power in places without electricity)?
6.   Does the fieldworker's equipment include satellite capability, for email and phone contact from a remote field site to any part of the world?
7.   Do you have backup equipment for crucial items, e.g. extra micro-phones, computer(s), recorders, etc.?

It is a good idea to use portable computers in the field which have state-of-the-art video- and audio-editing capabilities. In purchasing and planning, remember that quality is not something to be overly economical with – pay top prices if necessary to get top equipment. There are other areas to be frugal in, if that is necessary (and of course it always is).

Once you have found and purchased the equipment needed for your field research, spend some time familiarizing yourself with the hardware and software. It helps to acquire at least an intermediate level of technological skills prior to departure for the field. Design an effective (for you) filing system on your computer for your work. Treat it as a portable office. Make *sure* you have hardware to back up all your files and programs (fast-transfer portable hard disks are very convenient for this).

This technology is particularly important when documenting a language: it is impossible to do nearly as well without modern technological aids as you can with this technology. Documenting a language involves creation of a multimedia record of the language in use by native speakers. Analysing a language also benefits tremendously from, and often requires, technological support. Software and hardware for sound analysis, video-editing, transcription and preparation of data for long-term storage are essential to field research.[4]

Wherever possible, native speakers should be trained in the use of the equipment. This is important training for them and can be very helpful to you, even avoiding the need for you to return to the community as small samples of data could subsequently be collected by the native speakers.

Exercise 5.4

Search for online resources on tools appropriate for fieldwork. There are many websites by fieldworkers giving such information. New materials are added all the time, and as technology improves at such a rapid pace, it is a good idea to keep informed about the state-of-the-art equipment at the time of your study.

5.1.5   Financing your fieldwork

Even if you are a student or first-time fieldworker, there may be ways to finance your fieldwork. Sometimes, university departments or research centres have funding in place to support student projects. Sometimes these require you to be pro-active to qualify; in a few other cases such funding is already in place and part of the programme.

If such grants are not available, there may be other ways of financing your fieldwork. Is there a project at your university or elsewhere that researches similar aspects? If so, do they have funding, and would there be the opportunity for you to work in that project, conducting fieldwork? A way to find out is by searching online or asking other researchers. It is invaluable to get in touch with those working in the field you want to work in. They will probably be pleased to hear that others find their work exciting. If they do not have funds available to hire you (even for a short time), they may think of you the next time they apply for funding.

There are other ways of funding projects, namely by asking other organizations involved with the language or the speakers. Such organizations could be NGOs, as in the case of the Mosetenes (2.1). For example, there may be developmental agencies that could fund you to write teaching materials in the language. For studies like the one on Somali (2.2), you could ask local Somali organizations, the local city council, or existing research projects whether there are ways in which you could help them with your linguistic study or whether you could apply for funding together. This type of funding is less straightforward and demands a great deal of initiative on your part.

However, you may also start fieldwork without any funding in place. While it is generally a good idea to pay the speakers (see 4.4.2), you could buy presents for the speakers yourself. Many linguists start off like this. Once you have gained experience, it will probably become much easier to obtain outside funding.

5.1.6   Funding proposals for PhD theses and beyond

If you want to carry out a major fieldwork project, such as for a PhD thesis, there may be specific grants to apply for to cover the cost of your fieldwork. Writing a funding proposal can take a considerable amount of time. Unfortunately, funding is never guaranteed and the process of application is always highly competitive. The work and long wait involved in a funding proposal will more often than not end in a rejection letter from the funding agency. So why should one subject oneself to this? The reason is simple. You need money to do field research, and well-funded projects can produce better results than poorly funded projects. In terms of your career, well-funded projects also bring money and student support to your home institution. They are also necessary to underwrite team research and to enable you to train new fieldworkers.

The first step in preparing a proposal is to identify an appropriate funding agency. Agencies differ widely in the kinds of research that they fund, the kinds of methodologies that they favour, the amount of additional personnel, indirect costs, etc. they will fund. And they differ in their constraints on the form of proposals. So before writing a proposal, familiarize yourself with the agencies most likely to be interested in your work.

All funding proposals will be evaluated by at least the following criteria:

1.   *Track-record of the principal investigator*: do they deliver what they promise? Are they active, publishing researchers? Is their work respected, as of high quality?
2.   *Evidence of preliminary preparation*: e.g. contracts and permissions obtained ahead of the proposed project start date, and so on.
3.   *Budget*: is it reasonable, non-lavish, yet well thought out, covering all likely expenses (from batteries to hotels)?
4.   *Criteria for success*: how will the scientific community know when the project is a success? How and when will project personnel, including the principal investigator, know this? How will the funding agency know this? What are the follow-up plans if things do not go exactly according to plan (they will not)?
5.   *Deliverables*: has the principal investigator promised too little or too much from what they expect to learn from this project (publications, websites, blogs, community contributions, etc.)?

6.   *Intellectual quality of the proposal*: the reviewer wants evidence that the principal investigator is fluent in their speciality and the matters to be investigated, that they have outlined an interesting problem that the referee would like to know the answer to as well (ideally), and have contextualized it appropriately within the field of study.

With regard to your track record, if you are a new PhD with few or no publications, reviewers will be willing to give you the benefit of the doubt, depending on how long it has been since you received your PhD and how well written the current proposal is. The larger and more ambitious the project, the more reviewers will require from previous publications of the principal investigator. Your track record, as mentioned, will also be extremely important. If the principal investigator says 'We will publish the results of our findings in *Language*, *Natural Language and Linguistic Theory*, and *Linguistic Inquiry*', the readers will ask if they have ever before published in these journals.

It is also important, once the principal investigator has identified a funding agency, that they contact the relevant administrative personnel of the agency to discuss their potential project with them, to confirm that this agency is interested and to request advice on what the agency looks for in a successful proposal. Occasionally, it is even worthwhile to travel to the headquarters of the agency to meet the programme officer in person or to attend the relevant professional meetings, e.g. the Linguistic Society of America annual meeting, where linguistic funding agencies and programme directors often agree to meet with potential principal investigators.

It is also useful to bear in mind that for many agencies the submitter has the right to request that some individuals *should not* be asked to review the proposal or that some individuals *should* be requested to review the proposal. If you know someone opposes your type of research (or, worse, hates you), then you should say simply 'I prefer that the following people not be asked to review my work.'

Exercise 5.5

Look at ways in which you could fund your fieldwork project. You could check out the funding available at your university or venture out to read about funding agencies and other sources of support. Note down things such as deadlines for application and what information needs to be included. (If you are feeling courageous, you can then try to write an application for funding of your project.)

5.1.7   Ethics application

Most types of fieldwork, often even short student projects, require applications to an ethics committee. This is usually the ethics committee of the university, but funded projects usually also have to seek approval from the funding agency's ethics committee. This process has been put in place to make sure that the research is not taking advantage of speakers, and that you have clearly thought about the way in which you are going to deal with the speakers (see 4.4 on fieldwork ethics).

Most ethics committees have their own procedures for these applications. If you are applying for the first time, you may be able to ask more experienced researchers at your institution about the procedure. They may let you review their applications as a guide.

Some ethics committees are open for discussing issues with you as they arise during the fieldwork process. It is good to keep in close touch with them. Ethics committees are not a hurdle on the way, but there to help you and the speakers to get the most out of your fieldwork, without causing any harm or damage.

Exercise 5.6

Look at the ethics guidelines of your university, or funding agency (if relevant), and those governing the country or area in which you want to work (see also exercise 4.8). Then, fill in the ethics paperwork for ethics approval (whichever of the above types are required) for your project.

5.1.8   The place and timing of fieldwork

Whether you go far away or stay near home, you will have to carry out your work somewhere. Of course depending on your project, you could interview speakers as and when you meet them, wherever that may be, but you may need a suitable setting where you can carry out linguistic experiments.

Exercise 5.7

Why do you think place and time of fieldwork play such a vital role in some projects? Which places and times would you consider most appropriate, which ones are less suitable?

The best places, especially when doing audio- or video-recordings, are those that are relatively quiet and free from disturbances. Recordings pick up on background noise. Good places could, for example, be a room at your university, a room at a local community centre or at participants' own homes. In your fieldwork preparation you will have to consider this and make arrangements, if possible.

Make sure your speakers will be comfortable as well. If you want them to give you naturalistic language data, a highly formal setting might be too much for them and they may not be able to relax. Finding a good medium that suits most needs is important.

When handing out questionnaires to be filled in, the place of study may not matter as much, but again you want people to be able to concentrate and fill in the questionnaires to the best of their abilities, not being disturbed all the time. Also, people filling in questionnaires in noisy, busy places may give different answers from those working in quiet places. If you want your data to be comparable, this is an important point to consider.

For fieldwork in remote, rural and prototypical settings, this may be difficult to achieve: it may be impossible to find sound-protected locations that are comfortable, bug-free, dry, free from distractions and with running water and electricity! Still, there may be compromises you can find. It is vital that the site chosen be as close to ideal as the fieldworker is able to get in the community. This could mean little more than taking a couple of folding chairs and table out of the village, or busy neighbourhood, etc. to a relatively calm, isolated area.

Dan Everett

Peter Ladefoged and I once commandeered a hut in a Pirahã village to carry out phonetic investigations and I simply asked people to keep the children and dogs away and to keep the general noise level as low as possible. They kindly accommodated us.

Like any field activity, selecting and developing a location for your work can have unintended consequences. At a later stage I built a small wooden structure about 100 metres outside the Pirahã village, raised above the ground, and screened in, with a lockable door. I discouraged people from looking in during sessions and tried to allow in only the teachers working in a given session, rather than them and all their friends. The Pirahãs do not mind this. But a Brazilian government agency investigating the activities of a 'gringo' in the area asked the Pirahãs about this small structure when I was absent from the village. The Pirahãs, in their nearly non-existent Portuguese, were able to communicate that I spent a lot of time in there and that few people were allowed in. The agency representatives wondered what sort of fiendish experiments I might be running out there. Finding out about this, I quickly visited the agency headquarters and gave them a full explanation.

Likewise the timing of fieldwork will have to be thought about, taking into account the constraints of the community and those of the language teacher. When is it best for the community and for the teacher for sessions to take place? It is important that the linguist keeps appointments, to show that they take these times seriously. You may work with teachers and speakers who find time-keeping difficult. If that is the case, you can discuss the problem with the participants involved, clearly stating your expectations. In some cultures time-keeping may not be taken as seriously as in others. Still, if the problem persists you may have to find alternative things to do or alternative speakers to work with (in order not to waste too much of your own time). It's good to have things prepared for yourself to work on 'in case a speaker does not turn up'.

5.2   Considerations for remote fieldwork

Apart from the issues directly related to the linguistic aspects of fieldwork, there will be a number of non-linguistic issues to take into account during your preparation phase. This certainly applies to remote fieldwork settings, though some of the points will also be relevant to fieldwork closer to home. Before setting out on your quest, try to learn as much as possible about the group whose language you will be studying: their history, geography, foods, language, culture and laws, especially those governing foreign researchers (e.g. the constraints on research authorizations and visas). There are significantly more considerations for a remote fieldwork setting than when, for example, conducting fieldwork in your home environment. For this reason, most of the discussion below will deal with issues highly relevant for remote fieldwork, while they may not be pertinent to other situations.

5.2.1   Culture and relations

Before going to the field, it will be advantageous – and in some cases necessary – to be aware of the group's relations with the culture you belong to, as well as relations with other cultures relevant to the speakers. In a remote setting, such as the Mosetén study (2.1) this would be the Mosetenes' attitude towards your culture (do they expect you to act in a certain way?) and home country (if there are animosities, how could they be handled so that your fieldwork will still be a success?). Also relevant would be the relations between the Mosetenes and other indigenous groups in the area, and with the general Bolivian population.

Yet, such preparations are also beneficial for fieldwork closer to home. Even if you are doing fieldwork on your own language, you may face cultural issues that are worth considering beforehand. For example, is it culturally appropriate for a male linguist to work with women? Is it inappropriate for you to record older members of the community? You may encounter such cultural restrictions when working with speakers. Yet there are ways to record the language of 'inaccessible' speakers.

Early in the history of North American linguistics, linguistic studies were seen as a branch of anthropology. Today, however, most linguists would probably not think of themselves as anthropologists, nor would most anthropologists identify even descriptive linguistics as a subfield of anthropology. Nevertheless, because in many cases doing field linguistics is doing linguistics in a natural cultural setting, you cannot avoid culture. You can approach the cross-cultural linguistic experience ignorantly or informed – that is the only choice. Good introductions are general texts such as Foley (1997) or Duranti (1997), which you can follow up by reading on topics of personal interest via the references in these texts. Or, if you already have a background in anthropological linguistics, you can read in the major journals, for example the *Journal of Linguistic Anthropology*, *Journal of Anthropological Linguistics* and *Current Anthropology*. We also recommend reading Sapir (1921) and work by Lucy (1992a, 1992b) and others on the neo-Whorfian approach to the language–culture interface, as well as Enfield (2002) on the connection between culture and grammar.

Likewise, it is advantageous to correspond with anthropologists who have studied the people whose language you plan to study or with anthropologists who have worked nearby.

Exercise 5.8

Think about the cultural issues that could come up in your fieldwork situation and how you could prepare for these.

5.2.2   Paperwork and bureaucracy

When going to 'the field' means crossing political boundaries, it often entails getting two broad types of authorization: authorization to enter the country and authorization to do research. These permissions usually require the fieldworker to apply for special visas, to get medical checks, criminal checks, official translations of diplomas, etc. It will take time.

Many countries will not allow fieldwork on a tourist visa. And in some countries tourist visas restrict the tourist so that they cannot visit minority communities outside of major cities. Most funding agencies require evidence, in advance, that the researcher has secured or will secure from the local government the proper legal documents for undertaking research.

In some countries, e.g. Brazil, you also need permission from a government department responsible for minority affairs. Additionally, your scientific project may need authorization from the national research or science foundation. The latter may require that you have a national partner, i.e. a linguist from the country, or other appropriate specialist, who is personally supportive of your research and is willing to be your academic sponsor. In most countries these processes are all made easier and faster if you know the people responsible for the authorizations. If you find that you need such permits, it is a good idea to get to know local researchers who can help you in the application process. If you have the funding, you could go to the country on a tourist visa to make connections with people. These people may be able to help you with the research permits and provide you with a letter of introduction, if needed.

5.2.3   Vaccinations and medicals

It is essential to have appropriate vaccinations in remote field sites. Some countries will check your vaccination card upon entry or when leaving, to make sure you do not carry dangerous diseases. Some places may even require a medical before giving you permission to carry out your fieldwork.

It is very important to read up on the requirements and suggestions for the country and area of your study in the early stages of your preparation phase.[5] Some vaccinations need to be given months in advance or require boosters at a later stage. In many areas it is wise to take malaria pills and to carry other medication.

5.2.4 Medical training

In very remote fieldwork situations, it may be necessary to have basic training in first-aid and treatment of diseases common in your chosen area. Ideally, if you are going to be working in extremely isolated situations, consider some training in suturing and bone-setting. Books such as Werner (1993), *Where there is no doctor* and, Dickson (2009), *Where there is no dentist* can be extremely helpful, as is knowing emergency numbers to call locally and internationally (by satellite) for consultants' help if necessary.

Dan Everett

One afternoon among the Pirahãs, I was pursuing my never-ending quest to understand the structure of the Pirahã verb. Suddenly, I heard yelling at the river. When I looked, the Pirahãs were running towards the river, talking loudly. Someone came to tell me that a man from the village, *abagi* 'Toucan', was hurt. Sure enough, as they brought him up into our house, his left arm was bright red, amazingly swollen, and oozing pus. He had had an accident in his canoe and an arrow had entered his forearm just above the wrist and emerged on the opposite side, below the elbow. He had a fever and was in obvious pain, something the Pirahãs only admit to in extreme circumstances. He freely admitted that the pain was nearly unbearable.

What was I supposed to do about this? It was clear that every Pirahã there expected me, the outsider, to have some Western medicine and to know what to do. So I did what any courageous, knowledgeable, and resourceful field researcher might do – I called my wife, Keren.

Keren was able to treat Toucan and he fully recovered. How? Well, before we ever set foot in the Pirahã village we both took courses in first-aid. We also asked various people – doctors, nurses, missionaries and others – what kinds of health problems we were most likely to encounter. We then purchased medicines accordingly. In Brazil, as in many countries, a much wider and more potent range of medicines can be purchased over the counter than in the UK or USA. So we purchased several hundreds of dollars worth (this in 1978) of malarial medicines, analgesics, snake anti-venom (antiophidic serum), local anaesthetics, syringes, sutures, and so forth. During our first couple of days among the Pirahãs, we organized our medical equipment and supplies on shelves, with our most useful medical manual, *Where there is no doctor*, by David Werner, in the front.[6]

There are many field locations where the fieldworkers would not be expected to provide health care. There are many places where unlicensed people dispensing medicines would be in violation of local laws. But in many isolated communities, a linguist or anthropologist may be the only hope for health care. Certainly you may need to care for your own health, or your partner's or children's, depending on where you are. Therefore, training, reading, equipment and medicines are all crucial components of any fieldworker's kit.

5.2.5   Basic fieldwork equipment

The equipment a fieldworker takes to the field can play a significant role in the success of the project. This is particularly important when going to a remote location, where you may not be able to get some of the items you could have brought from home. In remote places that are culturally very different from your home community, you would ideally take things that enable you to feel a sense of 'continuous identity'. As Wengle (1988: 20ff) makes clear, 'identity maintenance' in the field is crucial for successful fieldwork (or, at least, it is crucial for a healthy fieldworker). Wengle (1988: 7ff) advocates the idea that '... the stability of an individual's sense of identity depends directly on the "innumerable identifications" he has established with the familiar, personal and impersonal, concrete and abstract, animate and inanimate objects of his past and present existence'. Judicious selection of mementos, photos, books and music, for example, can help you to maintain a connection with your life outside of fieldwork.

Items that are useful to take to the field in a tropical area (adjust accordingly!):

1.   Three changes of clothes (one to wear, one to wash, and one drying), hat, flip-flops, closed shoes, and gym shorts for bathing. This would obviously not be an adequate wardrobe for fieldwork among the Inuit. What you take varies on where you are going. But the principle is to travel lightly.

2.   Medicines (for first-aid and treatment of serious village health problems).

3.   Multivitamins if you do not anticipate having access to fresh vegetables or fruit in your field site.

4.   Food (again, depending on availability in the field).

5.   Hammock and mosquito net.

6.   Entertainment: books, music and pictures from home.

7.   Linguistic equipment: laptop, recording devices, books.

8.   Money, or merchandise for paying language teachers when money is not wanted. Cloth, machetes, files, hoes, axes, munitions, fish hooks, sewing needles, flashlights, batteries and so on are all useful.

9.   Toiletries and bathroom supplies.

10.   Tools.

If there are special treats that you like to eat to cheer yourself up, be sure to take an adequate supply. However, there is an important caveat to consider before you decide what to take: things you take, no matter how innocent-looking to you, could and probably will, be desired by people in the language community. This can lead to theft, hard feelings, jealousy, demand for equal treatment. Plan to take things to give as presents, to share your coffee and sugar (for instance), to give away most of what you have taken there before you leave the village, and to make sure that nothing you take is too important to lose, be destroyed or be taken. Never let 'things' come between you and the community. If things appear to create interpersonal problems, best go without them. Try not to argue about them. And that entails avoiding taking along anything you would be prepared to argue about.

As for tools, the authors found that a multi-use knife comes in handy (such as a Swiss Army knife). The tools you choose will depend, obviously, on your particular field situation. Whatever essential equipment you take, it is very valuable to know how to repair it and have the right tools and replacement parts to carry out such repairs.

Two items that are useful in most situations are duct tape and durepox. The former can fix most broken things. Durepox (which comes in two clay-like sections, to be mixed together) forms a chemical bond which is strong enough to repair holes in boats and cars. It is very valuable in the field. A flashlight, e.g. one that can be attached to your head for hands-free lighting when trying to read or repair something, is also useful.

An essential in many far-flung places is a water-filter system, so that you always have fresh drinking water. You cannot always buy water in remote field sites. In many remote places it is easier to get Coca Cola than clean drinking water!

The field is usually rough on equipment. Whatever you take with you is likely to be exposed to some combination of the following: high humidity, sand and dust, bugs, rain and temperature extremes. As you travel and pack and repack, heavy bags and other objects are likely to be put on top of delicate equipment, your equipment will be dropped, perhaps even in a river, and will otherwise be treated very differently than it might, say, at your home institution.

You could choose to use waterproof bags, widely available for canoeing, for example. There are also special carrying cases with adjustable foam linings and quality rubber seals for laptops and other sensitive electronic equipment. These cases, when maximally useful, are of metal or hardened plastic (yet relatively lightweight), waterproof, and able to hold equipment tightly in place and secure, without rattling around inside. There must be room in the equipment case for a desiccant of some sort if you are going to be in a wet or humid environment. One popular desiccant is silicon gel.

Exercise 5.9

Make a list of equipment for your fieldwork project. Try to find websites that list suitable fieldwork equipment appropriate for your area of study.

5.2.6   Additional equipment

Depending on your fieldsite, you may be able to take additional luxuries, such as a folding table and chairs, a backpacking stove, kerosene, solar panels and so on. If you have electricity, you may take movies with you. Choose programming that will entertain and relax you, but not offend the community's sensitivities. Also, it is important to remember that movies and other programmes can be great educational tools for the community. So take a selection of DVDs just for showing the community. The Pirahãs, for example, tremendously enjoy material about other indigenous communities and their daily lives, as well as about animals of all kinds. National Geographic movies are very useful. On the other hand, the most popular film among the Pirahãs is the old John Wayne film *Hatari*, about capturing wild animals in Africa.

For fieldwork in remote areas, a satellite phone is a great investment. There are several options on the market and most of them, though quite expensive with high per minute charges, can allow you to maintain contact with friends, colleagues and others in the most remote locations. Some people find this very useful. For example, with a satellite phone you can call for linguistic help, phoning or emailing your home institution to get expert advice on how to analyse or collect data on a particular subject (not to mention emergency help). In general, though, satellite phone communication is expensive, so will not be a way to chat freely with your friends at the weekends.

In areas where there is no electricity you may be able to bring your own portable power systems. There are a number of small, relatively inexpensive (but fossil fuel-consuming) generators available in most countries. These are useful and convenient tools. But generators have severe disadvantages: (i) they are environmentally harsh (use of fossil fuels); (ii) they require significant quantities of fuel; (iii) they are noisy; (iv) they require maintenance and careful storage and they break down.

A small solar-powered system may be more practical in many situations. It would not have to be large if used only for charging a camcorder, computer, audio-recorder, or for small light bulbs.[7]

Other possible equipment in places without electricity include wind-up radios, torches and laptops. These are often inexpensive and can make great gifts at the end of your stay.

5.2.7   Consumable study supplies

You will also need to take pens, paper and other office supplies, even if you rely more on the computer than on paper. Consumable study supplies include:

1.   *Flashlight batteries and AA-size batteries.* Buying alkaline batteries saves space as they last much longer than other batteries.
2.   *Blank DVDs* are important for backing up data or making copies of lab sessions, songs, etc.
3.   *Indelible, acid-free, waterproof ink pens.* It is a good idea to buy enough for one a week, minimum.

4.   *Pens in various colours* are useful for colour-coding data and have a range of other uses.

5.   *Paper and notebooks.* The authors found it useful to take sheets of paper (with side holes) to use in notebooks. You can use one notebook for every major division you want to make (e.g. when writing a grammar: 'Verbs', 'Nouns', 'Transitive clauses', 'Subordinate clauses', and so on). Take plastic binders for loose papers which are not yet in particular notebooks.

6.   *Paper clips, staples, stapler, clear adhesive tape and plastic bags of different sizes* may come in useful as well. The plastic bags will be vital, especially in rainy and humid areas, for preserving your notes and many other supplies (e.g. matches) from the effects of humidity and leaky roofs.

7.   *Back-up computer battery, memory cards and other equipment.* Computer batteries and other electronics do fail, especially in a humid climate. It is highly recommended to take extra supplies to the field.

5.2.8   How long to stay

The length of the first stay in the community should be based not only on the fieldworker's available time, but also on a realistic assessment of his or her ability to withstand the separation, newness, anxiety and work responsibilities of the initial visit. The general rule is to underestimate your staying power, rather than to overestimate it.

The authors find that an initial visit of about a month's length is ideal. There is a psychological as well as cultural issue involved in this recommendation. In general, when you give a date that you plan to leave the community, whether only to yourself or to others, this date is taken as a sort of promise, a kind of moral commitment.[8] So if you overestimate your staying ability for the initial visit, then you can feel that you are breaking a promise or 'wimping out', having failed in some way. In fact, anyone who goes to the field and stays for a reasonable period of time should feel pride in their accomplishment, not guilt. If you leave after the first visit feeling guilty, this would be an unnecessarily inauspicious beginning to your field programme.

The estimate of the length of the entire project clearly depends on several factors, including the nature of the project (e.g. to collect data for a grammar, dictionary, text collection, partial study of phonetics, phonology, constituent order typology, etc.), the degree of physical isolation of the community (from the fieldworker's perspective), the degree of bilingualism in the speech community, the state of documentation and description of the language of study, the state of documentation and description of related languages or languages of the area, the goodwill and cooperation of the community, and so forth. Consider the following extract, from Samarin (1967: 71):

> Criticizing linguists because they have not had enough time with informants is like condemning shipwrecked sailors for not having provided themselves with food and water. What we can more wisely do is evaluate how much was accomplished in the time a linguist had at his disposal.

It is generally the case that most linguists would like more field time than they have had before writing up their results. For example, a *rough* estimate of how long it would take to write a comprehensive grammar (no dictionary, no carefully compiled text collection) depends again on the availability of other sources on the language. An Amazonian language which has not previously been researched would take, after all permissions are received, in the neighbourhood of two full years of near-daily work and contact with the community. The writing up of the grammar would take at least an additional six to twelve months, including follow-up visits to gather, verify or clarify data. For a language of North America, where at least some in the community speak English and related languages are well-described, the time for data-gathering might be somewhere between six and ten months, again of regular, daily work with language teachers. We base these estimates on an assumption of three hours per day of *good* fieldwork sessions, excellent language teacher help for data-processing in the field, good health and no undue interruptions in the work routine.[9] Of course, it is highly unlikely that everything goes so smoothly, and it is good to plan for interruptions such as no transport available (e.g. due to flooding or strikes), disease (you or the speakers you work with) or other circumstances (such as harvest time, where everybody has to work long hours).

The timeframes of most projects can be estimated by comparing your study to those of others – how long did it take them? Talk to other linguists with similar experiences, and ask them about their estimates.

Exercise 5.10

Think about the length of your fieldwork project. If you are 'going far away', how long would you be able to stay in your fieldsite? Even if you are working closer to home, make estimates of the appropriate length of your fieldwork necessary to achieve your research goals.

5.2.9 Accommodation

Unless you live nearby, you will have to arrange for accommodation during your field visit. Depending on your budget, you could book an expensive hotel or stay with a friend. In many remote fieldwork situations, however, there are no hotels. What to do?

You may be able to arrange for accommodation prior to your first visit, by asking your contacts (if you have any) whether anybody would be willing to rent you a room. This may be a good way of getting to know the village, living among the people whose language you study.

Sometimes you will stay in dwellings with very little privacy. Depending on the geographical area you are going to, you are wise to take a hammock or a good sleeping bag. You may need mosquito nets and similar devices (see above).

Be aware that when staying with – or among – speakers, problems based on false expectations can arise. For example, the people you are staying with may expect that you exclusively work with their family, or that you will always stay with them. It is good to be honest from the start in this case, and to be aware of these issues so that you can avoid them, where possible. Sometimes, issues about accommodation arise that are not anticipated at all, as is seen in Sakel's experience described below.

Jeanette Sakel

When I carried out fieldwork in Greenland, I was staying at a boarding school for adults, a popular place to spend a gap-year for many Greenlanders. When I first contacted the school I was promised the guest-apartment. However, it was unexpectedly occupied by a local poet at the time I arrived. I was given a room for myself on the ground floor of the school among rooms of other students, which I much preferred. I settled in well and started my work, studying voice structures like 'the door opened'. Now, when I asked people how to say this in Greenlandic they all looked at me with wide eyes, asking 'really'? I did not give it too much thought, but soon there were other strange reactions, such as people refusing to enter my room, and a lot of interest every morning and enquiries about my night's sleep. I remembered Greenlandic friends of mine in Denmark warning me about a ghost at the school. As I did not believe in ghosts, I jokingly asked one of the speakers if there was one. To my surprise I learned that the room I had been allocated was actually generally locked and no-one 'in the know' wanted to stay there as that was where many people had experienced paranormal activities. Thus, the ghost was not at the school 'in general', but rather exclusively in my room! At first I thought 'okay, that's fine – I'll set my tape-recorder to noise-triggered auto recording and if the ghost comes I may be able to record some Proto-Eskimo!' However, after a long day's work, lying in bed at night things looked very different indeed! I couldn't fall asleep at all. The next morning, absolutely shattered, I forced myself to go through the daily routine of 'how did you sleep' interrogation and I kept replying 'really well!', as I felt that I had to keep up 'an image'. I felt that I had to keep my authority as a fieldworker, even though I confided in one of the speakers (the one who told me about the ghost in the first place). For the remaining week in Greenland, I did not really sleep. It was November, and for much of the time a heavy snowstorm was raging outside, so fierce that one could barely stand up. On other days the skies were gleaming with northern lights. It actually could not get much more spooky.

I never saw the ghost, who I later learned was supposedly an old lady, nor did I record any proto-Eskimo.[10]

5.2.10   Travel arrangements

Travel arrangements can be a major part of preparing for remote fieldwork. Some universities require you to book your journey through a particular travel agent. This may be fine for getting to the country or area of your research, but how about local travel? This is often for you to arrange on site. The authors have travelled to many remote places. In some, a backpacker's guidebook (such as the *Lonely Planet* series) can give valuable information. In others, you have to ask around locally to find ways to get to your final destination. Many remote places have connections to bigger cities, e.g. by pick-up truck, boat, taxi plane or similar. For example, the Mosetenes can be reached by a weekly bus service from a major city, and by pick-up trucks at other times. More isolated communities, like the Pirahã, may not have any transport. You may have to hire a boat or car, charter a plane or – in some cases – even walk to reach your fieldsite. In some cases, employing a guide may be called for, especially when you do not know the area well or have to go a long distance on your own.

5.3   Summary and further reading

This chapter dealt with fieldwork preparation, ranging from formulating research questions to what to take to the field. We discussed finding the relevant literature, making best use of technology, applying for funding and ethics approval, as well as various aspects of dealing with fieldwork in remote settings, such as vaccinations, paperwork and how long to stay. Indeed, some of the issues particular to remote fieldwork can, in a minor way, also be applied to other types of fieldwork. For example, taking into consideration the culture of the people whose language you study is of vital importance in any fieldwork situation. Official paperwork may also become an issue when working on an immigrant language in your community.

Further information on fieldwork preparation can be found on a number of linguists' helpful websites, for example Keren Rice's website http://projects.chass.utoronto.ca/lingfieldwork. Chelliah & de Reuse (2011) have a detailed chapter on fieldwork preparation. For the preparation of language documentation, see Austin (2006).

6 Fieldwork methods

This chapter deals with the methods of different types of fieldwork. Fieldwork can involve naturalistic, controlled or reported data; methods can be qualitative and/or quantitative, including elicitation, recording of spoken language and linguistic experiments. Still, even the most distinct types of fieldwork often make use of similar processes, such as recording metadata.

In this chapter, we will discuss the different methods employed in fieldwork. How you employ these methods largely depends on your goals. If your aim is to write a grammar, you may well use all of the methods. If your aim is to look at a particular structure in a well-described language, you may be able to get away with just one method.

Likewise, the timescale of your studies depends on what you are doing. For example, when conducting a pilot study (like the Somali study in 2.2) you may be able to collect your data in short sessions arranged to suit your and your speakers' availability. When writing a grammar, some field linguists work with language teachers eight hours a day, seven days a week, the entire time that they are in the community. Others find that a less intensive schedule works better. It is up to you to find a way that works for you, your teachers and your project. The authors have found it appropriate to work for two to six hours each day of sessions in intensive fieldwork projects, including verification of data collected with multiple teachers. The remainder of the day would then be used for data-processing, analysis, hypothesis formation, language practice and planning the next session. Linguistic experiments can be conducted in much shorter timeframes and leave more freedom to arrange timings.

6.1 Types of research method

A common distinction in research, not just in linguistics, is that between qualitative and quantitative methods. Depending on what you want to study and what your desired outcome is, you would employ either of these methods, or indeed a combination of both of them: mixed methods.

6.1.1   Qualitative methods

Qualitative methods are generally concerned with naturalistic language use among a small number of speakers. Qualitative studies can and often do make use of a wide range of language data, such as stories, conversations and interviews. The sample size is generally small, though of course this depends on the project. In qualitative studies, the focus is on the behaviour of individuals and in particular the subjective behaviour of individuals, rather than comparing variables across a range of speakers. This can leave the researcher with a fair amount of interpretative freedom. The preparation phase of the research does not necessarily have to be extensive, as methods may evolve over time. This includes finalizing research questions, which may be vague at the beginning of the research or change later due to different findings during fieldwork and analysis.

Prototypical fieldwork is inherently qualitative. Still, quantitative and mixed methods are equally commonly applied in fieldwork, and a considerable number of linguists work in far-flung places using other than qualitative methods.[1]

6.1.2   Quantitative methods

Quantitative methods are appropriate for studies looking at one or several variables across a range of speakers. They can also involve manipulation, e.g. giving one group a certain treatment and testing them afterwards, comparing the results with a control group that has not had that particular treatment.

Typical quantitative studies could, for example, be 'the pronunciation of /r/ among speakers of language x', 'the degree of contact influence in structure y' or 'speakers' grammaticality judgements of construction z'. Ultimately, quantitative data are meant to be boiled down to numbers. In the first study mentioned above, findings could be '/r/ is pronounced [r] by 80% of the speakers, [ʀ] by 15% and the remaining 5% use a variety of pronunciations'. This means we learn about the variable that the majority of speakers adhere to, while individual differences (e.g. the remaining 5%) may go unexplained. In order to get valid generalizations, larger samples are usually needed (i.e. data are collected from a variety of speakers). Tools to collect and analyse the data involve standardized procedures, such as questionnaires, experiments and statistics. This means that the results can be replicated, and researcher subjectivity be cut out or at least decreased considerably. In this way the data will give you a good idea of what a population's language use is like. In order to achieve this, however, the quantitative data-collection needs very careful preparation. For example, you need to make sure a questionnaire is appropriate before you go out and collect data, otherwise you run the risk of the data not being comparable or asking the wrong questions. It would be difficult to rectify your mistakes, as you would have to go back to all the people you had interviewed. A way to ensure you have got everything in order is to carry out a pilot study. That way you can test your methods prior to embarking on the actual study. From the authors' experience, there are always unexpected issues one wants to change following a pilot study.

Many fieldwork projects aim to combine both types of methods in so-called mixed methods.

6.1.3   Mixed methods

The term *mixed methods* refers to the combination of both qualitative and quantitative methods. This can lead to more solid studies than mere qualitative or quantitative studies on their own. There are various ways of combining methods. One could, for example, carry out a questionnaire-type study collecting quantitative data, while at the same time asking for further written explanations which could be analysed qualitatively. Or when writing a grammar, one could supplement qualitative data with quantitative studies on specific structures that require further clarification. The Mosetén study in 2.1 is a qualitative study. The Somali study in 2.2 is a mixed methods study: making use of structured, though relatively free, interviews at the same time as using picture stories to collect similar texts from a range of speakers. The stories are comparable and could be analysed statistically. At the same time, the qualitative part of the study involves looking at the actual language materials and studying how the language of individuals is influenced by language contact.

6.1.4   Cross-sectional and longitudinal studies

Qualitative, quantitative or mixed methods can be employed in different timescales: cross-sectional, i.e. all at one time, or longitudinal, i.e. over a period of time, comparing data from different points in time.

Which one of these you would choose, again depends heavily on your research project. When looking at a speaker's language attrition, a longitudinal study may be valuable, comparing the speaker's language use now to their language use in five years from now. One could imagine similar studies on language acquisition. Other data-collection, e.g. for a grammar, does not necessarily need a longitudinal perspective. This does not mean the research can be completed there and then – the actual fieldwork may still take several years, as long as some longitudinal attrition studies. Thus, the length of the data-collection phase does not necessarily have much to do with the cross-section versus longitudinal divide. Some studies, such as student projects, will be less suitable for longitudinal studies. Others may start out as cross-sectional studies but go back to the same speakers in the future to collect longitudinal data.

6.2   Metadata, recordings and field notes

An essential part of fieldwork is the careful annotation of the data for storage. This is usually referred to as 'metadata', a term that is often used with computational connotations, which is not the intention here. We suggest you carefully log the following points together with your linguistic recording (these are based on Samarin 1967; see also the EMELD project, http://emeld.org).

1.   *Code*: This gives the genre of the text (e.g. narrative, conversation).
2.   *Sound file number*: Where the text is found in your audio database.
3.   *Topic*: What the text is about (e.g. 'fishing story', 'story about jungle spirits').
4.   *Dates*: When the text was collected and when the tape was transcribed.
5.   *Speaker and language teacher information*: Who produced the text; who helped transcribe and translate the text; sociocultural information on language teachers (e.g. age, gender, marital status, occupation, birthplace, knowledge of other languages, religion, language of parents, societal status, etc.).
6.   *Team member information*: Which linguists worked on the text and what was the contribution of each?
7.   *Place*: Where was the text recorded (village, city, university, etc.)?
8.   *Any notable characteristics of the text*: for example 'this ritual text includes prosodic phrasing that appears quite unusual'; 'the speaker uses expression *x* a great deal', and so on.
9.   *Other comments* the linguist believes are relevant.

This background information will be important when it comes to analysing your data. For example when you look at the language of different speakers, a speaker's age or even gender may play a role in their language use. If you are doing a longitudinal study, the time of the recording will be highly relevant, and so on.

It would be good practice to treat recording ethical consent as part of the metadata process, making sure you have considered all ethical issues prior to embarking on your fieldwork. It may also be advisable to record, or at least plan for recording, metadata prior to embarking on your actual fieldwork. Having said this, you may wish to spare your speakers too many questions not directly related to the core of the study at the onset, and reserve such questions for later (also the discussion on questionnaires in 6.5.1).

An approach the authors have found helpful is to note important metadata briefly on tape at the onset of a fieldwork session. You should list the information on a piece of paper or state the participants and the setting of the work at the beginning of the recording. It will make it easier to organize data at a later stage. This way you can also ask for ethical consent from the speaker, either having ethics forms ready or recording the speaker's consent on audio or (even better) video. The latter can be the only way to record such consent if the people you are working with are illiterate.

Many fieldwork projects can benefit from video-recordings, as they preserve the verbal as well as the non-verbal cues. You can see who is speaking in case there are several speakers at the same time. You will be able to see what was going on in the situation (e.g. if someone comes in and everybody stops talking). You will have to take care to place the video camera in such a way that everybody is visible. You may have to buy a good microphone to go with your video camera, or do an audio-recording at the same time as the video-recording. It is essential to try out all recording equipment prior to the first session.

The disadvantage of video-recordings is that some speakers may not want to be recorded, or may not feel comfortable being recorded. The authors have found that – in particular when eliciting narratives, conversations, etc. – recording the session on video can be a hindrance, as speakers inevitably tense up (and the language becomes formal and scarce). You could try to get the speakers used to the camera first, or you may just decide that recording the story on tape is enough.

Exercise 6.1

Take one of your class mates, best friend, neighbour or any other person familiar to you and record them on video (this could be, for example, on your mobile phone). Ask them to tell you a story or to tell you about themselves. Afterwards, note down how the recording of the person is different from how you know that person. What is the length of the text they gave you? How does it differ from them talking normally, when not being recorded? Next, ask your friend to record you on video telling a story. How do you feel?

The exercise will probably show you that you are tense when being recorded, even if the person recording you is someone familiar. The same holds for audio-recordings, which may not be appropriate in all settings, even though most people are more relaxed when recorded on audio. Again, a lot depends on the setting: put a tiny microphone up and they may forget it is there after a while; put them in a recording studio with flashing lights and you may not get the relaxed language data you were after (see also 6.3 below on recording texts).

Viveka Velupillai

When conducting fieldwork on tense and aspect in Hawaii Creole English, she used small clip-on microphones for her recordings. While the speakers were generally aware of the equipment at the beginning of the sessions, on a number of occasions they wandered off later on, offering to make coffee, etc. Only then would they realize that they were actually wearing a microphone. She took this as a sign that they had become less aware of being recorded, and that their language was closer to 'naturalistic'.   (personal communication)

No matter if you record or not, it is a good idea to take notes during the fieldwork session. These are usually referred to as *field notes*, and are essential when not recording on audio or video (most people do not have a good enough memory to recall everything discussed after the session; notes during the session can help you both to sort your data and to remember what it was about). Even when recording, it may be a good idea to take notes for the same reasons, but also to see which parts of recordings are essential, e.g. if you record a lot of data in case something important comes up but do not have the time to go through it all afterwards. In this case it may be a good idea to note down the timing given on your recorder (if it shows timing – solid state recorders and other digital devices generally do). You could use your computer for field notes, or use pen and paper (little books are good, as they keep pages in order, rather than dealing with random, and inevitably messy, sheets of paper).

6.3   Text data

Most types of qualitative linguistic fieldwork make use of text data. There is a wealth of texts you can collect, ranging from narratives (old stories, fictional stories, etc.) and other monologues (e.g. speeches, presentations), to interactions between speakers of the language. Different texts give you different kinds of data: you can observe discourse strategies such as turn-taking in discussions, while this may not be possible in stories. On the other hand, stories can give you longer chunks of data that are more appropriate for looking at reference tracking, among many other things.

Thus, the kind of texts you would aim to record depend again on the study you are doing. Still, independent of your project, if you have the time it may be a good idea to look at different types of text data in order to get an overview of the language. Sometimes you find unexpected structures in other styles or types of data, so it can pay to be more inclusive when it comes to figuring out which data to record. The following are the main types of text you may encounter:

1.   NARRATIVE: This includes stories told by the speakers. They can vary between very informal pieces and highly formalized texts of cultural significance, i.e. recognized oral literature using archaic language. Some speakers prefer to give traditional stories rather than informal narratives. Such material is of course wonderful and the linguist certainly must collect a good deal of it. However, for a wide range of fieldwork projects you also need informal narratives of the type 'what I did for my summer vacation', 'how my fishing trip went today', 'what I told my son to do to avoid jaguars' and 'how my little girl made her dress'. Different speakers will have different abilities and preferences for different kinds of narrative texts. There is no magic answer. One simply has to experiment with different methods and speakers.

2.   PROCEDURAL: This kind of discourse is easier to collect, because it involves a speaker telling the linguist how to make something, following a specific order of activities, e.g. a recipe, how to make a bow and arrow, and so on. These were the first texts Everett ever collected among the Pirahãs, and they are among the easiest to understand,

since you can pick out individual parts of the process and figure out fairly easily how the overall structure of the text works. It is an excellent genre for collecting imperatives, temporal connectives, and other natural features of recipes, etc.

3.   EXPOSITORY: These are explanations, ideally of culturally important information. So a language teacher might explain how a man becomes a shaman, what the village headman was talking about last night in the text you could not understand, and so on. Again, these are usually not too difficult to collect. They have characteristic aspects, tenses, and other features which set them off.

4.   HORTATORY: These types of text urge the listeners to take some sort of action. They can be difficult to elicit from speakers. Some planning can help you record text of this type.

Jeanette Sakel

The Mosetenes held regular meetings, at which it was easy to come across hortatory texts. For example, the *cacique* (leader or mayor of the village) would give a speech on the main square every Sunday morning. While there was usually some day-to-day administrative business, much of the rest of the speech would be occupied with things he wanted the Mosetenes to take care of, so there was plenty of hortative language use. These speeches tended to be in a mixture of Mosetén and Spanish (depending on the person who was cacique at the particular time).

---

5.   CONVERSATIONS: Conversations are both the most important genre of text to collect, because they contain natural, everyday use of the grammar, and the most difficult. To put two or three speakers together and then say to them 'converse' is not conducive to natural discourse.

Dan Everett

In July 2004, for example, I was able to record a natural, long (thirty minutes), and linguistically rich conversation from two Banawá men, Sabatao and Bido. They each wore headsets with high-quality unidirectional microphones and were recorded onto separate channels on a digital tape-recorder. The conversation was then transcribed, glossed, and filed. It is the best data I have ever collected from the Banawá.

At the same time, it proved much harder to collect a similarly natural conversation from the Pirahãs, whom I know much better. I tried various strategies after it became clear that just asking two people to converse was not going to give useful results. I have just sat with people in their huts, with the recorder running, often getting natural conversation. However, since they are obviously not wearing headsets in such circumstances, the sound quality of such recordings is far inferior. Nevertheless, it is good enough for prosodic and morphological analyses in most cases.

In order to record texts, you will have to make sure that you stick to the ethics requirements, such as not recording people without their knowledge. A good way of eliciting texts for recording is to put the speakers at ease to begin with: make sure they are comfortable, have a chat with them first. Let them see the recording equipment, tell them about what is going to happen. The speakers will probably be 'nervous' for the first few minutes until they forget that there is recording equipment, or become more comfortable with it. This is perfectly normal, and being aware of it, you can make sure that whatever is crucial to your study is recorded after the first nervousness has passed (see also 6.2. above).

Recording a text is not always as simple as putting a microphone in front of one or more speakers. That way you may not end up with any language data at all or in the wrong language. There are various strategies to obtain texts. You could simply ask the speaker(s) to tell you a story. Imagine someone asks you out of the blue to tell a story. Would you be able to do it? You may not be able to think about anything worth telling. It may be easier to ask 'tell me about yourself' or to be even more specific, e.g. 'tell me about your hunting trip', 'can you tell me how to weave a basket', etc. That is, open-ended questions that probably will involve multi-sentence answers and can give you at least something text-like.

Alan Vogel

One thing I do is always carry a list in my pocket of stories I want to record. When I am talking to people, and I hear a reference to some experience or story that sounds worth recording, I make a note to myself to record the story later, jotting down the person's name and something about the subject matter. And I ask the person if he would be willing to record the story another day. Then later, when we both have time, I record it. This is a good way of avoiding the problem of sitting down with someone and asking them to tell you a story, and they don't tell a good story, because you don't know what stories they know (or maybe they are not a good story teller).   (personal communication)

Exercise 6.2

Many of the exercises in this chapter are designed for you to try out a number of fieldwork methods. For this purpose, you will need to find a speaker of a language you do not know. The language does not have to be exotic, but it may be good to know nothing or only little about it. Ideally, the speaker should be easily accessible to you, for example an exchange student on your course, a neighbour or a friend, and should be willing to help you in your quest. You do not have to take up too much of the speaker's time, but you will have to get back to them from time to time to carry out further exercises. Make sure you inform them about your study and stick to the ethics guidelines (see 4.4).

Record at least three different types of text with your speaker(s). They can be very short (even a few minutes may suffice). Ideally you would record a variety of genres.

Which genres are more straightforward to elicit than others? Listen to the texts to see what you understand, and in which ways they appear to differ. Note down your observations, as we will get back to these texts again in later sections.

Once you have recorded texts, you will have to prepare them for analysis. Recording a huge number of texts may be a good idea when documenting a language, where the emphasis is on collecting as much material and as many diverse aspects of the language as possible. However, in other types of study it may be better to restrict the recording of an overall volume of texts and focus on those that you can prepare for analysis. This preparation may include the transcription, translation and glossing of your texts, as discussed in the following sections.

6.3.1   Transcription

As a rule of thumb, never estimate less than a 4:1 ratio between transcription and recordings. That is, for each hour of recording, it will take the linguist at least four hours to transcribe the data, if they are already highly familiar with the language and its sounds. If you are just beginning in a new language with unfamiliar sounds, the ratio is more likely to be 5:1 or 6:1, or even more, until you get used to transcribing this particular language.

Where possible, you can work with speakers who can read and write their own language and who can help you transcribe your texts. In cases where such help does not exist, you could transcribe the text on your own, using phonetic symbols if an orthography has not been established yet. Then read the transcription to a native speaker. With a different colour ink, write in that speaker's correction of your transcription, as you pronounced it. Where doubts and confusion arise, you can play the original recording of the text and ask the teacher to tell you what was said and what it means. From the authors' experience, it is a good idea to use your own pronunciation initially, because it is the best and most immediate check of your ability to pronounce and transcribe the language. The native speaker will almost always easily understand the original text, since it is by another native speaker. But this way you can see if *you* have it right. You can then indicate whether you think any correction is of the actual phonetics or whether it is a 'prescriptive' correction, i.e. that it reflects what the second speaker believes that the first speaker *should* have said if speaking correctly. It is very common for speakers to make fun of one another and to think that the other's use or knowledge of the language is inferior to their own. Likewise, speakers tend to 'correct' their own language in a similar manner when faced with the recording.

Also, in cases where a speaker can help you transcribe the text, it is a good idea to discuss 'what it should have been like', and to make the person helping you transcribe aware of the fact that you are interested in both the way it was said, and the way it 'should have been' said according to their judgement.

While you can transcribe using just pen and paper or a word processing program, there are various good tools specifically designed for transcription, most of which are free (though you may need to register with the developers). The program Transcriber (http://trans.sourceforge.net) has been developed to transcribe speech. It works by importing the sound file, which is linked to the transcription as you are writing it in. This is very useful, as you can easily go back to any transcribed part of your data without having to listen to the entire recording. Another program, ELAN (www.lat-mpi.eu), can be used to annotate both audio and video. It has been developed by the Max Planck Institute for Psycholinguistics and has been specifically adjusted to linguists' transcription needs. Like Transcriber, it links sound and video files with the transcribed text. ELAN can also be used to gloss and translate the data (see the next two sections).

A program originally designed to build a corpus of child language is CLAN (http://childes.psy.cmu.edu/clan/), which can be used for transcription, as well as annotative and statistical analysis of the data. CLAN has an annotation tool called Chat, which links the recording to the transcribed text. While CLAN was specifically designed for work on first language acquisition, it can be used in various fieldwork settings (see Meakins 2007 for a review).

Exercise 6.3

Transcribe one of the texts you recorded earlier, using pen and paper or a word processing program. You may first try to do this without the help of your speaker, but you may have to try to get your speaker (or another person who knows the language) to help you.

Then, download one or more of the programs mentioned above and try to transcribe the remaining texts in that way. You will have to read the instructions for the specific program first. Initially, this may take considerably longer than when you transcribed your text directly. Getting used to the program, can you find ways in which it could be helpful in your fieldwork?

6.3.2   Translation

When the transcription is finished, the next step is generally to translate the text – that is, unless you speak the language under investigation, in which case you may be able to skip this step. Still, even in this case you may not get around the need for a careful annotation and translation of your examples, since if you were to publish in a journal you would generally be expected to translate (and gloss) any examples you are giving unless the language under investigation is the language of the publication.

If you are studying a well-known language, or if your speakers are able to read and write, this aspect of the study may be straightforward. You could employ someone to carry out the translation for you. If such help is not available to you, you will have to work on the translation yourself.

For most studies it is advisable to translate the text as a whole as well as the individual lines or sentences of the text. This helps you to grasp the overall story, as well as giving you an understanding of the individual words and morphemes of the data. It is a good idea to carefully translate and gloss at least a few texts even when the language is already well-described. The available grammars and other materials will help you during this process, and you will learn a lot about the language under investigation.

The translation of the overall text can be approached by asking the teacher to retell the story in the other language, or by asking for a summary of what the text is about. This will give you a general understanding of the story, rather than getting caught up in details, as more often than not the individual word-by-word translation can be very different from the overall meaning. This can easily lead to misunderstandings.

Exercise 6.4

Again working with the texts you recorded previously, translate the individual words with the help of your speaker or alternatively a dictionary. If you are working with the speaker, make sure you tell them what this exercise is about, so that they do not 'help' you too much when it comes to the overall understanding of the text. For now, we merely want to know what each individual word means.

Once your word-by-word translation is finished, try to figure out the overall meaning of the text. Retell it to your speaker and check whether you got it right. If not, where did you go wrong?

(The key to the exercise is available at www.cambridge.org/Sakel-Everett.)

While essential for understanding what the text is about, an overall translation would not tell us much about what is going on at the level of the word. Such information is essential for most studies, not just those dealing with grammatical aspects. For example, studies of discourse structures, language contact, second language acquisition or sociolinguistic variation all require or at least benefit from some knowledge of what is going on at word level.

A word-by-word translation could be carried out with the help of a speaker or a dictionary. If you are working with a speaker, you may be able to ask further questions (indeed, sessions of translating texts can easily turn into elicitation sessions on other things, sparked by some or other structure that appeared in the text).

A helpful way to approach the word-by-word translation is to divide the text up into 'sentences'. Such sentences are not always clear at the outset, as spoken language does not work in the same way as written language. You can look for pauses in what is said, or try to find natural breaks in the story, or turns between speakers in a discussion, in order to establish smaller chunks of text. You may change your mind about these chunks again later, but for now it is easier to work with shorter sections than with a whole long text. It is a good idea to number the chunks (henceforth referred to as sentences, with the understanding that they are not necessarily sentences!).

It may be useful to translate the individual sentences (as a whole), and then proceed to translate the components in a word-by-word translation. The same caution given in relation to 'sentences' applies to what a 'word' is: you may write them down as words, but careful morphological and phonological analysis may reveal that they are morphemes, or vice versa. For now, it may be easiest to accept that this is part of the game and you can always change it later, marking your data as 'will have to be looked at again once I know more about this'. For now, it is not so important to get it all 'right'. More than likely, getting it all right at the beginning is impossible anyway, especially if the language is only little-described.

Exercise 6.5

Follow up from the text you recorded and transcribed and do an overall translation, then divide it into 'sentences'. Now compare your findings with your word-by-word translation. What did you learn from each stage of the process?

6.3.3   Glossing

Preparing a text for analysis, the next process is usually to gloss the examples. Glosses are essentially translations of morphemes, so yet a level further down from word-by-word translations. Again, depending on the type and circumstances of your study, you may not have to gloss your examples. For example, if you study aspects of the overall discourse structure of the text, you may get away with a rough word-by-word translation without too much detail (1):

(1)   *Ich habe ihn   auch gesehen AND HE SAID TO ME*
          I   have him   also   seen

          "DON'T TELL THEM!" aber ich habe ihn   trotzdem verpfiffen.
                               but   I   have him   anyway   denounced

          'I also saw him, and he said to me "don't tell them!" but I denounced him anyway.'

If you are working with bilingual data, you can present different languages with different fonts, e.g. capital letter for English as in (1).

In other fieldwork situations glossing is essential. For example, if you study a language that is not well-described, early glosses may be very basic, speckled with question marks, which you will gradually be able to eradicate as you become more confident. Once you know more about how the language works, you will be able to use more elaborate glossing.

Usually, glosses are given below the language data and above the translation (2):

(2)   *Mi'-we*   *miñ-i*   *ji'-chhae-yi-ti.*
3M.SG-DOWNRIVER go-VERB.M.SBJ CAUS-know-VERB-REFL.M.SBJ
'He went there to study.'

It is general custom to give lexical elements as translations and grammatical elements as abbreviations, often in small caps, but you will encounter a lot of variation in the literature. There has been an effort to establish conventions for glossing, referred to as the 'Leipzig glossing rules', see www.eva.mpg.de/lingua/ resources/glossing-rules.php. These rules aim to make frequent glosses more easily identifiable, standardizing common practice among linguists.

A number of other conventions are generally used in glosses. Words are aligned in the data and the gloss, separated by tabs. This way it is easy to see which gloss belongs to which word. Within each word, morphemes are divided up to correspond to one another in the data and the gloss. Morpheme boundaries are indicated by '-', and there should be a direct correspondence between the number of morphemes in the data and below in the gloss. For example, the dash between *mi'* and *we* in (2) indicates a morpheme boundary; there are two morphemes, *mi'* and *-we*, presented in the gloss as 3M.SG and DOWNRIVER.[2] The gloss of the first morpheme consists of three elements: third person, masculine and singular. These are all expressed by the single morpheme *mi'* in the data. In order to show that there are not three different morphemes for each meaning, these three aspects are divided up by a full stop. To make things ever so slightly more confusing, it is common practice not to write a full stop between person and number or person and gender, i.e. 3M rather than 3.M.[3]

While the Leipzig glossing rules give abbreviations of frequent grammatical categories, you may have to find a way to present glosses for less frequent categories. You could try to get away with not abbreviating the category label at all and presenting it in small capitals (or a significant part of the category name), e.g. DOWNRIVER in the example above. However, if a category is common, a long form like that may make glosses too long, so a shorter form may be preferable (e.g. DR). You will have to decide what works best for your language and/or the format of the output. For this reason, it is very important to give a list of abbreviations (3) whenever you present glossed examples. They may be presented in a footnote to the first example where such glosses appear, or they may come at the end of a paper or prelude to a book.[4]

(3)   List of abbreviations for example (2)
         3   third person
         CAUS   causative
         DOWNRIVER   downriver associative motion marker
         M   masculine
         REFL   reflexive marking in the verb
         SBJ   subject
         SG   singular
         VERB   verb marker

Sometimes detailed glosses can obscure the overall meaning of a word. For example *mi'we* in (2) above is glossed as 3M.SG-DOWNRIVER, while it could simply be translated 'there'. Yet, it implies that there is a third person singular masculine antecedent and that the location is downriver from the deictic centre. It does not, however mean 'he is downriver', or any other possible combination of the morphemes for third person singular masculine (= 'he') and *downriver*. In the same way as the overall meaning of a story can differ quite significantly from the meanings of the individual words, morphemes can also express aspects not necessarily expected when looking at the overall meaning of words.

Once you have translated and glossed your data, take some time to go through your glosses, making notes of doubts you may have and structures that are unusual in content, form, linguistic complexity or cultural information. You may want to discuss these aspects with one or two other language teachers. If the text is particularly complex, it is a good idea to go through it with the original giver of the text.[5] If you have to correct previous translations or glosses, it can be helpful to do this by strikethrough, or alternatively to keep an earlier copy of your data. The original translations or glosses sometimes do, on subsequent reflection or investigation, turn out to be the more accurate versions after all.

There are a number of computer programs that can be used to gloss (as well as translate) language data. Two of these, ELAN and CLAN have been discussed above (6.3.1). Another one is Toolbox[6] (www.sil.org/computing/toolbox), a program developed by SIL International specifically to facilitate the annotation of (mostly) prototypical fieldwork data. By building a dictionary of lexical and grammatical items, the program eventually 'learns' to annotate new texts automatically. New lexical items and unclarities of analysis are set aside for the linguist to review, while the remaining text is analysed automatically, or 'interlinearized', which can save a lot of time if you have a substantial amount of data.

Exercise 6.6

Now gloss your texts using either one of the programs mentioned above or writing out your glosses in a word processing program, following the Leipzig glossing rules. Make sure you give a list of abbreviations. Try to work on your own (i.e. without the speaker) for now. We will go back to consulting the speaker in the next section.

Is anything unclear? Languages with *fusional* morphology tend to be more difficult to gloss than so-called *agglutinative* languages. The latter often have clear morpheme boundaries and direct morpheme-by-morpheme translations, while the former may have only one morpheme with many different translations, as well as fuzzy morpheme boundaries.

6.4   Elicitation

Elicitation can be described as an interview process between you and one or several speakers. You may want to use your computer and recording devices during elicitation sessions, although many field researchers find simple pen and paper the most important tools to make notes of their findings. These can be detailed accounts of what is said, or merely short notes. It is highly dependent on what you want to achieve. You may choose to record an elicitation session. This is possible if you carry out only a few or short elicitation sessions or have an infinite amount of recording time (e.g. a solid state recorder and many batteries or solar power). However, be aware that you may not ever listen to what you have recorded. Elicitation sessions can be long, and it may be far easier to make notes during the process, without having to go through everything again afterwards. Of course, in case you should miss something or want to review a pronunciation later, recordings can come in very handy.

Elicitation is not just the unplanned activity of sitting down and talking about the language. Rather, a successful elicitation session benefits from careful planning. First of all, make sure you have a point! It is advisable for each session to begin with a well thought out, measurable objective.

Peter Ladefoged

. . . when in the field spend more time thinking what you want to record than making recordings. I so often see students and others wasting time recording masses of useless stuff, hoping they can use it later when in fact it will simply delay their later work by their having to go through it all. **Think hard first, record later**. [emphasis DE]   (personal communication)

Additionally, you should have back-up plans. As Mick Jagger reminds us, 'You can't always get what you want.' The secondary goals need not be related to the primary goal. But time with the language teachers is precious, literally, and it should ideally be fully and productively utilized.

There are two strategies for what to do when you have run out of planned material. Some linguists favour stopping the elicitation session here, and sending the speaker away. Their argument is that there is no sense in paying someone to watch you 'sputter and spin your wheels'. In fact, you could give them evidence that you have no idea what you are doing, which is not a good impression to give. Other linguists prefer to let the elicitation session take them to new grounds. This can be very enlightening – often elicitation sessions lead you to things you did not think of before, and sometimes it pays off to follow on from things that have come up during elicitation. It is for you to decide which strategy works best for you. Of course, if you have completely run out of things to ask, it may be a better idea to stop than to carry on regardless!

6.4.1   Types of elicitation

There are various types of what field linguists would call 'elicitation'. Much of the following is based on Samarin (1967: 112ff), where some of these types were first spelled out.

1.   *Questionnaire-based*: It can be useful to follow a questionnaire. There are two basic types of questionnaires: (i) lists of categories of the type 'does language x have structure y?', e.g. the Lingua Descriptive Studies questionnaire (www.eva.mpg.de/lingua/tools-at-lingboard/questionnaire/linguaQ.php) or the phonology questionnaire presented in appendix 2, and (ii) lists of questions to ask speakers during an interview. Questionnaires of the first type may be helpful tools when investigating a topic in great detail, e.g. when writing a grammar, but they have little to do with elicitation itself and are therefore disregarded in our discussion below. The second type of questionnaire is commonly used in elicitation.

There are a wide variety of questionnaires that are already written and available for fieldworkers to use. Some are very specific, e.g. dealing with a particular grammatical structure, while others are general and aim to cover a wide variety of sociolinguistic and grammatical information. A selection of questionnaires can be found on the following website of the Max Planck Institute for Evolutionary Anthropology in Leipzig: www.eva.mpg.de/lingua/tools-at-lingboard/questionnaires.php.

Questionnaires generally anticipate the sort of answers you want to get. For example, if you are studying the way arguments are referenced in a language (i.e. when you say *he walks* and *she eats cake* that the *-s* at the end of the word refers to the third person singular subject in each clause), you may have to include intransitive, transitive and ditransitive clauses in your questionnaire. You should probably also try to vary the persons in subject and object positions, e.g. *I walk* and *you eat cake* do not appear with an *-s* in the verb, so this means that there is a difference between first/second and third person in English. The way arguments are cross-referenced in the verb in the languages of the world can be very different from the way this is done in English, and a good questionnaire anticipates such differences. Of course, not all questionnaires do! You may also come across structures that are very rare or that have not been discussed elsewhere. Thus, while questionnaires can be helpful in planning your work, relying too heavily on them can easily lead to missing out on essential aspects of the language under investigation.

Questionnaires can be the main type of data-collection in some types of quantitative studies. We will discuss the methods used in these studies in more detail in 6.5.

2.   *Complementary*: In this type of elicitation you are looking for further examples of material already collected. This can be helpful if you have only got one example of a structure or word. You can ask the teacher to give you further examples of that particular word or construction. It is often a good idea to ask for the context (i.e. to give you a short story or a short context in which this word/structure would be used). Teachers can be very good at sensing a difference a word/structure makes, without generally knowing the linguistic expression or pinpointing the exact place where the difference occurs, unless, of course, they are linguists themselves.

3.   *Probing*: You can ask open-ended questions, looking for explanations and paradigms provided by the language teacher. You can, for example, give a verb in the present tense such as *John walks* and then say that this was yesterday and ask your teacher to tell you what John did yesterday, probing the past tense expression *John walked*.

While this type of elicitation can be great to fill gaps in paradigms, it is best taken as simply one form of input and never used to settle any issue with just the elicitation data. Of course, this holds for other types of elicitation as well.

4.   *Hypotheticals*: You can test lists of hypothetical words generated by computer (see William Poser's webpage (www.ling.upenn.edu/~wjposer/) for one such program). This is less good for testing grammatical constructions, but may come in very useful when, for example, eliciting possible word forms and looking at the phonology of a language.

5.   *Translation*: Translation elicitation involves getting translations for texts and other materials. Matthewson (2004) presents some of the pitfalls of eliciting translations. In spite of her well-taken warnings, getting translations of the data collected is vital. The fieldworker, however, must be careful to treat native speaker translations as only one source of data about the meanings of texts, sentences, etc.

6.   *Reverse translation*: Another way of getting at the meanings of texts is to ask one set of speakers to translate a vernacular text (a text in the language under study) into the national or local trade language and then ask a different set of speakers to translate the translation back into the vernacular. The fieldworker can then compare and contrast the different forms given and design further elicitation tasks to probe and test the resultant hypotheses.

7.   *Corrective*: This type of elicitation tests the linguist's understanding of a certain set of constructions, expressions, texts, constraints, rules, etc. by discussing examples that the linguist has devised based on his or her current understanding of the grammar. This is likely to have a low and unreliable rate of return but, so long as you bear this in mind, it can play a useful role in analysing the relevant structures.

As an example, in a language in contact with English, you may be analysing a suffix *-nuk*, which you have seen attached to a number of verbs, e.g. *walk-nuk*. In order to figure out what *-nuk* is, you may want to test whether it can be attached to other verbs, e.g. *kill-nuk*, *live-nuk*, and so on. Does it appear with different semantic classes of verbs or is it restricted to some classes? Furthermore, could English verbs appear in the language without this suffix, e.g. *walk, kill, live*? If not, this may be a verb-integration marker, making 'native' verbs out of loans.

8.   *Filling in gaps*: You may have to look for missing paradigm forms, gaps in phonetic charts, sentence types, different participant lists, etc. If you can not find these in your corpus, you will have to develop a way of asking about these forms. If your teachers are linguists themselves, they may easily answer a question such as 'what is the form of a first person plural acting on a first person singular?' However, most teachers will not be able to deal with such a request, and you will have to devise ways to get the information, e.g. by saying 'Imagine we are all in a boat, looking into the river – we are at such an angle that we can only see my reflection. How would I express this, saying "we all see me" in the language?' The authors found that such stories worked well with some speakers, but confused others. If you aim to 'fill in gaps' in your elicitation session, you will have to try out different approaches to see what works for you and your teachers.

9.   *Lexical elicitation*: This type of elicitation could also have been treated under the heading of 'questionnaires' above. Many linguists use lexical questionnaires to collect basic words when first trying to get an overview of a language. Until recently, the most prominent of such questionnaires was the Swadesh list, devised by Morris Swadesh in the 1940s and 1950s. Indeed, there are various Swadesh lists (including an initial 200-word list and a subsequent 100-word list, see Swadesh 1971). Many field researchers have found the lists helpful when collecting the basic words of a language, and various grammars and other major publications on languages present such a list in the appendix.

Since 2009, there is a new option to use instead of the Swadesh list, namely the Leipzig-Jakarta list of basic vocabulary (Haspelmath & Tadmor 2009). This list is based on a large-scale empirical study of lexical borrowing in a typological sample of languages. In contrast to the Swadesh list, the 100 basic words on the Leipzig-Jakarta list can be used for the classification of genetic relationships between languages.

There are other types of elicitation. These overlap with other methods, such as experimental elicitation, where the linguist carries out small (e.g. psycholinguistic) experiments in order to answer questions about the language. The latter type will be treated in detail in section 6.6. Elicitation on translation, as discussed above, overlaps with text analysis (6.3.3). Very often, elicitation sessions encompass various methods within one session: you may be following a questionnaire, but the teacher may give you an answer that needs more probing, and perhaps you will be using corrective elicitation at the same time, making up your own examples based on what you have learnt.

Exercise 6.7

Go back to your text and look through your glosses. Even though you know what the words and the overall translation mean, you will probably still have many questions regarding the glosses. Find some of these questions and go back to your speaker to shed light on them in elicitation. You can try to use different techniques, such as writing out a questionnaire prior to elicitation, using probing and filling gaps (e.g. working on the verbal paradigm of the language under investigation).

6.4.2   Limits of elicitation

It is important to keep in mind that elicitation is but one tool of fieldwork, and not to rely too heavily on it. The reason is that elicited data may not always reflect actual language use – elicitation is artificial, and in real dialogues the data may look very different. It may not even be enough, in this case, to check your data with various speakers.

Imagine asking your speakers 'can I say this?' or 'can a speaker of your language say this?'. In the authors' experience, language teachers often say 'yes, you can!' without the slightest regard for the acceptability or grammaticality of the utterance. This is partially because the linguist is paying, so, to some language teachers, the linguist can say anything they want! None of these expressions can in fact be relied upon to give clear evidence of either the acceptability of an utterance or its grammaticality. There are simply too many variables for the fieldworker to know why a particular answer has been given – does the speaker's judgement reflect pragmatics, semantics, syntax, phonology, lack of concentration, desire to please, or feelings of different status? There is no foolproof way to know the answer to these questions.

So what can the fieldworker do? Well, one thing is to get the speaker to confirm his or her broad assessment by uttering the sentence themselves. Then the linguist can repeat it slowly and ask for yet another repetition. The native speaker would usually not repeatedly utter an ungrammatical sentence. They will 'edit' it, i.e. change it slightly to make it grammatical. Or they will refuse to say it. (If the utterance is grammatical there often will be no problem for the speaker to repeat it.) The kind of correction made should identify what was wrong with the example structurally. On the other hand, if the example is *pragmatically* bad (roughly, if it is inappropriate in the environment of your elicitation session), it is quite likely that the speaker will still not say it. In this case, the linguist cannot tease apart the ungrammatical from the inappropriate.

Another problem concerning elicitation is reported speech. Consider the following anecdote from Danish, where a researcher asks speakers of the language how they pronounce the first person singular pronoun *jeg* 'I'. There are two pronunciations, the very formal and hardly used [jɑi] and the informal [jɑʔ]. Various speakers give the following answer:

(4)   [jɑʔ siːɐ jɑi]
        I   say I
        'I say [jɑi].'

This shows that the speakers think they use the formal form, while actually using the informal [jɑʔ] when speaking. These speakers may want to portray themselves as more formal in their speech than others, but such differences in actual use and reported use are very common. Similar precautions have to be taken with other reported data, be it of actual linguistic forms or sociolinguistic information: the speakers may think they are using a particular form, or they may want to be seen to speak a more formal variety than they do in reality.

Exercise 6.8

Try to compare reported speech with actual data. You could, for example, ask your teacher how often per minute he thinks he uses fillers such as *uhm* in his speech (if you have transcribed fillers in your recorded text together with your speaker, he or she may be aware of the amount and you may have to find another way of comparing reported and actual speech). If asked, many people play down the amount of *uhm*s they use, or are not aware of them at all. Make sure to adhere to research ethics, as the teacher could understand this exercise as an attack on his or her language use. You could compare it to a speaker being interviewed on TV or radio – most people other than professional journalists use such fillers frequently, especially in 'interview-type' situations that require them to think while speaking.

There are also other concerns with elicited data. While there may be contact influence from other languages present in the language of study (see 3.1.1), you will have to be alert that you do not superimpose the structures of the languages you speak, know or have analysed in the past on to the one you are researching! This is easier said than done, as many linguists tend to categorize the data they see. Gil (2001: 102) gives a nice analogy, citing a passage from *Alice in Wonderland*:

> In her adventures in wonderland, Alice fell into a deep pool of her own tears, and then met a mouse: '**O Mouse**, do you know the way out of this pool? I am very tired of swimming about here, **O Mouse**!' (Alice thought this must be the right way of speaking to a mouse; she had never done such a thing before, but she remembered having seen, in her brother's Latin Grammar, 'A mouse, of a mouse, to a mouse, a mouse, O mouse!')'

In this case, Alice models her own language on the pattern of Latin: having seen that there is a specific case marker for addressing people (and mice!) in Latin, she assumes that a similar structure must exist in her own language. She uses the closest equivalent in English, in this case *O mouse!*

Speakers easily make such analogies. Indeed, this is a case of language contact and could be investigated as such. However, as a researcher it is important to make sure you do not superimpose such categories on the language you are studying. There may be a way of marking the genitive in most Germanic languages, but that does not mean that all other languages have a genitive. Even if there is a similar morpheme that at a first glance looks like a genitive marker, it may have a very different distribution once you study it in more detail. Take our example from Mosetén (in 2.1), where *yäe-si' tse'* means 'my mother' (lit. I-*si* mother). You may assume that *-si* marks the genitive, just like the English possessive *my*. However, when looking through the data you may be confronted with the following forms from Mosetén (remember that Mosetén displays 'nasal harmony', and in some contexts vowels are pronounced in their nasal equivalent, indicated by two dots on the vowel):

(5)   *jaem'-si' tse'*
        good-SI   mother
        'a good mother'

(6)   *mö'   minsi'   chhïï-yë'-si'*   mi
        3F.SG woman know-VERB-SI 2SG
        'the woman that you know'

(7)   *jaem-tyi' mintyi' chhïï-yë'-tyi'*   mi
        good-TYI man   know-VERB-TYI 2SG
        'the good man that you know'

Exercise 6.9

Try to figure out the function of *-si* and the equivalent *-tyi'* in examples (5) to (7). Is this a 'genitive' in the sense of the English (possessive pronouns or the *-'s* marker on nouns as in *the man's house*)?

Indeed, you will find that this marker *-si'* is very different from the genitive in English and other languages. First of all, there seems to be a feminine marker *-si'* and a masculine marker *-tyi'*, depending on which antecedent they appear with (in the case of 'my mother' the possessed, i.e. the feminine 'mother'). Second, the markers not only appear suffixed to the possessor of something, but also with modifying adjectives (*jaem-si' minsi'* 'a good woman'), marking the verbs of relative clauses (*chhïï-yë-si'* 'that you know') and seem to be inherent parts of the lexical forms *mintyi'* 'man' and *minsi'* 'woman'. Sakel (2004: 105ff) analyses these elements as linker morphemes in the noun phrase. One of the functions is to link possessor and possessed, and in this way *-si'* and *-tyi'* are overlapping – in part – with the genitive case of other languages. Yet, calling it a 'genitive' would disregard the other functions of this marker.

6.4.3   Ethical considerations for elicitation

The success of elicitation sessions depends largely on the rapport, trust and mutual understanding of the linguist and the language teacher. Therefore, the elicitation session should be a meeting of equals. The language teacher must be fully confident that they are respected by the linguist, and vice versa. The arrangement of the physical space (chair, table, etc.) should ideally reflect equality rather than hierarchy. The linguist's facial expressions, tone of voice and body language should at once show professionalism, respect and enjoyment of the task at hand.

Frequently in the sessions the linguist will find a particular response puzzling, apparently irrelevant, or otherwise unhelpful. Receive any 'unhelpful' response with the same gratitude that should mark the linguist's attitude towards every response and help from the language teacher. Respect means allowing the teacher to offer information that does not always coincide with the linguist's request.

Dan Everett

As I have listened to some of my more than 25-year-old tapes of the Pirahãs, I have, with my hard-earned ability to speak the language, realized that some of these 'unhelpful' responses were in fact attempts to correct some of my mistaken impressions, offering, instead of what I had ignorantly asked for, a response that was much more helpful, had I only recognized the Pirahãs' ability to teach me, rather than to simply answer my questions. That is, had I realized that they were teachers rather than mere passive 'informants'.

Further, the language teacher will look for evidence that the linguist has understood or at least heard correctly their response. The best way to show this (and that the linguist is paying attention) is to repeat every example back to the teacher. Make it clear that you want to be corrected.

One source of potential pressure on the language teacher that can lead to less useful responses is for the linguist to reveal too much about his or her predictions and analysis before they have been carefully verified. This could bias the results, leading the teacher to, in a friendly way, look for examples to confirm what you are saying or otherwise bias the nature of the results obtained. (This excellent bit of advice is taken from Boas 1911: 59).

Finally, the linguist and teacher must know when the session should conclude. There are various criteria. First, conclude at the agreed time, unless there is mutual agreement that the session should continue for some reason. Second, conclude when the linguist runs out of material for the session. Third, the session should be concluded if this is a bad day for the teacher – or the linguist – and they cannot get focused. Fourth, conclude the session if there are too many distractions (e.g. a hunter has just brought back game and the language teacher is concerned about missing his or her share).

6.4.4   Monolingual elicitation

Let us consider some suggestions for beginning monolingual elicitation. You may choose to work monolingually even when you and the speakers have a language in common. In such a case, you would probably introduce yourself in the lingua franca, and start out working in that language as well. Once you have gained some knowledge of the language(s) under scrutiny, you may decide to work purely monolingually. In other cases, however, you may not have a language in common with the speakers and may be forced to work monolingually from the beginning. We will give you some ideas as to how to start this kind of work. The procedure below is very simple. Clearly, the resourcefulness of the linguist is the main ingredient. Your initial aim would be to gain a working knowledge of the language in order to be able to ask the right questions. This type of fieldwork is usually associated with a more prototypical setting, i.e. in a remote area and with the aim of documenting the language and/or describing aspects of the language. For this reason, our examples below are geared towards grammatical description of the language, but one could imagine other types of monolingual elicitation as well.

It is a good idea to begin monolingual elicitation with objects from nature. So pick up a leaf, stick, rock or some such item to begin with. Try to find out its name by pointing at it and saying what it is in your language. Don't just grunt. Use your language freely. This is natural. Then repeat back what you were given, for correction. Now say the word again as you let the rock, whatever, drop to the ground. Write down (don't use a tape-recorder yet – just you and your ears and paper) what you get. Now say it back again. Now pick up another object of the same type and roughly same size and colour. Show two fingers while letting both drop. Imitate. Write this down. Did the form of the verb change? Can you recognize any differences in the form of the nouns or noun phrase? You probably now have a form for plural or dual. Now pick up two other objects (same type, size, colour) and repeat the process from the beginning. Now do it all over again with three, then four objects. You should be getting numerals and grammatical number, articles, etc. Always build up slowly, so that you can feel in control of what you are getting. Look at how much you are learning! And this is all with just a few natural objects and a single verb.

Now work with colours, sizes and conjunctions (which you can get by mixing the object types, e.g. 'a rock and a stick fell to the ground'). After exploring these aspects of noun phrases for a bit, you can try some transitive verbs. Begin perhaps by having your language teacher hit you. You can do this by taking his hand (if appropriate) and hitting it lightly on your shoulder. Then you pretend to hit him. Work with this for a while until you feel fairly secure that you are getting a transitive construction. Now take a biggish stick. Hit yourself with this. Now pretend to hit your language teacher with it. Now have him hit you with it. Now have him hit someone else. For every single action, get a description by your language teacher. Repeat after him and make sure that you watch reactions. It is very easy to confuse 'I' and 'you' in these circumstances. But if you repeat as you perform the action, if you describe what you are doing with the wrong pronoun, you will almost certainly be corrected. But if you don't repeat and make sure you are following, you could easily confuse the pronouns and confuse yourself for a while.

You are prepared, if you haven't already learnt this, to get at the paradigm for pronouns (at least those corresponding to interlocutors in your environment). You can get at this, or add to your knowledge, by now switching to intransitive verbs, e.g. 'jump', 'stand up', 'walk away', 'crouch down', 'sit down', and so on.

Let us review the implications of the fact that when working in a monolingual situation there is no 'metalanguage' (Matthewson 2004) to use. So how does one come to understand verbal or other meanings? One thing is certain – you cannot tease apart or even discover the full range of verb meanings (including affixal meanings), e.g. tense, aspect, valence, aktionsart, argument structure, case, etc. by simply going through texts. In a monolingual situation you cannot get translations for texts, for one thing. The best you can hope for are paraphrases. But since analysis of verbs requires subtle and accurate distinctions of verb meanings, you must come up with a method to help you obtain them.

Here are some suggestions. First, act out scenarios. Let's say you're following a guide, e.g. the Lingua Descriptive Studies Questionnaire, and you want to try to distinguish directional actions or to see whether such distinctions are made on the verb in the language. Try this. Assemble a few objects from the local environment – sticks, rocks, leaves, bones, tools, necklaces, etc. – things that are all in regular use and seen as normal objects that one would handle within the community. Next, begin work initially with individual teachers, moving later to work with multiple teachers. It is important to use culturally relevant objects and tasks at the beginning of the research to build on people's confidence in their knowledge of their culture (there is so much opportunity for uncertainty on all sides in any case).

So take, say, a necklace, some beads and the string (or whatever) used to make necklaces. Place the necklace on yourself. Get the description of what you did. *Record and film all of this.* Place the necklace on your language teacher, on a child, on a man, on a woman. That is, as you have time and opportunity in this session, try to act out paradigms. (Always be careful to obey cultural constraints.)

Place the necklace on the ground. Place it on a table. Hang it from the roof. Drop it. Throw it. Toss it up and catch it. Take the beads and place one on the string. String several in succession. Let one bead fall off the string to the ground. Let another fall off on to a table or chair. Let all of them fall off on to the table, chair, ground, etc. simultaneously. Get various (three to six) speakers to describe each one of your attempts.

Filming and recording all of this will give you good data, help you find directionals, numbers, positions, aspect, valency, transitivity, etc. And this is just a trivial example. Tremendous amounts of high-quality data can be collected in this way. But you need a plan, and it may be a good idea to follow a questionnaire (see above). You can also use films, of the type prepared by the Max Planck Institute for Psycholinguistics in Nijmegen. Using films, rather than acting things out, has both advantages and severe disadvantages. The advantages include the fact that film can do things you cannot (like make a bowl of beans suddenly appear on a table where there was nothing before).

There are, however, a number of points to consider when using films instead of acting out scenes for elicitation, especially when conducting fieldwork among speakers that are culturally very different from you. Some language teachers may have a difficult time following two-dimensional electronic images. They may not recognize the gender of the person on the film (many peoples consider long hair a sign of femininity or flat-chestedness a sign of masculinity, both problems the authors have encountered) and this is surprisingly distracting. Finally, some of the activities may make little sense to language teachers watching the films. To compensate for this, films and other media could be piloted before using them with the speakers, or you could have alternative strategies in place, e.g. acting out (see 6.6).

In monolingual fieldwork it is equally important to check your findings with different speakers. Sometimes crucial corrections are only given on the third or fourth repetition to different native speakers. Inexperienced language teachers often find it hard to know what the linguist is after (so does the linguist at times!) and find it even harder at times to correct the linguist, as they may think that as the linguist is paying their salary, he should have the 'right' to say whatever he wants. So checking the data with speakers other than the one who provided the original data is crucial to processing the data. Get these other speakers to paraphrase what the previous speaker said, as well as saying it back identically. This way, you have pronunciations of the same data by different speakers, as well as various alternative syntactic expressions of the same or similar (usually, but not always) content. Make sure you get paraphrases of difficult to understand data. Almost always, paraphrases will vary from the original's meaning in subtle, yet significant and revealing ways.

If you overhear something and speak no language in common with the speech community, describe the context in a few lines next to the transcription (e.g. time of day, who was speaking, what they were doing, what you think they were saying). Then test your understanding by trying to use the expression, as you understand it, when and where you think it would be appropriate to do so. Almost certainly you will discover that your initial guess was wrong (and if it wasn't, congratulations, but you might not know one way or the other at this stage anyway) and people will laugh at you.

The next step would be to take the expressions you want to study and generate paradigms from them. Imagine that someone uttered the word *squeat*.[7] What does it mean? Well, to get at this we write its context as uttered by someone, say, as they rise to leave, about 12ish, and as they walk towards the cafeteria. You could ask someone else to paraphrase it and they say 'he's hungry and he thinks you are too'. Then ask someone to say the phrase slowly and they say something like *Let's go eat*. Ask someone else to repeat this and they also say *Let's go eat* or, perhaps, *Let us go eat*. Now we can try to build some paradigms from this expression. To do this, we divide the utterance into positions or 'slots' and try to put other words we have learnt in each of these slots. An example of what someone studying English for the first time might do is given in (8):

(8)   a. Let us go eat.
        b. Try us go eat.
        c. Make us go eat.
        d. Help us go eat.
        e. See us go eat.
        f. Believe us go eat.
        g. Run us go eat.

(9)   a. Let me go eat.
        b. Let you go eat.
        c. Let him go eat.
        d. Let them go eat. etc.

(10)   a. Let us do eat.
        b. Let us try eat.
        c. Let us make eat.
        d. Let us can eat.
        e. Let us want eat.
        f. Let us be eat. etc.

(11)   a. Let us go run.
        b. Let us go fish.
        c. Let us go please.
        d. Let us go work. etc.

Next, we work through all of these in (8) to (11), asking whether each is acceptable/pretty/crooked/etc. (in the way a Pirahã teacher might reply), and how they compare to one another, i.e. which would the native speaker think that they are most likely to use. Never be satisfied with an answer that simply says a form is 'good'. Get the native speaker to say it themselves. If they will not, then the form is almost certainly not 'good'. If they do, do they say it with natural speed and intonation and a solid sense that they understand it?

We can now ask what the linguist is supposed to learn from these paradigms? First, they learn that the verbs that can go in the first slot are limited. *Try* and *believe*, for example, are not allowed. Why not? What makes these verbs different from *let*, *make*, and the others? Let's say you hypothesize that *try* and *believe* are excluded because they are interpreted as second person imperatives by native speakers. How could you test this hypothesis? That is, what data would you need to refute it, do you have such data, and is it refuted?

The point, of course, is not whether this initial hypothesis is right or wrong. All your initial hypotheses will probably be off to one degree or another. The point is that by developing these paradigms, you generate grammaticality differences and different hypotheses about the grammatical structure of the language.

The development of paradigms should ideally be restricted so that the initial data used to generate them come from *natural texts*, not elicitation. Using elicited data, which itself can be artificial, can *propagate artificiality* throughout the examples. Hence you may get reported data again, rather than actual use data, as in the *I say 'I'* example (4) from Danish.

Next, test each paradigm with several speakers. If you see little or no disagreement in judgements between speakers, then you can move much more quickly to the next paradigm. If you do encounter disagreements (say, for example, that some speakers allow *try* and *believe* in the sample paradigms above) then ask them about this, as *in*directly as possible, never directly. For example, what does the controversial example mean to the speakers who claim that it is acceptable to them? Can they be got to say it with intelligibility? What does the same example mean to those who reject it?

Now let's assume that you have worked your way through a paradigm and that you now believe that you have a reasonable understanding of what the morphemes in the examples mean. What next? One example of what to do next comes from the beautiful study by Lowe (1990) in which he shows how to 'track' the morpheme through texts, as reported above. Can the morpheme be isolated? In fairly mechanical terms, does the same sequence of segments occur in different positions in the utterance? Can it occur with other segments, e.g. in answer to a question? Does this sequence correlate with a constant meaning in the utterances in which it occurs? Consider in this regard another example, from English:

(12)   They were running but stopped suddenly.
(13)   When I am done eating, I'll talk to you.
(14)   I would rather be playing my guitar.
(15)   Q: Are you done?
         A: *No, I am **ing**.

Does it appear in some parts of texts more than other parts (e.g. introduction versus conclusion; denouement versus setting versus build up, main theme 'line' versus subsidiary information lines, etc.)?

You could produce photographs of your family and of items, places or people important to you, in order to trigger questions from your teachers. If you are in a remote, non-Western setting, you can deliberately show people things from your baggage that you do not think they will have had previous experience of. If they allow it, you should have a video camera, preferably, or an audio-recorder (keep it running as you unpack, settle, etc, and keep it pointed at the people speaking).

Listen as you unpack, try to imitate, go back over your tapes later and try to figure out what was being said. Test your hypotheses by trying out phrases, based on your understanding of what they mean, with the people. Do you see or hear question-like behaviour? Look for things like hand-gestures, eyebrow-raising, intonational changes, and question-like actions that might provide clues. Do any of these seem to be focused on potentially novel items among your possessions or your photographs? In particular, listen out for things like 'what is that?', 'what is he doing?', etc. These are vitally useful phrases for your research, for getting along with the people, for negotiating your way through the community and the language. These are not usually easy to get by direct elicitation, yet they are uttered spontaneously in exactly the kind of situation your initial arrival in the community will create. Pay attention. Linguistically, such phrases are vital even if the linguist otherwise plans to work bilingually (i.e. using a trade language for fieldwork).

6.4.5   Third-party interpreters

In some field locations, it may not be possible to engage in either monolingual or bilingual work directly with the language teacher. In such cases, it may be necessary to employ a third-party interpreter (see also Samarin 1967). Such a situation arises when the linguist and the language teacher do not share a common language and the monolingual method is impractical for some reason (e.g. when the time available to the linguist is too short, the teacher is one of a few survivors of a moribund language, etc.).

There are some special precautions to take when working with interpreters. First, the linguist must be clear in all instructions given. It can be safely assumed that all questions asked through an interpreter will be distorted to one degree or another. Ambiguity or vagueness in questions will create more severe problems when asked through an interpreter. Second, the linguist should be suspicious of the quality of the question, the translation, or both if short questions to the interpreter become very long questions or conversations between the interpreter and the language teacher. Answers in such circumstances should be viewed as highly suspect. Third, be equally suspicious of short answers by the teacher which require apparent circumlocutary translations to the linguist or for which the translations are hesitant or unclear. Finally, since the interpreter has a closer linguistic connection than the language teacher to the linguist and, perhaps, more formal schooling, there may be a tendency for the language teacher to perceive that they have lower status. Avoid this. Neither the linguist nor the interpreter should communicate any attitude of superiority to the language teacher.

In some situations, however, interpreters (and other helpers, e.g. main teachers sitting in on sessions where some help with interpreting is required) can be extremely useful.

Jeanette Sakel

When I started doing fieldwork on Greenlandic, I set out to record a number of texts. I spoke some Greenlandic, but was not very fluent (and could not understand a lot of the texts I was given until I had had a chance to transcribe and translate them together with my main teacher). I worked with a friendly man in his forties, who spoke very little Danish. I interviewed him and asked him to tell me about himself, all entirely in Greenlandic. He started telling an animated story, of which I understood very little. I was nodding and smiling all the way through in order to encourage him to continue. When he eventually stopped, he took in a long breath and looked at me. I thanked him profoundly for telling me his story. He looked a bit puzzled when he left, and later I found out why! When I worked through the text with my main teacher (transcribing, and translating it) he laughed out at this stage of the story, even though the matter was not very funny: the nice speaker had told me about his life, as predicted, but then he had said 'actually, I was in prison once, it was a very bad experience, but let me tell you about it [deep intake of breath]' and then there was me saying 'thank you very much for telling me your story, goodbye'. Had my main teacher been there during the recording of this text, he would have been able to intervene! Even better, he could have taken over the interviewing process himself, understanding what was said, rather than guessing and giving the inappropriate feedback I was giving. Indeed, from then on I asked him to accompany me when interviewing speakers or recording texts, and in subsequent fieldwork (e.g. on Mosetén) I made use of this strategy again. It can be far more rewarding to have a native speaker collect texts, especially from monolingual or older speakers. They can ask questions, give the right feedback and engage the speaker in conversation. They can also ask questions of clarification straight away in case they do not know words (e.g. old words for things). Otherwise, such questions will inevitably come up later when transcribing and translating the text.

6.4.6   Group teaching, serial teaching and individual teachers

Elicitation sessions do not exclusively have to be between one language teacher and the linguist. You could also work with multiple teachers simultaneously. It is often useful for the linguist to work with small groups as well as with individuals. Group sessions (three to four language teachers) have various advantages: (i) they can allow the linguist to put the language to use right away, by checking the data immediately, within the same session; (ii) they can easily provide the linguist with alternative phrasings and pronunciations of the data and alternative ways of telling and/or interpreting a short text; (iii) they give speakers a chance to discuss their answers and their understanding of the linguist's questions, developing linguistic sophistication and awareness of the linguist's objectives, at the same time also helping the linguist to learn more of the language and meta-language by listening attentively to the native speakers converse; (iv) they may help to put the teachers more at ease in some situations, though one could also imagine the opposite in other situations, where some speakers may feel that their language is being 'judged' by other speakers.

Jeanette Sakel

I have carried out group teaching as part of the different types of fieldwork. Sometimes this came naturally; for example in the Somali study my teachers found speakers to work with, we would meet at someone's home, and then we'd record everybody's speech, one by one. This made it easier, as I only had to explain the experimental setup once, and I had the impression that the speakers felt more at ease in a group.

Dan Everett

The Pirahãs have never developed a great deal of patience for sitting and teaching me their language. So rather than have one person sit for long sessions, I schedule different language teachers for every 20–30 minutes for the entire morning, giving myself a coffee break or two in between sessions. This breaks up my day, keeps language teachers from getting bored, and provides many opportunities for clarifying and checking other teachers' data.

Serial sessions also have another significant advantage over working long periods with a single teacher. Speakers who only work 15–20 minutes per day will not usually see the linguist as substantially in debt to them for their time and services. They can see their participation as a break, as 'fun', as a change, etc. rather than serious work. And this lightened attitude and environment can translate into better exchanges and more openness between the linguist and the teachers.

6.5   Quantitative questionnaires and structured interviews

Two types of elicitation discussed above are interviews and question-naires (6.4), yet elicitation is often perceived as a qualitative method. There are also quantitative interviews and questionnaires, which are regularly employed in some fields of linguistics, for example psycholinguistics, applied linguistics and sociolinguistics. Also, studies in other fields successfully make use of question-naires for quantitative purposes as well as clearly structured interviews.

You may choose to work quantitatively with these two methods, or you may complement qualitative studies with quantitative data of this type. For example, if you are studying contact phenomena in an immigrant language dominated by English, you may collect text data and carry out elicitation with a few speakers, but then decide to study the distribution of some remarkable phenomena quanti-tatively. For this, you could use questionnaires with a wide range of speakers, or conduct structured interviews. The data you end up with can be compared, i.e. quantified, so you may be able to gain an overview of frequencies and information on cause and effect (see 6.1.1, above).

Quantitative studies generally benefit from very careful preparation. Thus, whether you use questionnaires or structured interviews, you may want to carry out a pilot study to test your methodology prior to embarking on the actual study. Pilot studies are a way to try out your questionnaires, experiments or other methods on a few selected speakers. What is their reaction? Is there anything they do not understand? Do they bring up issues other than those covered in your material? Do they have new ideas? Pilot studies are great ways of testing your methodology, without compromising the actual study. The idea is that by the time you are ready to carry out the study, most mistakes and inconsistencies will have been eradicated. There are several additional advantages. You will collect some initial data, which will give you an understanding of potential outcomes of the main study. These results may also help you to formulate other questions previously not thought about (for more detailed information on pilot studies, see 2.2, on Somali in Bristol).

6.5.1   Questionnaires

Questionnaires are very versatile and can be used to study many different topics, such as language attitudes, use of languages by bilinguals, and even grammaticality judgements. Since the studies are versatile, the setup of your questionnaire will depend a lot on your individual study. Still, there are a number of points common to questionnaires of different types.

First of all, the data collected in questionnaires are inevitably reported. Rather than hearing speakers use the words themselves, questionnaires are written state-ments of what the speakers think they do. Thus, the results have to marked as 'reported speech', rather than actual speech recorded by the linguist. While this is a clear disadvantage of questionnaires, there are also a number of positive aspects. You can administer questionnaires in many different ways – if the speak-ers you are studying live far away you could send the questionnaires by mail or email. The other positive point is that you can also very quickly gather a lot of information, for example, if you are studying the language behaviour among a group of students, you could just give them the questionnaire (e.g. in class) and complete you data-collection within a very short time.

When it comes to putting together questionnaires, you have to consider two opposing factors. You may want to get as much information from your speak-ers as possible, packing the questionnaires with questions to cover all potential outcomes; the speakers, on the other hand, will probably prefer shorter ques-tionnaires – their attention span may dwindle after ten or twenty minutes. If you remember the ethics guidelines (4.4), your speakers may indeed drop out at any time if they wish to. Thus, if your questionnaire is very long and tedious, even the most polite and patient of speakers may lose interest.

In order to deal with these issues, it is advisable to make sure the questionnaire is as concise as possible, with an appealing layout. At the same time, you will have to try to fit all those important questions in. The way ahead is, we cannot stress it enough, careful preparation. Think about your research questions and hypotheses. Which data are essential for your study, which other data would be nice to have but are not as crucial?

A lot lies in the formulation of the questions, which should ideally be simple, clear and not misunderstandable. Even small changes in the questions can lead to very different answers. For this reason, it is a good idea to try out the questions in a pilot study (see below).

If you think back to cases when you have been filling in questionnaires in the past, be it for market surveys, course evaluations, scientific studies or even your tax return form, you may have come across the scenario where a number of answers are given, but none of them really apply to you. Maybe you felt that you had to clarify your points in more detail. It is easy in such cases just to answer at random, without thinking too much about the questions. Or not to reply at all. Or, alternatively, to scribble some notes on the back of the questionnaire to explain your case in more detail. Imagine in your study asking the question 'do you speak Spanish?' and the possible answers 'yes' and 'no'. Participants in the study may speak very little Spanish, and not know which of the two options to tick. If they tick 'yes' they may want to give more information on the degree to which they speak the language, such as: 'yes, I speak Spanish, but not very well and only ever once a year when I'm on holiday'. You could supplement every answer with points such as 'other', followed by a textbox where the participants can write in their specific points. This is useful in allowing for further points to be made, but on the downside the data are not quantifiable any more. The reason is that text data of this type are inherently qualitative, with all the advantages and disadvantages that brings. One of the participants may elaborate on a point, while others, who may have very similar concerns, do not. There is no way for you to know.

Another way to present possible, comparable, answers to the questions is by giving various points on a scale (generally referred to as a Likert scale). It could have five points:

> *Likert scale*
> strongly agree – agree – neither agree nor disagree – disagree – strongly disagree

Some researchers use scales with more than five points to record more subtleties. Some use scales with an even number of possible answers, so that there is not a clear default 'middle' one. In this case, participants will have to take sides one way or another. This is all something to think about when formulating the questionnaire, and ideally it would be tested in a pilot study.

You could also give various specific options, especially if there are a number of standard answers that could be given:

Where do you use Somali (please underline your answer):

At school:	all the time	some of the time	rarely	never
At home with parents:	all the time	some of the time	rarely	never
At home with siblings:	all the time	some of the time	rarely	never
At home with friends:	all the time	some of the time	rarely	never
In the playground:	all the time	some of the time	rarely	never

Finally, no questionnaire is complete without metadata about the participants, such as age, gender, background and whatever else is relevant to your study. Many researchers prefer to ask for such information at the end of the questionnaire. In this way, they do not run the risk of participants getting 'bored' prior to taking part in the actual study.

Exercise 6.10

Put together a questionnaire to use with your speaker(s) (and some of their acquaintances of the same language background, if feasible). Ask about the language background, such as which languages are spoken under which conditions and with whom, how proficient they think they are in the languages they speak, etc. Try to give different options in the answers, including a Likert scale, yes/no questions and questions in which the speakers can elaborate further. Find out which of these ways is the most, and which the least, appropriate for your study.

Once you have carried out a pilot study and carefully reviewed your methodology, you can start to administer the questionnaire (see 4.1.1, on sampling participants). As a rule of thumb, you would need at least thirty participants in order to do simple statistics with your data; ideally, you should aim for more participants. When it comes to filling in the questionnaire, you may or may not be present at the time. Of course, if your participants live far away you may not have a choice in the matter and you may have to send the questionnaires off by email. If your participants are nearby and if it suits your particular study, you can choose to be present at the time. If you do this, it may be a good idea to have a positive attitude! Participants are generally more inclined to help you out when they can sense your interest.

Jeanette Sakel

My first ever empirical study, when I was a student, was on the language maintenance of Greenlanders living in Denmark. I had established links with a Greenlanders' meeting house in my town (Aarhus) and decided to use it as the locus of my study. I left my questionnaires in the meeting area, with instructions on how to fill them in, a letter of introduction and a huge box of chocolates with a sign stating 'Help me in my study and help yourself to some chocolates'. The finished questionnaires were to be deposited in a cardboard 'post-box' I had built and decorated for the purpose. After a week I went back to collect the questionnaires and had managed to get an astonishing 50 replies!

When you have carried out the questionnaire study, it is time to analyse the wealth of data you have been given. It can be overwhelming as to where to start. A good way is to use a database program (such as FileMakerPro or Access) and enter all of your data (of course you would have to learn how to use these programs first). You can then compare different findings (see also 7.3.5). You may also want to use statistics, for which many linguists would draw on the program SPSS.

6.5.2   Structured interviews

Structured interviews can be regarded as an oral form of question-naire. In many ways, they are similar to questionnaires and most of the points discussed above (6.5.1) apply as well. In contrast to questionnaires, interviews have to be administered one-to-one, rather than a number simultaneously, and in this way it can take considerably longer to collect your data. Advantages are, however, that you can pick up on subtleties from the participants much better than when using questionnaires (in the latter case you may not even have seen the participants, whereas interviews allow you to build up a whole picture of the person in question). While structured interviews also result in reported language data, you may still be able to pick up on a number of issues that do not seem to be the same in the participants' actual language use. Indeed, you can use the recordings of the interview to analyse the actual language of the interview if that is relevant to your study – see the Danish example (4) in section 6.4.2. Additionally, structured interviews can be interrupted and inter-spersed with less structured elements. For example, when a participant has spe-cific information regarding a question, you can pick up on that and ask clarifying questions.

6.6   Experiments and stimulus tests

Other ways of conducting quantitative fieldwork include linguistic experiments and stimulus tests. These are good ways to gain reliable and com-parable data. These methods can be used in very different fieldwork situations, from the most to the least prototypical settings. In some fields they are prominent methods for collecting data. This is, for example, the case in psycholinguistics, second language acquisition and other applied fields.

Experiments are methods commonly applied in sciences. If you think back to our definition of fieldwork (1.1), experiments are probably among the least prototypical fieldwork endeavours. They deal with controlled language data, a highly controlled setting and so on. Nonetheless, even prototypical fieldwork can be complemented by and benefit from experiments. Such experiments may or may not follow the rules of true experimental design (see further, below). Experimental design involves two groups, the one under scrutiny (usually referred to as the 'experimental group') and another group that is used to compare the findings (usually referred to as the 'control group'). At the outset of the study, the two groups are supposed to be comparable, with a similar spread in age, gender, ability and other factors relevant to the study. Then, one group undergoes the experimental treatment, while the other does not. After the experiment the two groups are compared again to see if there are any differences that can be attributed to the treatment. You could imagine a laboratory study where the experimental group takes a dieting pill, while the control group takes a placebo. If the experimental group loses weight at a faster, statistically significant rate than the control group, the experiment would be deemed successful.

Linguistic fieldwork generally does not involve administering dieting pills to speakers, but you could imagine a similar setup, for example in second language acquisition: one group learns a pattern, while the other group does not. The results from the two groups are compared in a pre-test (prior to the experiment) and a post-test (after the experiment) in order to establish what types of changes have happened. For this purpose, the researchers would generally use statistics to establish whether the changes are significant. This type of study is indeed common in applied linguistics, generally referred to as *intervention research* (see Dörnyei 2007: 119). You could imagine some situations where such intervention research would be possible, in particular when testing cause and effect of learning methods. However, in linguistic fieldwork aiming to analyse parts of a language or a language contact situation, experiments are less useful. There may not be strategies or 'treatments' you can study, but rather your focus will probably be on actual or reported language data.

The big advantage of experiments is that hypotheses can be tested in a controlled setting, without the interference of, for example, the language used by the researcher. For this reason, linguists have found ways to carry out other types of experiments using stimuli, cutting out any interfering languages from the data-collection. Stimulus tests investigate linguistic behaviour by using props, not language, to elicit language data. The simplest use of stimuli would be to use pictures or point at objects to elicit nouns (see 6.4.4, on monolingual elicitation). You can also find out about verbal behaviour by using props. One way to do this is to make little video clips of verbal actions. For example, you could test how languages express the difference between 'cut' and 'break' actions by making videos in which materials such as pieces of cloth, sticks and carrot can be cut or broken in different ways, for example by hand, with tools such as knives or without outside interference. Indeed, this particular project was carried out at the Max Planck Institute for Psycholinguistics in Nijmegen (Bohnemeyer, Bowerman & Brown 2001). They originally devised 61 video clips to find out about the semantics of verbs across a range of languages used to describe cutting and breaking actions. Field researchers working in different parts of the world played the stimulus videos to their speakers and elicited language data. The resulting data were directly comparable, since the stimuli were the same. In this way, the researchers gained knowledge about the semantics and distribution of 'cut' and 'break' verbs not just in one language, but across a sample of languages, all with first-hand language data.

Researchers at the Max Planck Institute for Psycholinguistics have created many more stimulus kits, collected in annual field manuals. The materials are accessible on their website (you have to register for free in order to gain access): http://fieldmanuals.mpi.nl/. Another collection of experiment and stimulus kits can be found on the following website of the Leipzig Max Planck Institute for Evolutionary Anthropology: www.eva.mpg.de/lingua/tools-at-lingboard/stimulus_kits.php.

You could, of course, also make up your own stimuli in order to study particular phenomena in your fieldwork situation. For example, Peter Gordon carried out experiments among the Pirahã to test their numeracy, using batteries and other common objects (Gordon 2004). Mike Frank and Ted Gibson replicated this experiment at a later stage (Frank *et al.* 2008). You can, for example, play out stories by using dolls or other props. Good preparation is essential, and you may want to take appropriate materials with you to the field.

Other stimuli commonly used in fieldwork are picture stories. The two most common ones are the frog stories by Mercer Mayer and the pear story video (Chafe 1980). The frog stories are a series of children's picture stories from the 1960s and 1970s, including the titles *Frog where are you?* (Mayer 1969) and *Frog goes to dinner* (Mayer 1977). The books are entirely wordless apart from the titles, which makes them appropriate for use as stimuli. Indeed, frog story data have been collected from a wide range of languages and a wide variety of speakers. The resulting data are comparable texts, as they are based on the same picture story: they contain roughly the same vocabulary and describe the same actions, while the speaker is using his or her own words. With this type of stimulus you can test many different aspects of language, e.g. how the grammar of the language works, how speakers conceptualize the world, and so on (see, for example, Daller, Treffers-Daller & Furman 2010). On the downside, many picture stories, including the frog stories, are culturally and geographically specific, in that they involve dogs, frogs, restaurants, mirrors, etc. In most Western cultures that is not a problem, but if your fieldwork is in a different culture or a remote setting where such items are not even known, it can be difficult to gather data in this way.

Jeanette Sakel

In the Somali pilot study (see 2.2) I wanted to make use of picture stories in order to gain comparable texts in both Somali and English from a range of speakers. I liked the idea of using the frog stories, as they have been used for data-collection in a wide range of languages and language contact situations. However, I was concerned that the cultural setting of the frog stories was not necessarily appropriate. I ran it past my two main teachers, who struggled to find words for many of the central items in the book, and who agreed that a more culturally sensitive story would be preferable. We set out to find good materials and settled for a range of pictures taken from a story for second language learners of Arabic. These pictures formed a story when put together. Yet, the pilot study with a total of 19 speakers showed that this story was also not ideal, as a few speakers struggled to find the links between the pictures.

The pear story (Chafe 1980) was initially used to work on Native American languages in order to compare texts collected in these languages. It set out to be culturally more sensitive, being a video of a person of a presumably non-Western background picking pears, with a subsequent story arising when a boy comes by on his bicycle, seeing the harvested pears. Also this video does not make use of language. It has been used to elicit texts from a wide variety of languages (see the following website on a project of Chinese pear stories, where the video is available online as well: www.pearstories.org).

As with the frog stories, the pear story video might not be appropriate in all settings. It may be necessary to make up your own story (or find existing materials that you could use), which has the advantage of the material (hopefully!) working for your setting, but the disadvantage of your data not being comparable to language data collected by others. Good sources of material for your own experiments with picture stories are children's picture books, cartoons or animated children's stories, but you can also make up stories or videos from scratch.

Jeanette Sakel

When conducting fieldwork on Pirahã, the team I was working in was asked by a colleague to collect data based on video prompts specifically created for this purpose. The colleague had attempted to make the videos as 'Amazonian' as possible, setting them in a leafy background (a back yard). However, there were a number of problems: the setting was as far removed from Pirahã life and culture as possible. The background was leafy, but the types of plants were unknown to the Pirahã and they found them very exotic! They also found the people featuring in the videos interesting to look at: one had a big moustache, another was very tall and blonde – you get the picture. Indeed, when we played these video prompts to the Pirahã they commented on all those issues, rather than paying attention to the prompts, i.e. the actual point of the video. This was not good for data-collection, and while in the field we decided that the only way to get replicable data was to act out those stories instead. Acting out can be a good way of getting around this problem. Still, acting out has the disadvantage that the actors may do things slightly differently each time (without realizing), so careful video-recording of the actions is in order. Then, you can later see whether all the prompts were the same, or whether differences in the outcomes had to do with the way the experiment was presented.

Exercise 6.11

Set up a small stimulus test study with your speaker(s). You could use one of the stimulus kits (such as cut and break verbs), or try out the pear or frog stories. Furthermore, try to set up your own stimuli to use on a topic related to a question that has arisen in your study so far.

6.7   Participant observation

Participant observation could also be called 'fieldwork without language teachers'. Instead of working with teachers, the linguist would overhear what speakers say in natural discourse. David Gil gave an interesting answer to a question on working with language teachers.

David Gil

To be honest, for the last decade or so I've actually done very little informant work myself. Reasons are, I find other sources of evidence generally more reliable, and using other such sources more fun and more rewarding. In fact, I would go so far as to say that I haven't done any informant work at all in many years on any of the issues that REALLY interest me; the little that I have done sporadically is mostly to check things for other people, or for very mechanical things like collecting word lists . . . As a result, my main source of evidence is naturalistic speech (via either eavesdropping or recording and then transcribing longer stretches), with various types of experiments as an alternative.   (personal communication)

Eavesdropping can indeed be a useful resource. You can often find what you need by spending unstructured time with native speakers and engaging in directed, selective eavesdropping. That is, the linguist can have a specific question in mind and listen for it to come up (obvious examples would be greetings and leave-takings, verb forms, pragmatic conventions, phonological features of natural speech as opposed to elicited speech, etc.). You can also use eavesdropping for probing, i.e. looking for new structures that you have not encountered before (or do not remember encountering). In these circumstances it is a good idea to have a small notebook to hand to jot things down. You can also pre-arrange recording your speakers spontaneously, which may make it easier to record naturalistic language data. For this, you would have to ask all possible participants beforehand if they would allow you to spontaneously record their speech when they are unaware. If they agree, do your recording and tell them straight away that you have recorded them, to make sure they are happy with it.

6.8   Integrating ethnography and fieldwork

All fieldwork, be it prototypical or non-prototypical, should ideally take into account cultural issues. Culture and language can interact in ways that go beyond standard sociolinguistics and may even affect the formal grammar of the language. In this respect, Sapir (1921: 172) writes of the need to understand the 'genius' of each language. By this, Sapir refers to that which makes each language unique, the essential core of a language, that part less subject to historical change (a sort of Heraclites-inspired question of what changes versus what remains). Sapir undertook a study of Nuu-Chah-Nulth (then known as Nootka, Wakashan, Canada) consonant alternations and observed that in this language there are extremely interesting consonantal alternations that cannot be explained grammar-internally:

> It is possible and often customary in Nootka to imply in speech some physical characteristic of the person addressed or spoken of, partly by means of suffixed elements, partly by means of 'consonantal play'. Consonantal play consists either in altering certain consonants of a word, in this case sibilants, to other consonants that are phonetically related to them, or in inserting meaningless consonants or consonant clusters in the body of the word. The physical classes indicated by these methods are children, unusually fat or heavy people, unusually short adults, those suffering from some defect of the eye, hunchbacks, those that are lame, left-handed persons, and circumcised males.   (Sapir 1915: 181)

Sapir exemplifies this 'consonantal play', concluding that to understand the grammar of a language, we must therefore understand the culture in which that grammar is found. This is the kind of study that illustrates the solid connection between culture and language.

6.9   Summary and further reading

This chapter took into account the different methods of fieldwork, from working with texts, conducting elicitation and linguistic experiments, to participant observation and the inclusion of ethnographic aspects.

Recommended references for further reading include the website of the Max Planck Institute for Evolutionary Anthropology in Leipzig (http://lingweb.eva.mpg.de/fieldtools/tools.htm) and that of the Max Planck Institute for Psycholinguistics in Nijmegen (www.mpi.nl/tools).

On the differences between qualitative, quantitative and mixed methods, see Dörnyei (2007). For metadata, consult the Electronic Metadata for Endangered Languages Data (EMELD, http://emeld.org) and various papers in Grenoble & Furbee (2010).

Further reading on working with texts and conducting elicitation includes Bowern (2008), Crowley (2007) and Chelliah (2001), among many others.

For more information on quantitative questionnaires and structured interviews, see Dörnyei (2007) and Codó (2008). For information on linguistic experiments in a psycholinguistic framework, see Gonzalez-Marquez, Becker & Cutting (2007).

Participant observation is common practice in anthropology, with a large literature, including Dewalt & Dewalt (2002) and Jorgensen (1989).

For including ethnography in fieldwork, see Franchetto (2006), Hill (2006) and Heller (2008). Various modern approaches to linguistics take ethnographic considerations into account; these include Lucy (1992a, 1992b), Gumperz & Levinson (1996) and Enfield (2002), as well as the field of 'ethnography of communication', including Gumperz (1982) and Saville-Troike (2003). See also Everett's (2005) work on Pirahã.

For the methods employed in descriptive fieldwork and language documentation, see the series 'Language documentation and description': www.hrelp. org/publications/papers/volume7/index.html), published at SOAS, e.g. Austin (2010). These materials can be purchased directly from SOAS on the above link.

7 The outcomes

In this chapter, we want to look at the possible outcomes of your fieldwork. These will depend on your individual project goals, and may include a fieldwork corpus, archiving and the publication of your results. We also look at writing grammars and dictionaries and compiling language documentation. Some outcomes of fieldwork have already been discussed elsewhere, for example developing materials for the language community (see 4.4.4).

7.1   The fieldwork corpus

Talking about corpora, you may think of the British National Corpus with its 100 million entries. Your fieldwork corpus will (almost definitely!) be very different: it is made up of the collection of your data, in general all of the transcribed or written materials, as well as your field notes. Spoken corpora also exist, as do corpora linking sound and text, which are made possible by programs such as ELAN, Toolbox or CLAN (see 6.3.1 and 6.3.3).

The collection of all of your data may end up being a rather messy compilation: you may have data from stimulus tests and elicitation alike, as well as various types of texts. A good way to organize your fieldwork data is to have a main corpus containing all of your data, as well as various subcorpora. The latter can be a subcorpus of all of your elicitation data, another of all of your stimulus test data and so on.

Ideally, your corpus will form the basis of your analysis, but will also be accessible to others. In any case, it is highly advisable to include metadata with all of your corpus entries (see 6.2), such as where and when you recorded the data. The best corpora are, furthermore, carefully annotated, which makes it possible to search them for specific entries or structures. Again, programs such as Toolbox are useful in this case (see 6.3.3), as they can help you to annotate your data consistently.

You can also make your corpus more easily searchable by tagging certain constructions. For example, if you are interested in the constituent order of the language under scrutiny, you may want to tag the different parts of speech for being nouns, verbs, adjectives, etc. This would make it possible for you to search for very specific structures, carrying out statistical analyses on your findings from the entire corpus. If you wanted to obtain generalizable results, the corpus would have to represent the speaker population (see sampling, in 4.1.1) and include different genres of data (narratives, discussions, etc.).

If you have a corpus of texts, such as old stories or other narratives, you may consider publishing a text collection. You could do this for the speakers of the language or, for example, in translation for a more general audience (for how this can be done, consult van den Berg 2001).

We will go into more detail on corpora specifically for grammar writing in 7.4, below. For now, we will look at other ways in which you can publish your corpus, in the following section on archiving.

7.2   Archiving

Archiving is the process of keeping all of your primary and secondary fieldwork data in a safe place and in an accessible format. These data include the initial recordings such as sound files, video files or field notes (these are the primary data), as well as the analyses you have done based on the data (secondary data), including research papers.

You should, under all circumstances, keep your data safe in the short term by making sure you back up data (e.g. on external hard drives, DVDs or similar). However, such backups are only good for so long, and a longer-term solution would be to archive your data. Archiving has become popular in recent years, as linguists have been realizing that valuable data disappear that could otherwise be utilized for years, decades (or optimistically, even centuries) to come. Field notes can get lost, computers die, and materials disappear in other ways. If they are archived, they are safe.

The format of your data will have to be accessible so that it will be readable in the future. This holds for word processing programs (which tend to be updated every few years unless they are the simplest text programs) as well as audio and video formats, which also change rapidly. You will have to make sure that your speakers agree to the materials being archived. The same ethics guidelines apply to archiving as to other publications.

There are a range of archives that are open to fieldworkers to deposit their work. These archives usually have guidelines that take you through the future-proofing, and ways of keeping the data accessible long-term. An overall umbrella for archiving language data can be found on the website of Language Archiving Technology: www.lat-mpi.eu. A wide range of archives and internet databases are registered with the Open Language Archives Community (OLAC): www.language-archives.org. DoBeS (Dokumentation Bedrohter Sprachen / documentation of endangered languages) is an archive for the documentation of endangered languages: www.mpi.nl/DOBES. Another endangered languages archive is ELAR, hosted at the School of African and Oriental Studies (SOAS): http://elar.soas.ac.uk/.

Alternatively, there may be a data archive and repository of research papers at your university; these are usually associated with the university library. Some programs used in fieldwork already come with archiving possibilities. For example, when using CLAN (see 6.1.1 and 6.1.3), you are asked to make your data accessible via the CHILDES archive. At the same time you have access to other researchers' data in that way, which can be helpful for comparing your results with those of others.

You may be worried that if you archive your materials, someone else will work on your carefully produced and annotated fieldwork data before you have a chance to publish your results. This is a valid concern, and most archives have prepared for this by either not being openly accessible, or only releasing the data a number of years after the research has taken place or after the results have been published. Furthermore, there are clear guidelines for citations and so on when using archived data.

Still, when preparing materials for archives that are not open access, it is important to keep in mind the ethics guidelines and prepare the materials in a way that does not allow for anonymous speakers to be recognized, or the speakers to be compromised in other ways.

In addition to archiving your data, you may also choose to publish your data on the internet, for example in a database, so that they are directly accessible to others. This may be a good way of distributing materials developed for the language community (4.4.4). Again, it is important to keep ethics in mind when publishing data in this way.

Exercise 7.1

Access a number of online archives (e.g. using the links above) and find out how you can view the data. Do you have to contribute to the archive yourself, or can you access the data directly?

7.3   Presenting methodology and results

Whether you are giving a conference presentation or are writing an article about your findings, you will have to find ways to adequately present your fieldwork results. Also, any good publication using first-hand data includes some sort of information on how the data were collected, i.e. on the fieldwork methodology. This will differ somewhat in qualitative and quantitative studies (if your aim is to carry out language documentation or write a grammar, you are

Table 1 *Ideas for inclusion in the methods section of your study*

Place and participants of the study
- Who are your speakers and teachers?
- Who are the researcher(s)?
- How did you find your speakers and teachers? Did you give any consideration as to general practicality, ease of access, suitability for the study, age-range, other sociolinguistic factors, languages?
- Where did you carry out your study? What were your considerations in choosing a certain place or setup for the study?

Type of fieldwork methods
- Which fieldwork methods did you use (quantitative, qualitative, as well as details, e.g. elicitation and text analysis)?

Materials for the empirical investigation
- Which types of materials did you use and how did you prepare them (e.g. how did you build up your questionnaire / design your experiments)?
- What recording equipment did you use?
- What setup in the recording room did you use?

Mode of carrying out the data collection
- *Questionnaires*: Did you stay with the participants while they filled in the questionnaires independently? Did you give the speakers 'background information' about your study that could have influenced the results (e.g. positive attitudes)? Did the speakers know exactly what it was you were after or did you pose a general question?
- *Elicitation and text collection*: How did you carry out your recordings? Did you take part in your recording (as an active participant)? Did you (attempt to) trigger a certain language behaviour (e.g. code-switching) during or before the recording?
- *Experiments*: What was the setup of your experiment(s)?

Analysis of the raw data
- How did you prepare your raw data for analysis?
- Did you use a statistics program?
- Did you use a specific computer program (e.g. Transcriber, ELAN)?
- Did you transcribe and analyse all your recordings or only parts (how many minutes did you record altogether)?
- How did you transcribe and translate your data (with the help of a speaker?)
- How did you compare the results from your questionnaire study?

Ethics
- What were your general ethical considerations?
- Did you record the names of teachers – did they agree to this?
- Did you promise your teachers anonymity?
- Did you pay your speakers or teachers?

referred to sections 7.4 and 7.6 to complement the points given in the current section).

When you look at research articles based on quantitative studies, these often give elaborate explanations as to how the studies were carried out. That is to make sure the studies are replicable, i.e. another researcher can try to carry out the same study and get to the same results. If you look at qualitative studies, many will also state their methods, even though you may come across scholarly articles where this is done in a mere footnote. The reason for this difference is that qualitative studies allow for researcher subjectivity, while quantitative studies do not (see 6.1). Still, it is a good idea to be able to establish the exact fieldwork background in qualitative studies as well.

Table 1 lists a number of points you may include when describing your research methodology. These are just some ideas, and depending on the type of your study, you may include some and exclude others and possibly add a number of further points.

Exercise 7.2

Working through table 1, write down the methodological considerations for your own fieldwork project.

Exercise 7.3

Find a number of journal articles based on fieldwork (e.g. in the *International Journal of American Linguistics*) and observe what information (if any) the authors give about the fieldwork they carried out.

Then, find a number of descriptive grammars of languages (e.g. in the Mouton Grammar Library) and see what information the authors give about the methods of their fieldwork.

7.3.1   Presenting the results of qualitative studies

In qualitative fieldwork, you would probably present your results alongside your analysis. That means giving examples from your corpus whenever you want to show a certain phenomenon, while disregarding the rest of your data not directly relevant to the discussion. You can present a small corpus in an appendix, but if you have accumulated a large corpus you may just offer a selection of texts in the appendix. If the target language is different from that of the publication, you would also be expected to translate the examples as well as giving careful glosses (see 6.3.3 for when glosses are appropriate). It is a good idea to clearly number the lines so that you can refer to them in the text. See table 2 for a hypothetical recording of a conversation between two British students that might be placed in an appendix. If your study focuses on the discourse structure

Table 2 *The transcribed text*

Text 1
This is a discussion between two teenage girls, here coded as (A) and (B):
1. A. And, like, I really wanted to tell him, you know
2. B. hhm
3. A. And he said
4.   'yeah sure, I'll come round tonight'
5.   but then, of course, he didn't show up, right?
6. B. But didn't you say . . . (interrupted by A)
7. A. (interrupts B) hey, what on earth is THAT? (points at B's skirt)

---

of a language, you may have to go into much more detail in your transcription than shown in table 2, indicating the length of pauses and so on.

7.3.2   Presenting the results of quantitative studies

In quantitative fieldwork, you would be expected to give an overview of your results first, before going on to a discussion of the results and the implications that arise from them. This means that you may give an overview of your data in a table or a graph, generally presenting your results as numbers. If you have carried out a substantial study with a lot of different types of information, you may prefer to give the entire results (tables, etc.) in the appendix.

In most quantitative studies it is not enough merely to present the results – you would also be expected to relate them to one another. For example, if you studied the domains of language use among French–English bilinguals, you could correlate the results as in table 3. Correlating your results, you will be able to find tendencies in your data, which you then can evaluate further: why do people who speak more French in their everyday lives identify with French culture than those that speak more English?

A way to present basic quantitative data is by using tables and graphs. It is a good idea to think carefully about the presentation, to make sure the graphs are not too simple or to complicated: too-simple graphs are generally easier to present in a few words in the text, while too-difficult graphs are impossible to read, which defies the whole point of them. If you are dealing with a very complicated graph, it may be easier for the reader if you present the data in two graphs instead.

You could also present your data in table format. For example, if you had studied the domains of language use among French–English bilinguals as relating to their identity, you could produce a simple list as in table 4. The presentations given are simple examples. In most types of quantitative research, you would be expected to provide statistical evidence for your findings.

Table 3 *The correlation of results*

- 40% speak French at home, 60% speak English at home.
- 15% speak French at work, 85% speak English at work. 14% of those who speak French at work also speak French at home.
- 2% speak French in social networks, 6% speak English in social networks, the rest do not attend any social gatherings. The 2% who speak French in social networks also speak French at home and at work. There is a strong correlation in my data: when you speak French at work and/or in social networks, you are likely to also speak French at home.
- 19% say that they identify with the French culture, while 11% say they identify with the English culture. The remaining 70% identify with both cultures. In my data, those who identify with the French culture all speak French at home. The majority of these also speak French at work. All people who speak French in social networks identify with the French culture. Hence, when speaking French at home and at work you are likely to identify with the French culture.

Table 4 *How you can present your results: domains of language use and identity*

	French at home	French at work	French at school	French at church
French identity	67	45	43	1
English identity	65	53	56	4
Mixed identity	23	2	32	2
Other identity	1	5	3	1

Exercise 7.4

Find a number of research articles based on quantitative fieldwork: how are the methods presented? How does this differ from the way in which fieldwork methods are represented in qualitative studies (see exercise 7.3)?

7.4   Grammars

If your intention is to do fieldwork in order to write a grammar – be it a grammatical sketch or a comprehensive grammar – you will have to evaluate your corpus and find generalizable information about the language.

Ultimately, a grammar is the linguist's theory of how a specific language works, atomistically and holistically, i.e. what are its 'bits' and how do these 'bits' fit together. A grammar is the result of careful methodology, lots of hard thinking, innumerable conversations with native speakers, boldness (to propose connections or to say that 'x' does not exist in language 'y', etc.), lots of luck, and huge amounts of reading, planning, testing and interpreting.

So how does one do fieldwork with the object of writing a grammar? First, it is helpful to have a basic outline of a grammar in mind from the start of your fieldwork. One such outline is the Lingua Descriptive Studies Questionnaire by Norval Smith and Bernard Comrie (this can be found on the Department of Linguistics website for the Max Planck Institute for Evolutionary Anthropology: http://lingweb.eva.mpg.de/fieldtools/linguaQ.html). Another is Everett's phonology questionnaire: (see appendix 2).

Exercise 7.5

Look up the Lingua Descriptive Studies Questionnaire and compare it to a number of descriptive grammars, for example Fortescue's (1984) grammar of West Greenlandic and Sakel's (2004) grammar of Mosetén. Is all information presented in the questionnaire included in the grammar? How is that achieved? What are the advantages of arranging the table of contents according to the Lingua Descriptive Studies Questionnaire, and what are the disadvantages?

Another way to do fieldwork guided by questions relevant to writing a grammar is to read grammars that are considered exemplary by other linguists, either for a given region of the world or in general.

Let us now turn to the fieldwork corpus. If your aim is to write a grammar of a language, your corpus will have to be representative of all the structures of the language, which means it is going to be large and will contain a wide range of data. For some linguists, such data will be mainly texts, although texts are but one type of data that is essential for a good corpus. Other data such as those collected using stimulus tests, participant observation and elicitation form part of many corpora. Certainly, texts are highly important because they can shed light on the interaction of language and culture and they provide natural data, often showing examples and structures that the linguist would never have discovered on his or her own. It is important to include as many genres as possible, such as narrative, procedural, hortatory, expository, and any other type that the fieldworker identifies as relevant for the language. Also, it may be advisable to include texts that cover all significant cultural topics, e.g. life, death, harvest, hunting, dealing with the outside world, creation, fiction, history.

Different genres will reveal a wide range of linguistic information. Different moods, aspects, tenses, participant coding and tracking, different kinds of logical connectives, etc. all are associated to a greater or lesser degree with text genres. And anthropologists, ethnographers of communication and linguists will all benefit from a rich array of text topics, linked to the culture (which implies that the linguist must understand the culture more than superficially, in order to know which topics to ask for texts on).

Table 5 *The phonetic consonant*
segments of a hypothetical language

[p]	[t]	[k]
[b]	[d]	
[m]	[n]	[ɴ]

To write a grammar of any type requires a significant corpus of data. What is the nature and size of an 'adequate' corpus for a grammar? The answer is simple: an adequate corpus must be varied (containing the greatest possible number of distinct form, meaning and construction types), natural (providing data that native speakers utter in the appropriate context), and big enough. But when do you have enough data? Samarin (1967) gives a number of useful suggestions in this regard. We have borrowed some of them and added some of our own.

A complete corpus is obtained when:

1.   All the closed classes of linguistic elements are fully accounted for.

2.   There are no 'holes' in the data needed for analysis (partially, therefore, the answer depends on theory).

3.   There are multiple tokens of all types.

4.   It is maximally useful for other disciplines, as well as linguistics.

5.   All new material collected only contains structures and meanings already found in the corpus collected.

Let us consider each of these points in more detail. First, what does it mean to say that all the closed classes are fully accounted for? This simply means that when you have all the prepositions, all of the adjectives, all of the verbs, i.e. classes with a small number of members that do not expand in membership. In some languages verbs will be in the open classes of lexical items (e.g. English), while in others they will be among the closed classes (e.g. Mosetén; Sakel 2004). How do you next determine that there are no 'holes' in the data? Well, you have to have a view of how language works, partially based on general principles shared by most linguists and partially based on any particular theory that you are most influenced by. And you must be able to argue for your conclusions.

If you were trying to establish the consonant phoneme inventory of a language, you might end up with table 5. There is a missing segment in table 5, i.e. a voiced velar, [g]. Is this an accidental gap or an actual asymmetry in the segmental inventory? The linguist will need to look for examples of [g]. At some point, you might conclude that the system is indeed asymmetrical, which is certainly not all that uncommon. But until you can say with confidence that this is the case, the corpus is incomplete.

It is also important to ensure that for every segment, prosodic pattern, syntactic construction, suffix, etc. in the language, that the corpus includes multiple tokens of each. And the linguist's analysis must be the guide as to when there are enough tokens of each. One useful criterion in answering this question is: 'Are all tokens I am now recording simply repeating the patterns that I already have?' If so, then there are probably sufficient tokens in the corpus. However, one cannot simply rely on texts to magically produce all the tokens and their distributions that are necessary for a complete corpus. You have to *think*, based on your analysis and ask questions like the following: 'If my analysis is correct, then there will be forms of interpretation/shape *x* but never forms of interpretation/shape *y*.' Then you can look for the missing forms, both those you predict to be missing (no matter how long you search) and those which you predict to be found eventually, but which are currently absent (i.e. accidentally) from the corpus. You must be able to assure the readers of the grammar that the corpus is complete by this metric.

The corpus should also be maximally useful for other disciplines. You may be working on a rare language that few people are likely to have access to. In this case especially, but in all cases ultimately, it is a good idea to collect texts and data relevant to other disciplines insofar as you have time and knowledge to do so. Text collections should include all important cultural values, to the degree that the community is willing to allow access to these. Claims about numerals or counting should be accompanied by experimental evidence corroborating the claims (even if this means bringing in an expert consultant). And so on. Finally, once all new data appear to contain no new structures, you can consider that, with respect to your current working hypotheses and purposes, the corpus is complete. But, as we have been saying before, the 'complete corpus' is a relative, never an absolute, concept.

7.5   Dictionaries

The traditional view of the dictionary in linguistic theory up until a few decades ago, and still widespread, is that the dictionary is an asylum for the misbehaved, i.e. where we put forms that are not derivable by regular rules of syntax or phonology. People who work under this view may be tempted to produce trivial dictionaries that are little more than lists of words, idioms and morphemes. But this would be a mistake, even for those with the 'asylum' (or 'jail' – see Williams and DiSciullo 1987) view of the dictionary, because it renders the dictionary less useful. A dictionary is formed by a view of its potential users, not merely by a particular theoretical perspective.

In their volume, *Making dictionaries: preserving indigenous languages of the Americas*, the editors address the purpose of making a dictionary:

> A reasonable person might . . . ask, Why do it? One way to read the contributions to this volume is as personal answers to this question. But a more general response can be discerned in all the chapters and, indeed, in the

work of every lexicographer. There is something at once both marvelous and practical about producing a guide to the mind, world, and behavior of a group of people. The benefits that accrue from such a handbook – literacy, preservation, history, discovery – only add to the excitement of seeing the published dictionary standing upright on the shelf.   (Frawley, Hill and Munro 2002: 2–3).

Indeed, when producing a dictionary, you can have various different goals, or a combination of these: a dictionary may serve the community to develop literacy, as well as to preserve the language for the future. It may be a tool for the linguist to collect grammatical, phonological and other data on the language alongside each entry, or it may be a bilingual dictionary that makes each language more accessible to speakers of the other language. It is important to think about your goals when putting together a dictionary. You may end up with two or more types of dictionaries, all aimed at different audiences or serving different purposes. This can make sense when having very different users of the dictionaries: a speaker who struggles to read and write will not have much use for detailed linguistic information; at the same time, a linguist looking for pronunciation rules may not need illustrations of the entries.

You may first have to develop an orthography for the language in order to put together a dictionary that can be used by the speakers. Some linguists use IPA to note down the language they study, but this is not necessarily appropriate for materials aimed at the language community.

One of the other issues to consider is which entries to include in a dictionary. Would you use just 'basic forms' and how, in this case, would you define those? According to Frawley, Hill and Munro (2002), the choice of entries for a dictionary will ultimately result from a ' . . . trade-off between the pressures for maximal explicitness and the desire to match the users' minds to facilitate their inferences as they fill in what must be left implicit' (Frawley, Hill and Munro 2002: 5).

Another question is regarding the format of the dictionary. You may want to publish it as a booklet or book, but you may also opt for an electronic version. There are a number of advantages to constructing an electronic dictionary, whether as a complement to a print dictionary or as the sole dictionary. Just a few of the things that an electronic dictionary can do better and more cheaply than a print dictionary are: better graphics, audio files (providing pronunciations of each entry and many examples), easier dissemination, easier connections and cross-references from entries to the text or portion of field data from which they come, much greater and easier searchability, permanence (if done properly, an electronic dictionary can last forever), accessibility (more people have access to the dictionary), lower cost, easier to look for and predict trends in semantic change of lexical entries, and much greater interactivity – changes, corrections and updating the dictionary become much easier when it is in electronic form. Anyone who has consulted an online dictionary source that one finds on internet sites such as Yourdictionary.com (www.yourdictionary.com) knows that being able to listen to the pronunciation of entries, being able to find entries almost instantly, are tremendous advantages of electronic media dictionaries.

7.6   Language documentation

In the development of linguistic fieldwork, notions of *documentation* and *description* have perhaps not been as carefully distinguished as they ought to have been. Until recently, they seemed to be used nearly interchangeably. To write a grammar of a language, for example, was to document a part of the language. Likewise a dictionary was a form of documentation. More recently, technological advances allow us to create interactive databases for long-term storage and usage of *primary* data on languages, i.e. audio and video files. Such databases refine our concept of documentation (though of course in the selection of data for such databases the researcher intrudes and obscures). In our opinion, 'primary documentation' is the recording of audio and visual data. Secondary, and perhaps tertiary, documentation may be thought of as data in increasingly interpretative matrices (e.g. grammars, theoretical articles, and so on). The more interpretative the documents produced, the farther removed they are from primary documentation, in the view advanced here. Again, in times past, description doubled for documentation, as primary sources were not made available to general linguists and all that we have/had on many languages were data as selected and interpreted by linguists, explorers, anthropologists, missionaries, and others.

Today, there is a recognized field of language documentation and a range of sources for funding, making language documentation possible and accessible. Various linguistics departments and institutions have specialized in the subject (e.g. at SOAS in London, see: www.hrelp.org).

Language documentation can preserve a language for future generations. This can be important not just for the field of linguistics, but also for the language community itself. Future generations may want to learn about their ancestors' language, or they might even want to revive the language, making use of the language documentation data.

7.7   Summary and further reading

In this chapter we looked at the possible outcomes of linguistic fieldwork, including corpora, scientific articles, grammars and dictionaries.

For further reading on compiling corpora and archiving, see Backus (2008), Johnson (2004), Trilsbeek & Wittenburg (2006), as well as in Gippert (2006). Further information on writing up the results of qualitative or quantitative studies can be found in part four of Dörnyei (2007), as well as in Moyer & Li Wei (2008). On grammar writing, see Payne (1997), Ameka, Dench & Evans (2006) and Payne & Weber (2007). There is also more information on the webpage of the Max Planck Institute for Evolutionary Anthropology [www.eva.mpg.de/lingua/tools-at-lingboard/tools.php], including links to Unicode for making orthographies. See also Gippert, Himmelmann & Mosel (2006) for developing orthographies. On making dictionaries, see Frawley, Hill & Munro (2002) and Landau (2001). For further information on the outcomes of language documentation, including revitalization, refer to the collections by Gippert, Himmelmann & Mosel (2006), Austin & Sallabank (2011), Grenoble & Furbee (2010) and Himmelmann (1998).

Appendix 1 Perspectives on the history of fieldwork

Linguistic fieldwork has as many histories as there are countries in which it has been carried out. And there is no global history of fieldwork (and virtually no local histories either). Nor is this the place to write one. This appendix focuses on the history of field research in Brazil and the USA, as examples of the kinds of issues, problems, and solutions faced by both individual field researchers and the general enterprise of field linguistics.

Arguably, field linguistics in the Americas, as field linguistics most places, began as an extension of colonial activity – specifically, missionary work. Let us first consider the case of Brazil, then move on to consider the USA.

1   Fieldwork in Brazil

1.1   The colonial era (1500–1822)[1]

On April 22 1500, a flotilla of ships commanded by Pedro Álvares Cabral appeared off the coast of what is today the city of Porto Seguro, in the current-day state of Bahia. Almost immediately, the sea-weary sailors of Cabral's ships spotted men and women on the shore, looking out at the ships. A group of sailors rowed to shore and were greeted warmly by those people bold enough to remain and not flee into the jungle. Thus occurred one of the first contacts between Europeans and South American Indians, in this case the Tupinambá. Cabral eventually sailed off towards his intended destination of India, around the Cape of Good Hope, finally arriving back in Portugal with news of the new land, to be called 'Brasil' (for the *pau brasil*, a tropical redwood that came to be highly valued in Europe). As it had begun with Ignatius of Loyola (1491–1533), the founder of the Jesuits and the modern missionary movement, the Church recruited missionaries to take the gospel to the newly discovered heathens of Brazil. One of the earliest missionaries to reach Brazil was the Jesuit Padre José de Anchieta (1533–1597). Anchieta turned out to be a brilliant linguist (and administrator – he was co-founder of both the cities of São Paulo and Rio de Janeiro). Anchieta began his work near what is today the city of São Vicente, between Rio de Janeiro and São Paulo. The original people contacted by the Portuguese explorers were the Tupinambá, a language of the Tupi-Guarani family.

Along with the very closely related language, Guarani, spoken to the south, in what is today southern Brazil and Paraguay, Tupinambá was spoken along a sizeable portion of the Brazilian coast, from São Vicente to what is today the city of São Luis do Mararanhão. Wherever the Portuguese landed their ships north of São Vicente they encountered the Tupinambá, eventually coming to refer to their language as the 'Brazilian language'. It was to this language and people that Anchieta gave most of his attention during his missionary career in Brazil. Anchieta produced a grammar, a dictionary and translations of catechisms. His grammar and dictionary still rank among the best ever produced of a Brazilian language, nearly 500 years later. Although his missionary activity was partially responsible for the complete extinction of the Tupinambá people (largely because the Jesuits increased the size of Tupinambá villages, thus increasing mortality rates when European diseases infected local populations), Anchieta was a dedicated linguist whose work can be considered the beginning of Amazonian linguistics (indeed, it would not be stretching matters too far to call his work the beginning of linguistics in the Americas).

In addition to Anchieta, Tupinambá was also the object of some study by the French Calvinist Jean de Lery (1534–1613), who originally went to Brazil to establish a French Protestant colony. Lery's principal contribution was to record in written form some naturally occurring Tupinambá conversations. These enhance the picture of the language presented in Anchieta's grammar and reinforce the importance of conversational data in the documentation of endangered languages, since Lery's data are now the only record we have of the living form of this language in use.

Several decades after Anchieta and Lery, another Jesuit, Padre Antonio Ruiz de Montoya (1585–1652) arrived in what is today the border region between Brazil and Paraguay to work among the Guarani people, speakers of a Tupi-Guarani language very closely related to Tupinambá. Like Anchieta, Montoya was a brilliantly talented and dedicated linguist who also produced a grammar and dictionary of the language (Montoya is a partial model for the composite character of the priest played by Jeremy Irons in the film, *The Mission*).

After these few examples of precocious linguistic studies of endangered languages (though Guarani has managed to survive this early troubled history), the field of Amazonian studies was to lie fallow for the next several hundred years, aside from reports and wordlists from a succession of European explorers, mainly from Germany, under the influence and example of Alexander von Humboldt (1769–1859).

So field research in Brazil began as a colonial activity. As such, its initial purposes were utilitarian: to serve the Church, to get catechisms and the gospel into indigenous languages. This story was repeated in country after country, around the world. Native speakers were often not necessarily valued for their knowledge and language but rather for their role as objects in the colonial (and personal) goals of the missionary linguist. They certainly played little active role in shaping the goals of the studies of Anchieta, Montoya and others, at least not that we have any record of or any reason to believe. In modern days, however, missionary efforts have been very important in the development of field research programmes and traditions in different countries. Yet, in a number of cases the attitudes have remained very similar, in the sense that the native speaker community plays no or very little role in shaping the missionary's objectives and activities among them. To see this, let us consider the modern history of field research in Brazil.[2]

1.2   The contemporary era

Brazilian linguistics in the modern sense arguably begins with Joaquim Mattoso Câmara Jr (1904–1970), who dedicated a significant portion of his life to the introduction of modern linguistics into Brazilian university (and pre-university) training. Câmara did not spend much of his illustrious career on the study of Brazilian indigenous languages, but he did encourage their study as part of the development of Brazilian linguistics. In terms of the study of Amazonian languages *qua* endangered languages, the pioneer in Brazil surely is Darcy Ribeiro (1922–1997), perhaps the first government official of the Americas to invest government resources specifically earmarked for the documentation and description (and for him, the 'preservation') of endangered languages. During his tenure as Chefe da Casa Civil for Brazilian President Jânio Quadros, Ribeiro invited the Summer Institute of Linguistics to Brazil in the late 1950s. Ribeiro states his motive in inviting SIL to Brazil as (translation by Everett):

> My objective was to save for linguists of the future, who possibly will know how to study them, the languages as crystallizations of the human spirit, in order that we might learn more about mankind.   (Ribeiro 1997)

Ribeiro's administrative and anthropological concern for the survival and welfare of the indigenous peoples of Brazil was admirable and extremely forward-looking. We return to the mixed results of his initiatives below.

In terms of personally conducted research, the modern pioneer of the documentation of Amazonian languages was Kurt Unkel (1883–1945), a German, later naturalized Brazilian. This famous explorer, linguist, 'indigenista' and anthropologist, known to most Brazilians as Nimuendaju – the Guarani name he was given in 1906 and used until his death in 1945, (partially) documented and identified a very large number of Amazonian languages. Amazonian languages are still difficult to access physically, culturally and linguistically. They were far more so in Nimuendaju's day. Yet he managed to visit the majority of Brazilian Amazonian languages personally, taking competent wordlists from the many groups he visited, which have been extremely valuable in the linguistic classification of these languages. Nimuendaju is today perhaps the most revered figure in the history of the study of indigenous languages in Brazil, making tremendous personal sacrifices to both study and support these languages and their peoples. Stories of his life are currently available only in Portuguese (to our knowledge) and even these are fairly superficial in their coverage. One hopes that one day Nimuendaju's life and contribution to the study of Amazonian languages will receive the attention it deserves. His concern for endangered languages and peoples motivated not only his professional career but his entire life, from about 1906 until his death. Nimuendaju was not motivated by the desire to change the people he studied, so in this sense his work was an ethical improvement over earlier missionary efforts. He wanted to provide a record of the peoples' languages and cultures. But his activities still represent an intermediate level of ethical relationships with the communities, because they still fall far short of engaging the native speakers as co-shapers of the records about themselves. Native speakers did not sit with Nimuendaju, for example, and guide his studies in any significant way – at least all records indicate otherwise, namely, that he approached his studies with pre-determined objectives that were not negotiated in the local context.

To most linguists, however, the true beginning of modern linguistic studies of Amazonian languages in Brazil, entailing historical and comparative research, emphasis on extensive grammars and dictionaries, begins with Aryon Rodrigues (1925–), who published his first articles on these languages before he was 13, as an eighth-grade student in his native city of Curitiba, Paraná. Later, Rodrigues was a friend and colleague of Darcy Ribeiro at the University of Brasilia when Ribeiro served as the University's first Rector (Rodrigues currently is a Professor Emeritus at the University of Brasilia).

Rodrigues combines most of the positive characteristics of previous figures mentioned above. Administratively, he has founded linguistics programmes, with strong emphases on Amazonian studies, at the University of Brasilia, the Federal University of Rio de Janeiro, the National Museum in Rio de Janeiro and the State University of Campinas (UNICAMP). Although Rodrigues has done little fieldwork of his own, he has supervised countless graduate students' research (including Dan Everett's MA thesis).

2   Fieldwork in the USA

In the USA, the Jesuits and other missionaries played a similar role to Anchieta and Montoya in beginning studies of indigenous languages. However, professional linguistic and anthropological fieldwork began with Franz Boas (1858–1942), who trained a core of linguistically aware anthropologists responsible for the birth and growth of North American linguistics. (Ruth Benedict [1887–1948], Edward Sapir [1884–1939], and in some classes and via Sapir, Mary Haas [1910–1996], among others). During the years of Boas's influence, roughly during his life and following his death until the 1950s, North American linguistics was concerned with describing specific languages in detail, producing integrated studies of texts keyed to cultural studies, grammars and dictionaries, providing exactly the kind of pragmatist study that has proved to be so important to knowledge of little-studied peoples and their languages throughout the intervening years. In fact, though this is not the place to attempt a more detailed intellectual history, a case can be made that these earlier descriptive linguists were heavily influenced by the pragmatist philosophy underlying much American intellectual endeavour until at least the death of John Dewey (1859–1952), a philosophy which itself was arguably influenced by Native American philosophy (Pratt 2002). Thus in a roundabout way, Native American thought influenced the way that Native American languages were studied and documented, at least until the 1950s. Consider some remarks of Boas in his 1917 introduction to the first volume of the new *International Journal of American Linguistics* (*IJAL*). According to Boas, one of the principal goals of the new journal was to provide what I would call a 'coherent' report of languages. For example, Boas (1917: 2) laments the fact that '... the available material gives a one-sided presentation of linguistic data, because we have hardly any records of daily occurrences, everyday conversation, descriptions of industries, customs, and the like. For these reasons the vocabularies yielded by texts are one-sided and incomplete.' That is, Boas felt that a full 'picture' of a given language was only possible by looking at the language in the cultural context. Or consider Sapir's (1915: 186) assertion that more studies are needed of cultural 'modalities of attitude' and consonantal alternations, thus explicitly connecting grammar with culture.

Boas (1911: 63–7), in his introduction to the *Handbook of American Indian languages*, provides perhaps the best statement of the relationship between language and culture ever given. For him, this relationship was directly related to the connection between fieldwork and theoretical research on the nature of language and the nature of culture:

> If ethnology is understood as the science dealing with the mental phenomena of the life of the peoples of the world, human language, one of the most important manifestations of mental life, would seem to belong naturally to the field of work of ethnology, unless special reasons can be adduced why it should not be so considered.   (1911: 67)

In the same passage, Boas proceeds to consider and reject several proposed 'special reasons'. He goes on in this section to consider ways in which culture may affect a language's morphology, lexicon and grammar, concluding this section by stating (1911: 67):

> It does not seem likely, therefore, that there is any direct relation between the culture of a tribe and the language they speak, except in so far as the form of the language will be moulded by the state of culture, but not in so far as a certain state of culture is conditioned by morphological traits of the language.[3]

Sapir carried on the Boasian tradition, describing languages as manifestations of culture, human psychology and local conditions. And more than any other person, with the possible exception of Bloomfield, he influenced the course of North American linguistics until the 1950s.[4]

Thus, for the first half of the twentieth century, the normal North American conception of the linguist's 'job' was to study little or un-studied languages in the field and to produce coherent bodies of data on the interaction of culture, lexicon, texts and grammar. But by the 1960s this had changed radically, with field research given more or less the intellectual status of butterfly collecting. Postal (1968) referred to previous linguistic theories as 'taxonomic', while even today fieldworkers can meet negative opinions about their work. What are the forces that changed the attitudes to field research in North America (and eventually the world) so dramatically? It is what we may call (with no pejorative intent), the 'Chomsky factor'. The twentieth-century withering of fieldwork began innocuously enough, in the restlessness of a graduate student at the University of Pennsylvania with his MA research:

> Harris suggested that I undertake a systematic structural grammar of some language. I chose Hebrew, which I knew fairly well. For a time, I worked with an informant and applied methods of structural linguistics as I was then coming to understand them. The results, however, seemed to me rather dull and unsatisfying. Having no very clear idea as to how to proceed further, I abandoned these efforts and did what seemed natural; namely, I tried to construct a system of rules for generating the phonetic forms of sentences, that is, what is now called a generative grammar.   (Chomsky 1975: 25)

Chomsky's intellectual frustration with (an extremely easy version of) standard fieldwork led indirectly to some of the most important developments in the more than two-thousand-year history of the study of language. Nevertheless, the very intellectual vigour and power of Chomsky's subsequent work sufficed to pull most linguistics students and departments away from the traditional emphasis on field research to theoretical work on, for the most part, the linguist's native language. Though there is nothing inherently anti-fieldwork in Chomsky's research programme, his attitude, as expressed in the passage just cited, and his rejection of the intellectual priorities of Boasian linguistics, led to an abandonment of fieldwork in the USA and a nearly five-decade neglect of the study of indigenous languages and fieldwork throughout the linguistics world, as his influence soon became massive and international. Over the past decade, as the spotlight has begun to shift to fieldwork once again, it has been primarily concerned with the study of endangered languages.

The resurgence of interest in linguistic fieldwork from the late twentieth century is largely linked to the concern for documenting and describing endangered languages. The interest in language endangerment itself had been an important motive for early field research (see the quote, for example, from Darcy Ribeiro, on page 154), especially for Boas and his students, but went out of vogue for decades, making a comeback in the early 1990s. It is perhaps best exemplified institutionally today by the Hans Rausing Endangered Languages Documentation

Project at the School of Oriental and African Studies in London, which was established after the 'endangered languages' movement began. Furthermore, various sources of funding fieldwork were established, alongside technological initiatives (e.g. ELAN and EMELD). Many university linguistics departments and the general public have begun to appreciate the fact that languages are dying daily and that with them die millennia of accumulated knowledge. From a hard-nosed linguistic viewpoint, however, all languages need to be better described and documented and the most important criteria for determining which languages should be studied, have to do with ensuring that the sampling of languages we document is sufficient to warrant linguistic claims about theoretical principles and typological universals of human grammars and languages. Although one can accept the claim that endangered languages are the most urgent priority, the long-term view of linguistics research must be to produce the best science it is able to do, and this means that we need diverse and robust data to better understand whatever it is about *Homo sapiens* that ultimately underwrites its ability to have grammars and language and use them. This entails more fieldwork, since so many areas of the world are under-represented in linguistic research and because certain types of linguistic phenomena are under-represented in the documentation of languages (e.g. intonation, information-structuring, the phonetics underlying the phonology of a given language, etc.).

In spite of the general belief in the scientific equality of all languages, there is a sense in which workers on little-studied languages need a guide more than those who study better-known languages. Consider that if someone makes a claim about, say, English syntax or French phonology, there are hundreds of scholars and millions of native speakers who are in a position to challenge analytical assertions they disagree with. But in work on little-studied languages it is often the case that very few people, if any, will be in a position to seriously test the actual data used by the linguist, unless the linguist has followed careful procedures that encourage, facilitate and promote as much replicability, soundness of presentation and analysis, and data-preservation as possible.

Appendix 2 Phonology questionnaire

The following questionnaire has been developed by Dan Everett for fieldworkers who face having to describe the phonology of a language. While there are a wealth of questionnaires on other aspects of linguistic work, there are only few materials dedicated to phonological analysis. For this reason, the authors decided to include the questionnaire in this book. It has been available online for some time, but this is the first published version.

We hope that the questionnaire can serve as a framework, a useful prod, for writing detailed phonologies of languages. It is not intended to be even nearly exhaustive and it requires some knowledge of phonology.

1   Segmental phonology

1.1   List the distinctive segments of the language. Give rules of allophonic distribution. Summarize the (articulatory) phonetic realization of each segment.

1.2   What are the non-allophonic restrictions on the distribution of these segments? For example, do any segments appear exclusively in loan words? Are any subject to sociolinguistic or cultural restrictions (e.g. 'Do not use /x/ in the presence of foreigners')? Are there differences in the segmental inventory according to gender (e.g. men use /s/ where women use /h/ or variation in points of articulation between women and men)?

1.3   Are some segments restricted as to which word class they may appear in (e.g. /b/ only in nouns and adjectives)?

2   Syllabic structure

2.1   What are the syllable types (e.g. CCV, CV, CVC, etc.)?

    2.1.1 Describe any restrictions on syllable distribution. Are some syllables allowed only in word/phrase-final position (or medial or initial)?

2.1.2 Discuss the evidence for these syllables.

2.1.2.1 Phonotactics:

- Are consonant sequences allowed? Where? Do allowable consonant clusters vary according to where they appear in the word (e.g. *st* only in word-initial position, but *ts* in word-final position)? Are there any restrictions as to the type of vowel/semi-vowel which may precede/follow consonant clusters?
- Are there word-final consonants?
- Are vowel sequences permitted? Where? Do allowable vowel clusters vary according to where they appear in the word (e.g. *ai* only in word-initial position, but *ia* elsewhere)? Are there any restrictions as to the type of consonant or semi-vowel which may precede or follow specific vowel clusters?
- How many vowels or consonants may appear in a single cluster, if clusters are allowed? In adjacent vowels, are there restrictions on vowel features (e.g. all the vowels have the same value for height and roundedness)? Are some sequences banned (e.g. *aa*)?

2.1.2.2 Phonetic evidence: Is there phonetic evidence in favour of syllables (e.g. chest pulses)?

2.1.2.3 Do native speakers segment words into syllables in slow speech?

2.1.2.4 Do phonological rules crucially refer to syllable structure, e.g. stress placement, nasal spreading, tone distribution, for example as in the following:

- Stress the rightmost (C)VC or (C)VV syllable in the word, otherwise stress the penult?
- Lower tautosyllabic, adjacent high tones to mid tones in (C)VV syllables.

2.2   Interpretation of glides

2.2.1 Do semi-vowels, such as [y] and [w], appear in both or either syllable-initial and syllable-final positions?

2.2.2 If the language allows vowel sequences and semi-vowels, may the first vowel be [i] or [u]?

2.2.3 In vowel or semi-vowel sequences, are any of the following orders prohibited? Preferred? In the following, X and Y are variables and thus may represent any segment type, for example:

X *iy* Y

X *yi* Y

X *uw* Y

X *wu* Y

X *yu* Y

X *uy* Y

X *wi* Y

X *iw* Y

2.3   What are the allowable sequences of segments within the syllable, according to their articulatory classification or generalizable acoustic properties? For example, are there ordering restrictions such as the following (just as a few suggestions):

- The onset of a syllable may begin with any consonant, but the second member of a complex onset must come from a more restricted class of segments (e.g. voiced continuant).
- In a complex nucleus, the first vowel must be a high vowel.
- In a complex coda, the order of consonants is more (or less) restricted than in a complex onset.
- The order of consonants in the coda is the mirror-image of the order in the onset.

2.4   If the nucleus contains a diphthong, can it also contain another vowel?

2.5   If the language has CVC syllables, can V be a diphthong? If so, are there any restrictions on the following C?

3   Tone

3.1   Does the language have contrastive pitches which distinguish lexical meanings of words?

3.2   Do contrastive pitches have a fairly constant F_0 or does their F_0 rise or fall or 'undulate' significantly?

3.3   If F_0 of pitches varies, yet is significant in distinguishing lexical items, does the variation correlate with position in the word, preceding or following segments, preceding or following pitches, or the word's position in the sentence or discourse?

3.4   Can consonants bear tone or only vowels? Which consonants? Under what circumstances (e.g. '*w* and *y* bear tone following a rule of asyllabification')?

3.5   Does consonant voicing affect tone? How?

3.6   Does vowel quality affect tone? How?

3.7   Can tone patterns of individual words vary arbitrarily or do there appear to be *tonal melodies* assigned on words or classes of words (e.g. High Low Mid for one class of nouns, HLH for another or LHL)? Do the tonal melodies change according to the number of syllables?

3.8   What happens to a tone if its associated segment is deleted? For example, does the tone delete or appear on another syllable?

3.9   If the language does not allow contour tones (those with an underivable but constant change in pitch, e.g. rise and fall) on short vowels or sequences, can they arise from morphological or phonological processes? Consider the Pirahã example in (i):

(i)   tíi Ɂísitoí Ɂogabagaí → tíi Ɂísitōogabagaí
         I egg   want

In the case of (i), in normal speech the direct object and the verb form a close phonological unit, deleting a verb-initial glottal stop and the noun-final vowel. Notice that the tone does not disappear, however. In the example in (i) no mark over a vowel indicates low tone and the acute accent marks high tone. The line over the first /o/ to the right of the arrow indicates that it bears both a low tone and high tone simultaneously. This is in my analysis the result of the high tone remaining even after its original vowel host, /i/, has been deleted. This is otherwise prohibited in the language.

3.10   Can a tone ever *shift* to the right or the left in a word? Across words? Can one tone ever replace another, e.g. in (i)?
3.11   Is there complementary distribution among the tones, e.g. H → M/L?
3.12   Are the frequency distances between tones (especially in a language with three or more tones) fairly constant or are some tones closer in frequency than others (e.g. M and H being closer in average frequency than M and L, in a three tone system)? Is frequency distance affected by how many different tone levels are present in a given word or phrase?
3.13   Is tone affected by phrasal intonation? How?
3.14   Does the language have other channels of discourse that exploit *linguistic* tone, e.g. whistle speech, drum communication or hum speech? Please describe this in detail, as well as the social/cultural restrictions on its use.

4   Intonation

4.1   What is the most common intonational pattern (e.g. rising, falling, fall-rise, rise-fall, etc.) at the end of utterances?
4.2   How are different intonational patterns distinguished? By end points? By beginning and end points? By relative height of the entire intonational phrase? By beginning, middle, and end points?
4.3   What functions does intonation serve? For example, does it distinguish:
         • syntactic phrasal types (e.g. interrogative, declarative)?
         • illocutionary acts (e.g. indirect request vs. direct request)?
         • other?
4.4   Is intonation affected by tone, stress, syllable patterns, or other phonological phenomena? How?

4.5   Does intonation affect tone, stress, syllable patterns, or other phono-
           logical phenomena? How?
4.6   What is the largest grammatical unit for which you can identify a dis-
           tinct intonational pattern? Phrase? Sentence? Paragraph? Discourse?
4.7   Does intonation serve to unite two or more phrases in parataxis?
4.8   Can intonation mark subordination/superordination relations between
           clauses?
4.9   Are there *step accent*s in the language, i.e. where the highest pitch of
           one intonational contour appears immediately prior to the stressed syl-
           lable, which itself bears a relatively low pitch? Are other correlations
           between stress and intonation placement observed? Describe these
           carefully, paying attention to the syntax, semantics, and pragmatics
           of the utterances as you do so.
4.10   What are the quantitative variations allowed in basic intonational con-
           tours? That is, can the same contour appear with more or less promi-
           nence by manifesting greater pitch distances between its distinctive
           points? When? What is the F_0 evidence like?
4.11   Is it more common for frequency to decline at the end of utterances?
           How many syllables or words are in the domain of this declination?
           Is there an accompanying rhythm (slow down, speed up, and so on)?
4.12   How can the different intonational contours be affected in their over-
           all ranges of pitch, amplitude, duration, etc. by different ways of
           speaking, e.g. 'speaking up' or whispering?
4.13   How is intonation manifested across different prosodic channels (e.g.
           whistle speech)?

5   Stress

5.1   Are some syllables in the language more prominent than others,
           for example, by using more acoustic energy, louder, higher pitch
           or longer?
5.2   Do such syllables appear in every word?
5.3   Is this prominence predictable? How?
5.4   Are there different patterns of prominence on different classes of
           words, e.g. nouns vs. verbs (if there are, describe them)? Or is it
           constant across all lexical categories?
5.5   Are there secondary (tertiary, quaternary, etc.) stresses?

           For example: mul*tipli***ca***tion*
                              2ary1ary

           5.5.1 Do n^{ary} stresses occur at regular intervals? How are these inter-
                 vals determined (e.g. every other syllable in the word from left
                 to right)?

5.5.2 Can primary or secondary (etc.) stresses ever appear on adjacent syllables in a word or phrase?

5.5.3 Does the stress of one word/syllable ever seem to move away from the stress of another word when it would otherwise be adjacent? Which of the otherwise adjacent stresses shifts, the one on the left or the one on the right? (e.g. *Thir'* teen + 'wo*men* → 'Thir*teen* 'wo*men*)?

5.6 Are 'heavy' syllables more frequently stressed than nonheavy syllables (e.g. (C)VC, (C)VV, vs. (C)V)? Under what circumstances, if any, can a lighter syllable bear primary stress if primary stress is normally restricted to heavy syllables?

5.7 What are the acoustic correlates of stress (e.g. loudness, pitch, length)? Are the correlates constant or variable across utterances or across speakers?

5.8 Do any (morpho)phonological processes interact with stress in a systematic way? What is the nature of this interaction (e.g. segmental lenition, voicing, vowel-harmony or vowel reduction)?

5.9 If heavy syllables bear stress, what happens if the syllable-final consonant or vowel of the stressed heavy syllable is deleted?

5.10 If stress shifts for any reason, in which direction does it shift, leftwards or rightwards? Is its 'final destination' predictable in such stress shifts? How?

5.11 Does stress behave identically in longer and shorter words or utterances?

5.12 Is there any evidence of native speaker sensitivity to stress, such as correcting your misplacement of it or tapping on stressed syllables as they say the word?

5.13 How does (or doesn't) stress interact with tone? Does stress shift also when tone shifts? Does stress placement perturb (raise, lower, metathesize, etc.) tones?

6   Morphophonology

6.1 Do affixes affect stress or tone patterns in words?

6.2 Do the affixes which do and do not affect stress (if there are such distinctions among affixes) fall into natural semantic, phonological, or morphosyntactic classes (e.g. syllable structure, inherent tone, prefixes vs. suffixes vs. infixes, derivational vs. inflectional)?

6.3 Do segmental rules (e.g. devoicing, assimilation, vowel-harmony and deletion) affect affix shapes? Which and how? Again, what are the differences between affixes which are affected versus those which are not?

6.4   Does the language have clitics? Like affixes, these are phonologically dependent on another word, never appearing alone. Unlike affixes, a single clitic can appear on a wide variety of word types, such as nouns, verbs, adjectives and particles.

6.5   Do these clitics appear in various locations within the sentence or do they cluster in a given position?

6.5.1 If clitics appear in different positions, does their placement depend on the phonology (e.g. stress) or the syntax (e.g. a clitic must appear on the word to the immediate left of the word with which it forms a syntactic constituent)? Consider English, where ( )s = phonological boundary and [ ]s = syntactic boundary: ([I]['ll) (go)].

6.5.2 If clitics cluster in a given position, which clitics may cluster and where does this take place in the phrase or sentence (e.g. 'all clitics expressing tense and mood appear following the first constituent of the sentence')?

6.6   Are some phonological processes peculiar to particular types of affixation (e.g. prefixation, suffixation, infixation, simulfixation, circumfixation)?

6.7   Is there reduplication?

6.7.1 Is reduplication monosyllabic, disyllabic, or larger or smaller (e.g. a single vowel, consonant or mora)?

6.7.2 Do the consonant–vowel sequences in the reduplicated morphemes follow a constant order and shape for all reduplicated affixes?

6.7.3 Are there subregularities of consonant–vowel patterns (e.g. CVC for one type of reduplication and e.g. CVVC for others)?

6.7.4 Does reduplication interact with any other phonological processes (e.g. stress, nasalization or vowel-harmony)?

7   Other prosodies

7.1   Do any other phonological elements take a domain larger than individual segments? Some possibilities are: aspiration, nasalization, labialization, voicing, vowel features, and so on.

7.2   Do such elements take larger domains only under certain circumstances? That is, can they 'spread' to surrounding phonological material?

7.2.1 In what direction can they spread?

7.2.2 What can trigger this spreading?

7.2.3 What can block this spreading (e.g. 'nasalization spread is blocked when it reaches a voiceless consonant')?

7.3   Is there a minimal word size (e.g. no word in isolation can be less than two moras in length)?

Notes to chapters

1 Introduction: what is linguistic fieldwork?

1 This generally coincides with qualitative as opposed to quantitative data-collection.
2 It legitimately might be if one finds oneself with access to a language one had not planned to work on, but which presents itself in a set of circumstances with interesting properties or which is endangered.

2 Fieldwork projects: two examples

1 It is worth mentioning that some people choose to make very detailed transcriptions, for example by measuring the length of pauses. It all depends on what you want to study. For example, the length of pauses is essential in discourse analysis, while for a grammatical description indicating all pauses may not be necessary. Having said that, pauses can tell you where 'sentences' begin and end.
2 In the past, researchers have also used wordlists of this type to establish genetic links between languages, though such a practice is not reliable, as language contact can skew the results.
3 More specifically, I wanted to follow current research trends to investigate two types of contact phenomena: the 'transfer' of elements from their L1 into their L2 and from their L2 into their L1. The former could be a foreign accent or unusual grammatical constructions. For example, a Somali person might say *he looked himself in the mirror*, using the reflexive pronoun 'himself' in this construction. In Somali, an equivalent structure to the reflexive can be used to convey this meaning, while native English speakers do not use a reflexive pronoun in this construction. The other type of transfer from L2 to L1 generally appears when immigrants have lived in the other country for a while. For example, Sakel has caught herself saying *worüber ist das?* (lit. 'what is this about?'), rather than one of the correct German equivalents, such as *wovon handelt das?* (lit. 'of what does this deal?'), modelled on the way this is expressed in English.
4 For example, some speakers had lived in the Netherlands for a long time, others had come straight to Britain.
5 Giving gifts is not always straightforward when working in bureaucratic environments. Many universities do not allow you to buy gifts, even if they are budgeted for in your own grants. In this pilot study, Sakel ended up buying the gifts out of her own money. Unless you are very rich, this is not possible with studies involving a larger number of speakers. It is therefore a good idea to find out about this before embarking on your study.

3 The languages

1 They are in part based on Everett (2001), from which this chapter borrows freely.
2 This excludes sign languages and special languages, for example secret languages that are only ever written.
3 The fieldwork setting plays a role as well, and the fieldworker may find it a struggle to record code-switching data even when aiming to record the appropriate language register (see 5.1.8 on creating a relaxed and appropriate setting).
4 This might be more difficult than you think. Take the UK, for example: would English qualify as an indigenous language, or would you list it as an immigrant language, considering only the Celtic languages to be original?

4 The people

1 However, this is not always the case and second language learners may sometimes prefer to use the strategy that is the furthest removed from the one they know.
2 In most fieldwork situations it is a good idea to learn to speak the language and to demonstrate regular and obvious progress at each meeting with the language teacher. It would be nice if others in the community complimented you and your teacher(s) for your progress (if complimenting is something they do).
3 In the film *Unforgiven*, Clint Eastwood shoots the unarmed owner of a brothel, in front of the local law officer, Gene Hackman. Hackman remarks that it is very cowardly to shoot an unarmed man. Eastwood says 'Well, he shoulda armed himself.' Opportunity does not always wait for one to arm oneself intellectually. A linguist needs to be prepared.
4 Many PhD dissertations in the USA, like much of the early work on Transformational Grammar, were funded by branches of the US military and the US Department of Defense. This is common knowledge. Although there apparently were no strings attached to these grants and although there was no involvement that we are aware of by the linguistics research of that time (1960s by and large), still, people in countries suspicious of the USA might want assurances that the funding behind the project has no connection with the US military. This is an extreme example, but not implausible.

5 Fieldwork preparation

1 Different methodologies, such as studying language in its natural setting, versus a highly formalized setting, are discussed in chapter 6.
2 If you struggle to imagine a fieldwork situation to work on, you could take one of the two situations described in chapter 2: (a) doing a study of the grammar of Mosetén in the Bolivian Amazon, or (b) studying language contact between Somali and English among Somali immigrants in your home town.
3 Unfortunately, grammars and research papers often omit this information or are imprecise in their description of it. For example, if an author says 'I have worked on this language for twenty years', what does that mean? Is the twenty years in question eight hours a day in the field collecting data or three months in the field every two years, followed by writing and reflection?
4 Several researchers have suggested that it is important to keep old versions of software for processing field data because there can be incompatibilities with newer versions

and the old versions may be necessary – so long as one still has hardware that will run them – to access the data properly. But care should be given to data-storage and the software used for this purpose. Proprietary software such as Microsoft Word may best be avoided and, instead, XML software could be used.

5 You might look online; for example, netdoctor has in-depth information on travel vaccines (www.netdoctor.co.uk/travel/vaccines_index.shtml).

6 Fieldworkers going to remote locations are advised to take a copy of this book. See publication details in the References. It can be ordered via the internet from Macmillan Education or from Hesperian Publications, www.hesperian.org. If not for profit, the pdf may be downloaded free: see publishers' details. This website also contains a wealth of information and material on health care in rural environments.

7 Two 32-watt solar panels (roll-up rather than rigid, for easier transport) could be connected by cables to a 12-volt, deep-cycle battery (e.g. the kind used on many small boats in the US. Deep-cycle batteries charge better and have a wider voltage tolerance.) This type of battery can be quite heavy, however, and needs to be replaced every year or two. Smaller batteries (e.g. a motorcycle battery) can be used, but these are unable to provide as much power. You will then need a voltage converter to change the power coming out of the battery to 110 (or 220) from 12 volt. A voltage regulator would be useful because it can keep your batteries from overcharging or running while undercharged. It will shut off the relevant input or output to protect the battery. If you choose not to purchase and connect a voltage regulator, you should get a voltage meter to check the power in the battery. It should never go above 13–14 volts and never below 11 or you will soon be without it.

8 This no doubt says more about Western culture's view of language than about fieldwork.

9 By this reckoning, a PhD programme with the projected output of a grammar as a dissertation, with courses, fieldwork, and writing up, should be estimated to take roughly four years in Britain or six years in the USA (where additional courses are required, making the whole process much more lengthy). Even if this may seem very difficult, it is a highly rewarding experience to write a grammar for one's dissertation!

10 Back at home in Denmark, after a good night's sleep, I was able to see the funny side of my experience. My local Greenlandic friends were in tears laughing when I told them about my trip! In the end I dedicated my MA thesis to the ghost in room 03.

6 Fieldwork methods

1 For example, work in many remote places all over the world by Steve Levinson and associates, e.g. Levinson (2003), as well as fieldwork on Pirahã numerals and other aspects by Frank *et al.* (2008).

2 The -*we* is a bound morpheme and hence written with a hyphen when presented separately.

3 See the Leipzig glossing rules for guidance on how to present non-overt elements, inherent categories, bipartite elements, infixes and reduplication.

4 For published resources, there are often clear guidelines as to where such a list would be expected to appear.

5 We recommend too that indelible ink (waterproof at a minimum) be used for all transcriptions, not just in the jungle, but also at your desk at home, where spilled coffee and other accidents may happen.
6 Based on its predecessor 'Shoebox'.
7 This example is taken from Kenneth L. Pike's lectures, University of Oklahoma, 1976.

Appendix 1 Perspectives on the history of fieldwork

1 Much of this chapter closely follows Everett's (2004) article on 'Coherent fieldwork'.
2 Pratt (2002) is a fascinating and largely convincing study of the influence of Native Americans on new world philosophy, which has been both profound and uncredited. The book *1491*, by Mann (2005), also demonstrates, very convincingly, the intellectual richness of pre-Columbian Native American populations.
3 This passage is particularly interesting in that it seems to contradict the linguistic relativity hypothesis often associated with Boas. Boas was probably concerned with something else here, namely, the classification of languages by culture, which he rightly attacked as quite erroneous. Nevertheless, Boas shows how the language–culture connection is bidirectional. This has obvious and important consequences for field research.
4 One influential linguist deeply impacted by Sapir was Kenneth Pike, who was both a professor of linguistics at the University of Michigan and the President of the Summer Institute of Linguistics (SIL) for over a quarter of a century. The rise of SIL in the second half of the twentieth century and its Sapirian influence gave a huge impetus to the study of American (and other) indigenous languages, as well as to the general enterprise of field research.

References

Abbi, Anvita (2001) *A manual of linguistic fieldwork and structures of Indian languages.* Munich: Lincom Europa.

Aikhenvald, Alexandra Y. (2007) *Linguistic fieldwork: setting the scene.* Special issue of *Language typology and universals* **60**(1).

Ameka, Felix, Alan Charles Dench & Nicholas Evans (2006) (eds.) *Catching language: the standing challenge of grammar writing.* Berlin: Mouton de Gruyter.

Austin, Peter K. (2006) 'Data and language documentation'. In Jost Gippert, Nikolaus Himmelmann & Ulrike Mosel (eds.) *Essentials of language documentation.* Berlin: Mouton de Gruyter, pp. 87–112.

  (2010) *Language documentation and description,* vol. 7. London: SOAS.

Austin, Peter K. & Julia Sallabank (eds.) (2011) *The Cambridge handbook of endangered languages.* Cambridge: Cambridge University Press.

Backus, Ad (2008) 'Data banks and corpora'. In Li Wei & Melissa Moyer (eds.) *The Blackwell guide to research methods in bilingualism and multilingualism.* Malden, MA: Blackwell, pp. 232–48.

Boas, Franz (1911) *Handbook of American Indian languages,* vol. 1. Washington, DC: Government Print Office, Smithsonian Institution.

  (1917) 'Introduction', *International Journal of American Linguistics* **1**: 1–18.

Bohnemeyer, J., M. Bowerman & P. Brown. 2001. 'Cut and break clips'. In S. Levinson & N. Enfield (eds.) *Manual for the field season 2001.* Nijmegen: Max Planck Institute for Psycholinguistics, pp. 90–6.

Bouquiaux, Luc & Jacqueline Thomas (1976) (eds.) *Enquête et description des langues à tradition orale.* 2nd edn. Paris: SELAF, CNRS.

Bowern, Claire (2008) *Linguistic fieldwork – a practical guide.* Basingstoke: Palgrave Macmillan.

Burling, Robbins (1984) *Learning a field language.* Ann Arbor, MI: University of Michigan Press.

Chafe, Wallace (1980) *The pear stories: cognitive, cultural and linguistic aspects of narrative production.* Norwood, NJ: Ablex.

Chelliah, Shobhana L. (2001) 'The role of text collections and elicitation in linguistic fieldwork'. In Paul Newman & Martha Ratliff (eds.) *Linguistics fieldwork.* Cambridge: Cambridge University Press, pp. 152–65.

Chelliah, Shobhana L. & Willem J. de Reuse (2011) *Handbook of descriptive linguistic fieldwork.* Dordrecht: Springer.

Chomsky, Noam (1965) *Aspects of the theory of syntax.* Cambridge, MA: MIT Press.

  (1975) *The logical structure of linguistic theory.* New York: Plenum Press.

Codó, Eva (2008) 'Interviews and questionnaires.' In Li Wei & Melissa Moyer (eds.) *The Blackwell guide to research methods in bilingualism and multilingualism.* Malden, MA: Blackwell, pp. 158–76.

Craig, Colette (1979) 'Jacaltec: field work in Guatemala'. In Timothy Shopen (ed.) *Languages and their speakers.* Cambridge, MA: Winthrop Publishers, pp. 3–58.

Crowley, Terry (2007) *Field linguistics – a beginner's guide.* Oxford: Oxford University Press.

Daller, Michael H., Jeanine Treffers-Daller & Reyhan Furman (2010) 'Transfer of conceptualization patterns in bilinguals: the construal of motion events in Turkish and German', *Bilingualism: Language and Cognition* **14**(1): 95–119.

Dewalt, Kathleen M. & Billie R. Dewalt (2002) *Participant observation – a guide for fieldworkers.* Walnut Creek, CA: Alta Mira Press.

Dickson, Murray (2009) *Where there is no dentist.* 3rd rev. edn. Hesperian Foundation.

Di Sciullo, Anna Maria & Edwin Williams (1987) *On the definition of word.* Cambridge, MA: MIT Press.

Dixon, Robert M.W. (2011) *Searching for Aboriginal languages: memoirs of a field worker.* Cambridge: Cambridge University Press.

Dorian, Nancy C. (1973) 'Grammatical change in a dying dialect', *Language* **49**(2): 413–38.

Dörnyei, Zoltán (2007) *Research methods in applied linguistics.* Oxford: Oxford University Press.

Duranti, Alessandro (1997) *Linguistic anthropology.* Cambridge: Cambridge University Press.

Enfield, Nick (2002) (ed.) *Ethnosyntax: explorations in culture and grammar.* Oxford: Oxford University Press.

Evans, Nicholas (2001) 'The last speaker is dead – long live the last speaker!' In Newman & Martha S. Ratliff (eds.) *Linguistic fieldwork.* Cambridge: Cambridge University Press, pp. 250–80.

Everett, Daniel L. (2001) 'Monolingual field research'. In Paul Newman & Martha S. Ratliff (eds.) *Linguistic fieldwork.* Cambridge: Cambridge University Press, pp. 166–88.

    (2004) 'Coherent fieldwork'. In Piet van Sterkenburg (ed.) *Linguistics today – facing a greater challenge.* Amsterdam: John Benjamins.

    (2005) 'Cultural constraints on grammar and cognition in Pirahã: another look at the design features of human language', *Current Anthropology* **76**(4): 621–46.

    (2008) *Don't sleep, there are snakes: life and language in the Amazonian jungle.* London: Profile Books.

Everett, Daniel L. & Barbara Kern (1997) *Wari'.* London: Routledge.

Foley, William A. (1997) *Anthropological linguistics: an introduction.* Oxford: Blackwell.

Fortescue, Michael (1984) *West Greenlandic.* London: Croom Helm.

Franchetto, Bruna (2006) 'Ethnography in language documentation'. In Jost Gippert, Nikolaus P. Himmelmann & Ulrike Mosel (eds.) *Essentials of language documentation.* Berlin: Mouton de Gruyter, pp. 183–212.

Frank, Michael C., Daniel L. Everett, Evelina Fedorenko & Edward Gibson (2008) 'Number as a cognitive technology: evidence from Pirahã language and cognition', *Cognition* **108**(3): 819–24.

Frawley, William, Kenneth Hill & Pamela Munro (eds.) (2002) *Making dictionaries: preserving indigenous languages of the Americas*. Berkeley, CA: University of California Press.

Gil, David (2001) 'Escaping Eurocentrism: fieldwork as a process of unlearning'. In Paul Newman & Martha S. Ratliff (eds.) *Linguistic fieldwork*. Cambridge: Cambridge University Press, pp. 102–32.

Gippert, Jost (2006) 'Linguistic documentation and the encoding of textual materials'. In Jost Gippert, Nikolaus P. Himmelmann & Ulrike Mosel (eds.) *Essentials of language documentation*. Berlin: Mouton de Gruyter, pp. 337–62.

Gippert, Jost, Nikolaus P. Himmelmann & Ulrike Mosel (eds.) (2006) *Essentials of language documentation*. Berlin: Mouton de Gruyter.

Gonzalez-Marquez, Monica, Raymond B. Becker & James E. Cutting (2007) 'An introduction to experimental methods for language researchers'. In Monica Gonzalez-Marquez, Irene Mittelberg, Seana Coulson & Michael J. Spivey (eds.) *Methods in cognitive linguistics*. Amsterdam: Benjamins, pp. 53–86.

Gordon, Peter (2004) 'Numerical cognition without words: evidence from Amazonia', *Science* **306**: 496–9.

Grenoble, Lenore A. & N. Louanna Furbee (eds.) (2010) *Language documentation – practice and values*. Amsterdam: Benjamins.

Grenoble, Lenore A. & Lindsay J. Whaley (1998) (eds.) *Endangered languages: current issues and future prospects*. Cambridge: Cambridge University Press.

Grinevald, Colette (1997) 'Language contact and language degeneration'. In F. Coulmas (ed.) *The handbook of sociolinguistics*. Oxford: Blackwell, pp. 257–70.

Grosjean, François (2008) *Studying bilinguals*. Oxford: Oxford University Press.

Gumperz, John J. (1982) *Discourse strategies*. Cambridge: Cambridge University Press.

Gumperz, John J. & Stephen C. Levinson (eds.) (1996) *Rethinking linguistic relativity*. Cambridge: Cambridge University Press.

Hale, Ken (2001) 'Ulwa (Southern Sumu): the beginnings of a language research project'. In Paul Newman & Martha S. Ratliff (eds.) *Linguistic fieldwork*. Cambridge: Cambridge University Press, pp. 76–101.

Haspelmath, Martin & Uri Tadmor (eds.) (2009) *Loanwords in the world's languages: a comparative handbook*. Berlin: Mouton de Gruyter.

Heller, Monica (2008) 'Doing ethnography'. In Li Wei & Melissa Moyer (eds.) *The Blackwell guide to research methods in bilingualism and multilingualism*. Malden, MA: Blackwell, pp. 249–62.

Hill, Jane H. (2006) 'The ethnography of language and language documentation'. In Jost Gippert, Nikolaus P. Himmelmann & Ulrike Mosel (eds.) *Essentials of language documentation*. Berlin: Mouton de Gruyter, pp. 113–28.

Himmelmann, Nikolaus (1998) 'Documentary and descriptive linguistics', *Linguistics* **36**(1): 161–95.

Hudson, Richard (1996) *Sociolinguistics*, 2nd edn. Cambridge: Cambridge University Press.

Hyman, Larry (2001) 'Fieldwork as a state of mind'. In Paul Newman & Martha S. Ratliff (eds.) *Linguistic fieldwork*. Cambridge: Cambridge University Press, pp. 15–33.

Johnson, Heidi (2004) 'Language documentation and archiving, or how to build a better corpus. In Peter Austin (ed.) *Language documentation and description*, vol. 2. London: SOAS.

Jorgensen, Danny L. (1989) *Participant observation: a methodology for human studies*. Thousand Oaks, CA: Sage Publications.

Karlsson, Fred (2007) 'Constraints on multiple initial embedding of clauses', *International Journal of Corpus Linguistics* **12**(1): 107–18.

Labov, William (1966) *The social stratification of English in New York City*. New York: Center for Applied Linguistics.

Landau, Sidney I. (2001) *Dictionaries: the art and craft of lexicography*. Cambridge: Cambridge University Press.

Lanza, Elizabeth (2008) 'Selecting individuals, groups, and sites'. In Li Wei & Melissa Moyer (eds.) *The Blackwell guide to research methods in bilingualism and multilingualism*. Malden, MA: Blackwell, pp. 73–87.

Laury, Ritva & Ono Tsuyoshi (2010) 'Recursion in conversation: what speakers of Finnish and Japanese know how to do'. In Harry Van der Hulst (ed.) *Recursion and human language*. Berlin: Mouton de Gruyter, pp. 69–92.

Levinson, Stephen C. (2003) *Space in language and cognition: explorations in cognitive diversity*. Cambridge: Cambridge University Press.

Loving, Aretta (1975) 'On learning monolingually'. In Alan Healey (ed.) *Language learner's field guide*. Ukarumba: Papua New Guinea: SIL, pp. 267–71.

Lowe, Ivan (1990) 'Cause and reason in Nambiquára'. In Doris L. Payne (ed.) *Amazonian linguistics: studies in lowland South American languages*. Austin: University of Texas Press, pp. 543–73.

Lucy, John A. (1992a) *Language diversity and thought: a reformulation of the linguistic relativity hypothesis*. Cambridge: Cambridge University Press.

(1992b) *Grammatical categories and cognition: a case study of the linguistic relativity hypothesis*. Cambridge: Cambridge University Press.

Mann, Charles (2005) *1491: new revelations of the Americas before Columbus*. New York: Knopf.

Matras, Yaron (2009) *Language contact*. Cambridge: Cambridge University Press.

Matras, Yaron & Jeanette Sakel (2007) (eds.) *Grammatical borrowing in cross-linguistic perspective*. Berlin: Mouton de Gruyter.

Matthewson, Lisa (2004) 'On the methodology of semantic fieldwork', *International Journal of American Linguistics* **70**(4): 369–415.

Mayer, Mercer (1969) *Frog where are you?* London: Puffin Books.

(1977) *Frog goes to dinner*. London: Puffin Books.

Meakins, Felicity (2007) Review of 'Computerized Language Analysis (CLAM) from The CHILDES Project', *Language Documentation and Conservation* **1**(1): 107–12.

Milroy, Lesley (1987) *Observing and analysing natural language: a critical account of sociolinguistic method*. Oxford: Blackwell.

Mithun, Marianne (2001) 'Who shapes the record: the speaker and the linguist'. In Paul Newman & Martha S. Ratliff (eds.) *Linguistic fieldwork*. Cambridge: Cambridge University Press, pp. 34–54.

Moyer, Melissa G. (2008) 'Research as practice: linking theory, method, and data'. In Li Wei & Melissa Moyer (eds.) *The Blackwell guide to research methods in bilingualism and multilingualism*. Malden, MA: Blackwell, pp. 18–31.

Moyer, Melissa G. & Li Wei (2008) 'Disseminating results: a guide to conference presentation and journal publication'. In Li Wei & Melissa Moyer (eds.) *The Blackwell guide to research methods in bilingualism and multilingualism.* Malden, MA: Blackwell, pp. 354–60.

Newman, Paul & Martha S. Ratliff (2001) (eds.) *Linguistic fieldwork.* Cambridge: Cambridge University Press.

Nida, Eugene A. (1947) 'Field techniques in descriptive linguistics', *International Journal of American Linguistics* **13**(3):138–46.

Nortier, Jacomine (2008) 'Types and sources of bilingual data'. In Li Wei & Melissa Moyer (eds.) *The Blackwell guide to research methods in bilingualism and multilingualism.* Oxford: Blackwell, pp. 35–53.

Payne, Thomas E. (1997) *Describing morphosyntax: a guide for field linguists.* Cambridge: Cambridge University Press.

Payne, Thomas E. & David J. Weber (2007) (eds.) *Perspectives on grammar writing.* Amsterdam: John Benjamins.

Pike, Kenneth L. (1967) *Language in relation to a unified theory of the structure of human behaviour.* The Hague: Mouton.

Postal, Paul M. (1968) *Aspects of phonological theory.* New York: Harper & Row.

Pratt, Scott (2002) *Native pragmatism: rethinking the roots of American philosophy.* Bloomington, IN: Indiana University Press.

Ribeiro, Darcy (1977) *Confissoes.* São Paulo: Companhia das Letras.

Saeed, John Ibrahim (1999) *Somali.* Amsterdam: John Benjamins.

Said, Edward W. (1978) *Orientalism.* New York: Pantheon.

Sakel, Jeanette (2004) *A grammar of Mosetén.* Berlin: Mouton de Gruyter.

Samarin, William J. (1967) *Field linguistics: a guide to linguistic fieldwork.* New York: Holt, Rinehart & Winston.

Sapir, Edward (1915) 'Abnormal types of speech in Nootka'; reproduced in Dell Hymes (1964) (ed.) *Language in culture and society: a reader in linguistics and anthropology.* San Francisco: Harper & Row.

(1921) *Language: an introduction to the study of speech.* New York: Harcourt, Brace and Company.

Saville-Troike, Muriel (2003) *The ethnography of communication: an introduction.* Oxford: Blackwell.

Seeger, Anthony (2004) *Why Suyá sing – a musical anthropology of an Amazonian people.* Champaign, IL: University of Illinois Press.

Swadesh, Morris (1971) *The origins and diversification of language.* Chicago: Aldine (edited *post mortem* by Joel Sherzer).

Trilsbeek, Paul & Peter Wittenburg (2006) 'Archiving challenges'. In Jost Gippert, Nikolaus P. Himmelmann & Ulrike Mosel (eds.) *Essentials of language documentation.* Berlin: Mouton de Gruyter, pp. 311–36.

van den Berg, Helma (2001) *Dargi folktales. Oral stories from the Caucasus with an introduction to Dargi grammar.* Leiden: CNWS.

Vaux, Bert and Justin Cooper (1999) *Introduction to linguistic field methods.* Munich: Lincom Europa.

Wengle, John L. (1988) *Ethnographers in the field: the psychology of research.* Tuscaloosa, AL: University of Alabama Press.

Werner, D. (1993/2010) *Where there is no doctor.* 2nd rev. edn. Oxford: Macmillan Education and Berkeley, CA: Hesperian Foundation. [11th rev. reprinting 2010.]

Index